IMAGES
of America

LINCOLN COUNTY

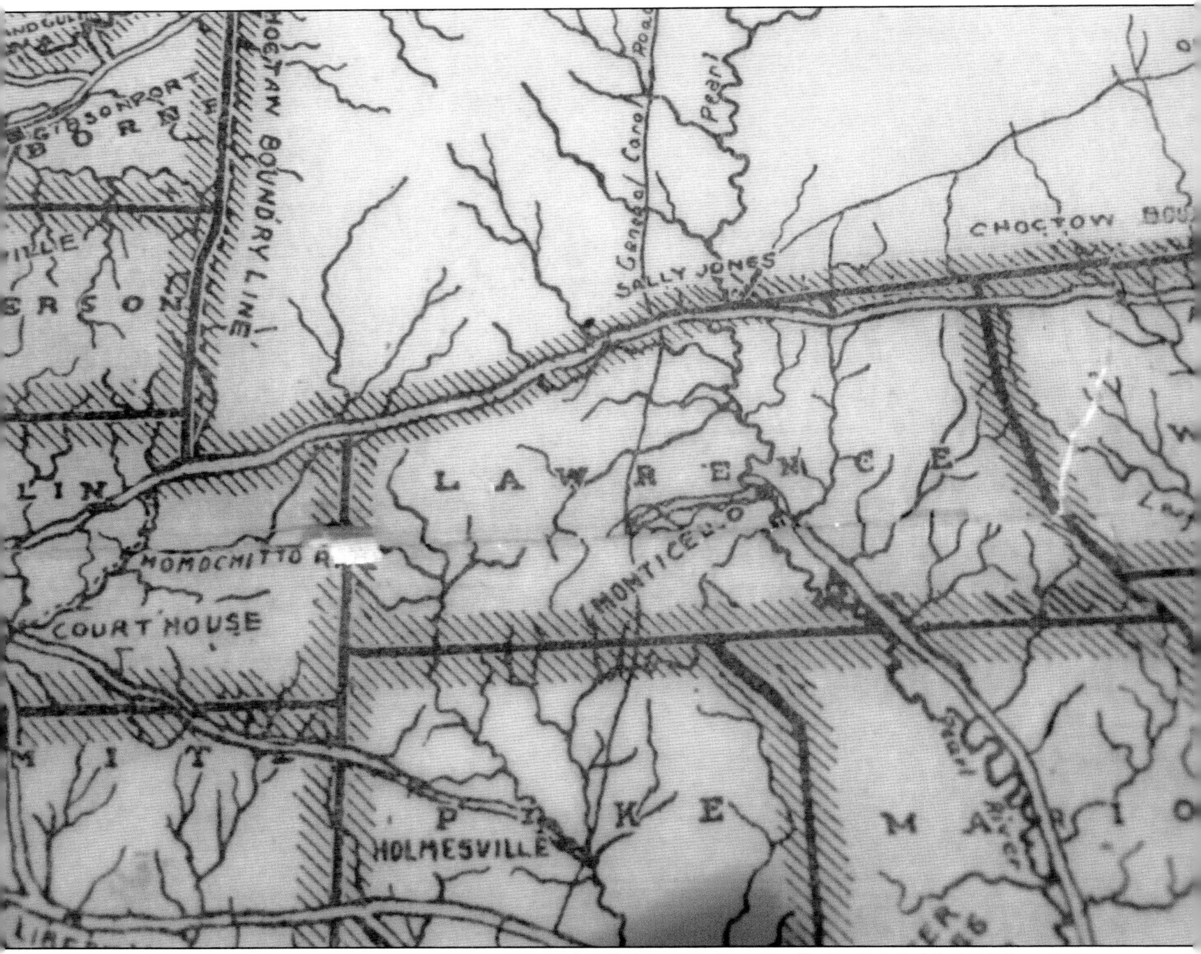

This detail of Mississippi Territory is from a badly battered copy of John Melish's 1819 hand-drawn map. The counties of Franklin, Lawrence, and Pike are clearly marked. Along with Copiah and Amite Counties, they are the counties from which parts were taken to form Lincoln County. Note St. Stephens Road, a common path for early settlers. (Marti Parker.)

On the Cover: Logging, the first industry in Lincoln County, grew as the railroad was built through the area. Bert Parnell (left) and his crew are shown with a load of longleaf pine being prepared for milling. (Lincoln-Lawrence-Franklin Regional Library.)

IMAGES
of America

LINCOLN COUNTY

Tammie Santos Brewer, Bettie P. Bullard,
Sue Dorman, and Marti Parker

ARCADIA
PUBLISHING

ISBN 978-1-4671-1495-0

Published by Arcadia Publishing
Charleston, South Carolina

Printed in the United States of America

Library of Congress Control Number: 2015941623

For all general information, please contact Arcadia Publishing:
Telephone 843-853-2070
Fax 843-853-0044
E-mail sales@arcadiapublishing.com
For customer service and orders:
Toll-Free 1-888-313-2665

Visit us on the Internet at www.arcadiapublishing.com

This book is dedicated to the memory of early Lincoln County settlers and the families who followed and helped the county grow.

Contents

Acknowledgments

Each day, a little bit of history is lost or disappears. We hope that, through our endeavors, a few photographs and memories of Lincoln County, Mississippi, have been preserved for you to enjoy.

Our sincere gratitude is expressed to the following individuals, without whose assistance this book would not have been created: Lincoln-Lawrence-Franklin Regional Library director Henry Ledet, board, and staff for the use of its vast collection of photographs and resources; all the individuals who participated in our scanning days by bringing photographs and information; Lincoln County Historical and Genealogical Society president Carroll Montgomery; Terry Pappas; Maxine Allen; Lincoln County Baptist Association and secretary Lisa Burt; countless individuals we called and visited who provided information; our title manager, Liz Gurley, and the staff at Arcadia Publishing; and, most importantly, our families, who love us and tolerate our endless pursuits of history.

Finally, to the historians and genealogists no longer with us who recorded times gone by and told their stories for future generations, we say "thank you."

Images from the following sources are credited with abbreviated forms: the Lincoln-Lawrence-Franklin Regional Library (LLF), the Lincoln County Historical and Genealogical Society Museum (LCHGS), and the Mississippi Department of Archives and History (MDAH).

Introduction

Lincoln County, Mississippi, was formed after men of the area had fought in the American Revolution, the War of 1812, the Mexican-American War, and the Civil War. By April 7, 1870, when the county was formed by legislative action, successful businesses had been established; Whitworth College for Women had offered education for over 10 years; major sawmills and lumber companies were supplying lumber to many parts of the nation, facilitated by a major north-west railroad through the center of the larger towns of Brookhaven and Bogue Chitto; and advances had been made in many other aspects of community life.

Lincoln County, named for Pres. Abraham Lincoln, was created by the subdivision of Lawrence, Franklin, Copiah, Amite, and Pike Counties to form the 574-square-mile area in the southwestern part of the state. The act located the county seat at Brookhaven, and it has always been the largest town in the area.

Lawrence County, on the eastern side of Lincoln County, was created on December 22, 1814, as one of the 14 original territorial counties. Over half of the land to create Lincoln County was taken from that area. Lands to the north were from Copiah County, to the west from Franklin County, and to the south from Pike County.

These boundaries, as described in the original act, are "on the east by R. line between ranges 9 and 10 east; on the north by T. line between townships 8 and 9, except sections 3 and 4, included in the present corporate limits of the town of Wesson; and on the west by the present boundary line between the counties of Copiah and Jefferson; on the south by the present boundary line between the counties of Copiah and Franklin, to a point one mile east of the point where said boundary line intersects the range line separating R. 5 from R. 6; thence due south to the township line, which separates T. 4 from T. 5; thence east along said township line to the commencing point."

Running in a north-south direction through the western part of the county is the Jackson-Liberty Road, which carried Andrew Jackson's troops to the Battle of New Orleans in January 1815. This battle was fought after the peace treaty had been signed ending the War of 1812, but the news had not reached either army.

The St. Stephens Road, first an Indian trail and later a wagon road, ran near the middle of the county, near the east prong of the Bogue Chitto River, about a mile and a half south of the present town of Brookhaven. This is the area where, in 1818, Samuel Jayne established a small trading post, which he named for his hometown of Brookhaven, New York. A watermill, tannery, and post office were later established. Soon, the small trading post grew into a regular stop for people in the area and those traveling from St. Stephens, Alabama, to Natchez, Mississippi. Families settled near the trading post and throughout the area well before federal land offices were established. Some families had established homes as much as 20 years before they could file legal papers. Many of those original groups have descendants in the area today.

The harvest of fine longleaf pine and other lumber began in the area around 1837 and continues today. Men originally used oxen to bring timber to market; with the completion of the Illinois Central Railroad in 1857, spur lines were built to move the cut timber to planing mills and to transport the lumber to northern areas and south to New Orleans.

Waters from the Bogue Chitto, Amite, Homochitto, and Bayou Pierre Rivers and their tributaries were used to move lumber in logging operations, run gristmills, and provide bottomlands for crops. Soil was fertile sandy loam, allowing the production of cotton, corn, sugarcane, rice, oats, peanuts, and potatoes, all kinds of vegetables, fruits, and melons in earlier times.

In the early 1850s, men arrived, looking for a way to build a continuous railroad from Jackson, Tennessee, to New Orleans, Louisiana. The original plan took the railroad through Samuel Jayne's land. Jayne was not interested and did not wish to give the railroad a right-of-way though his lands. Milton J. Whitworth offered other lands to the northwest, which the railroad accepted, to create one of the "ten mile stations" of Osyka, Magnolia, Summit, Bogue Chitto, and Hazlehurst in the area. Jayne realized his mistake too late to have his land reconsidered. While there are several versions of this story, these are the basic facts. This decision also placed the rail line through Whitworth's property, less than a half mile from Jayne's.

As the railroad was preparing to be built, Eben E. Seavey stated later that he, William Brooks, and James Ragsdale arrived by stagecoach from Atlanta, Georgia, to Samuel Jayne's for a stage stop and lunch. Liking the area, and hearing of the plans for the railroad, they stayed.

Whitworth was a planter, a lay minister for the Methodist Episcopal Church South, and a man with a mission. He wanted the railroad, and he wanted to build a college for women to reopen the Elizabeth Academy that had closed in the Washington area a few years earlier. The story is told that architect A.E. Moreton stepped off the first train to New Orleans, and Whitworth met him at the depot. Whether this tale is completely correct, Whitworth did meet Moreton and convinced him to stay in Brookhaven. By 1860, the new Whitworth College was opened for students. During the Civil War, the school was used as a hospital for both Northern and Southern troops. After the college was built, Moreton remained in Brookhaven, where some of his descendants live today.

By the 1900 census, only 30 years after becoming a county, Lincoln County was listed as having a total value of manufactured products of $1,767,239.

Images selected for inclusion in this book represent the variety of people and lifestyles in the area. Families from many nations came to this rich area, built homes and churches, and lived quiet and peaceful existences. Many of the larger homes still stand, and the streets of South Jackson and South Church lure visitors from many areas. Churches shared buildings with other denominations as needed; education was available in private and public schools throughout the county; the railroad provided easy access to larger commercial areas; Whitworth College offered higher education, first to young women and, later, to men and women; and a variety of programs were held for community entertainment.

One

Land of Longleaf Pine

The longleaf pine played a very important role in the history of Lincoln County and Mississippi, especially in the 1800s, when producers considered the supply of trees almost endless. It was widely reported that between 70 and 90 million acres of land in the United States were covered with the highly sought-after tree. Today, that figure stands at just over 3 million acres.

Several events in the mid-1800s contributed to the lumber industry's growth: the manufacture of railroad locomotives made specifically for logging; a steam skidder, which could haul more logs; and demand for the yellow pine soon after the Civil War ended. Railroads also made it possible to transport lumber from remote areas; sawmill owners began constructing spurs and dummy lines to and from mills to main rail lines.

Built around 1886 by Frank Norwood and John S. Butterfield, the Norwood & Butterfield Lumber Company was one of the earliest mills in the southern part of Lincoln County. Norwood left the company several years later. The Butterfield shareholders sold the mill around 1915 to the Denkmann Lumber Company. Another significant mill began acquiring lands in the northwestern part of Lincoln County and began milling operations around 1899. Like many sawmills of the time, Pearl River Lumber Company not only brought equipment to mill pine trees, it also brought men to work the mills. Houses were built for workers. Stores to supply the workers sprouted up, and hospitals and schools were also built.

According to the Mississippi Department of Archives and History, Pearlhaven was chartered as a village on August 7, 1901, with 310 persons. Pearl River Lumber Company shut down and was sold around 1910, and its village was annexed into Brookhaven in 1912. All of its holdings were either sold or disbanded and shipped elsewhere. Some of the old mill houses can still be seen on Railroad and Main Streets in the community.

Many other mills could also be found throughout Lincoln County. The once abundant longleaf pine was a contributing factor, bringing scores of people to Lincoln County in the 19th and the early 20th centuries.

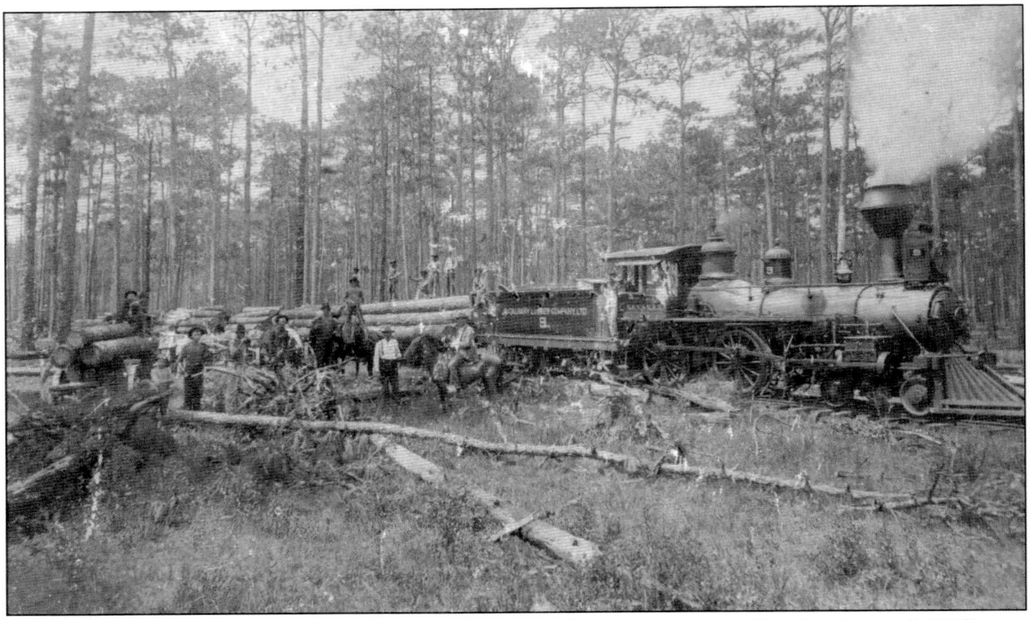

J.H. Williams (1850–1939), shown here in the white shirt at center, and his brother R.J. Williams were loggers in the late 19th and early 20th centuries. This photograph was taken about 1902. The name on the car behind the engine is "Natalbany Lumber Company, Ltd.," which was a division of Denkmann Lumber Company. (LLF.)

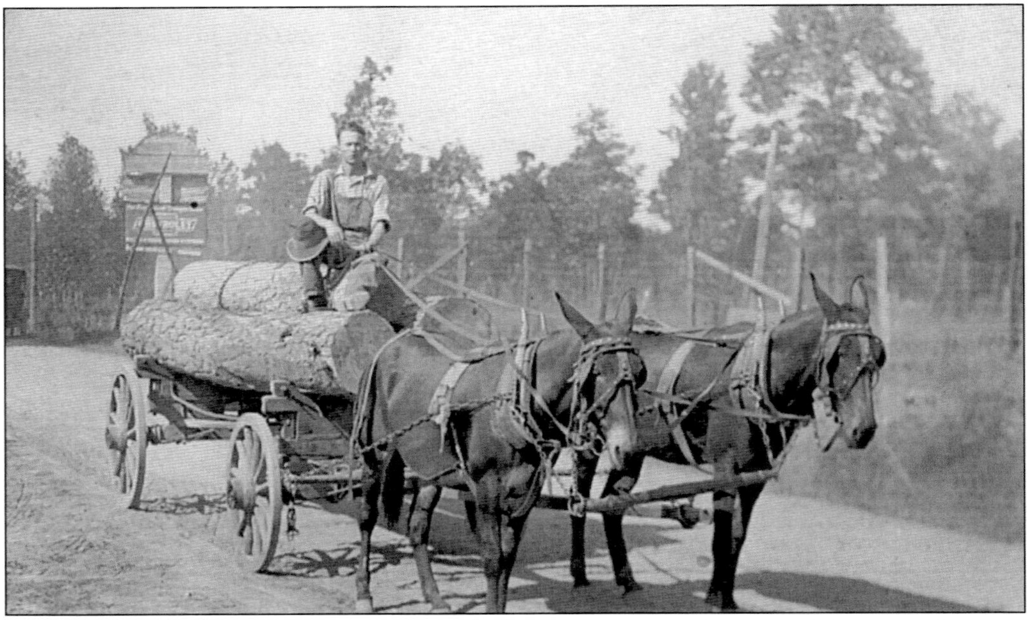

Troy Allen hauls logs to Brookhaven around 1925 using mules and a wagon. Note the Chevrolet advertisement in the background. (Seth Allen.)

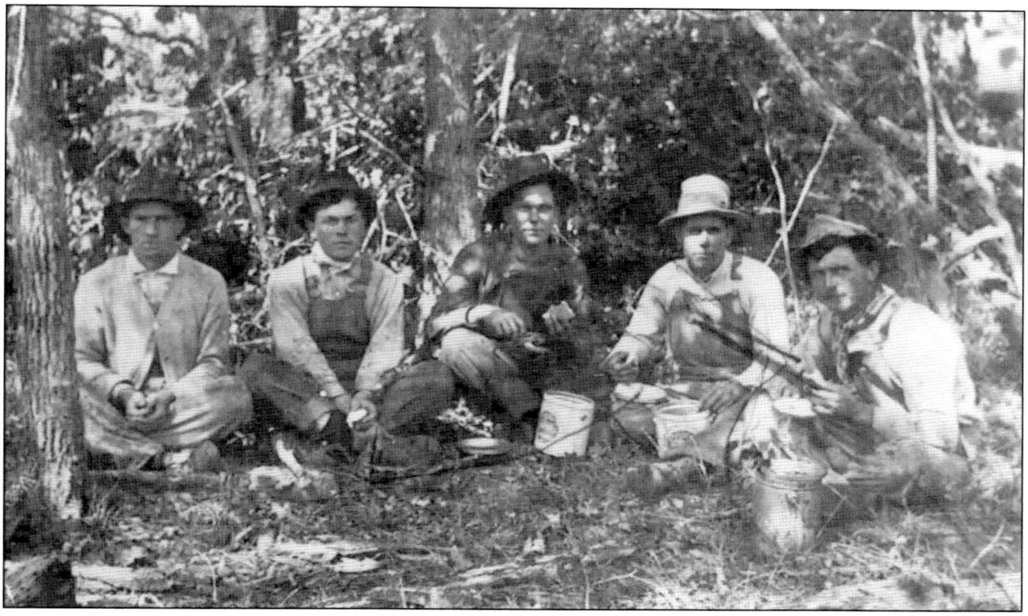

Cutting down large trees with only a crosscut saw was backbreaking work, and lunchtime was welcomed. These five men are taking time out to rest and eat their lunch. Charles Greer (far left) is the only logger identified. (Bonnie Cole Collection.)

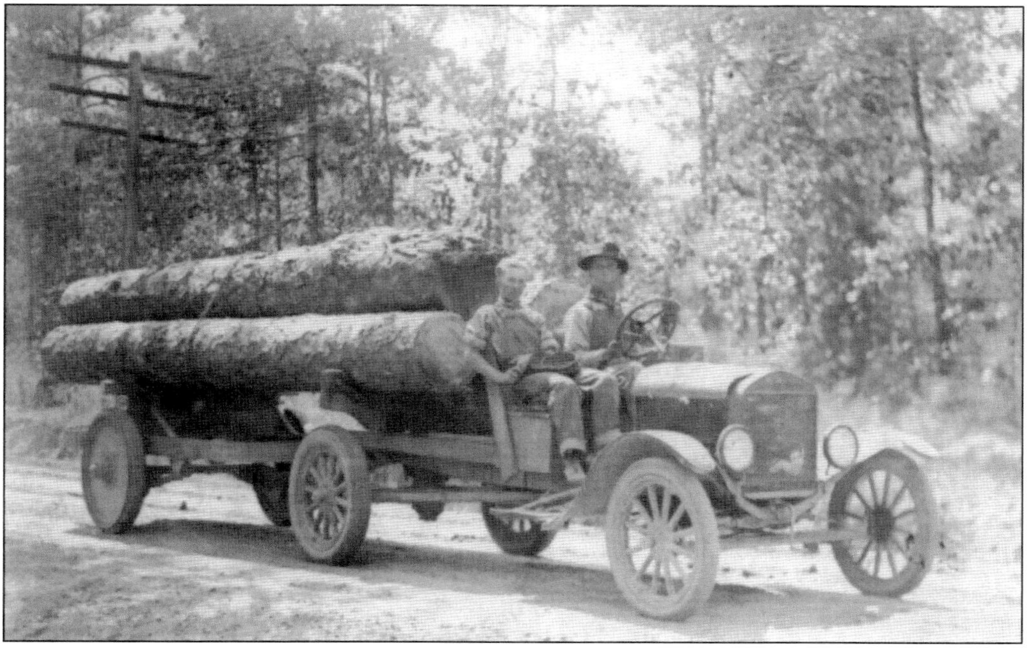

George Godwin (right), born in 1876, and Wroten Godwin, born in 1907, haul logs to a nearby mill. (Elliott Smith.)

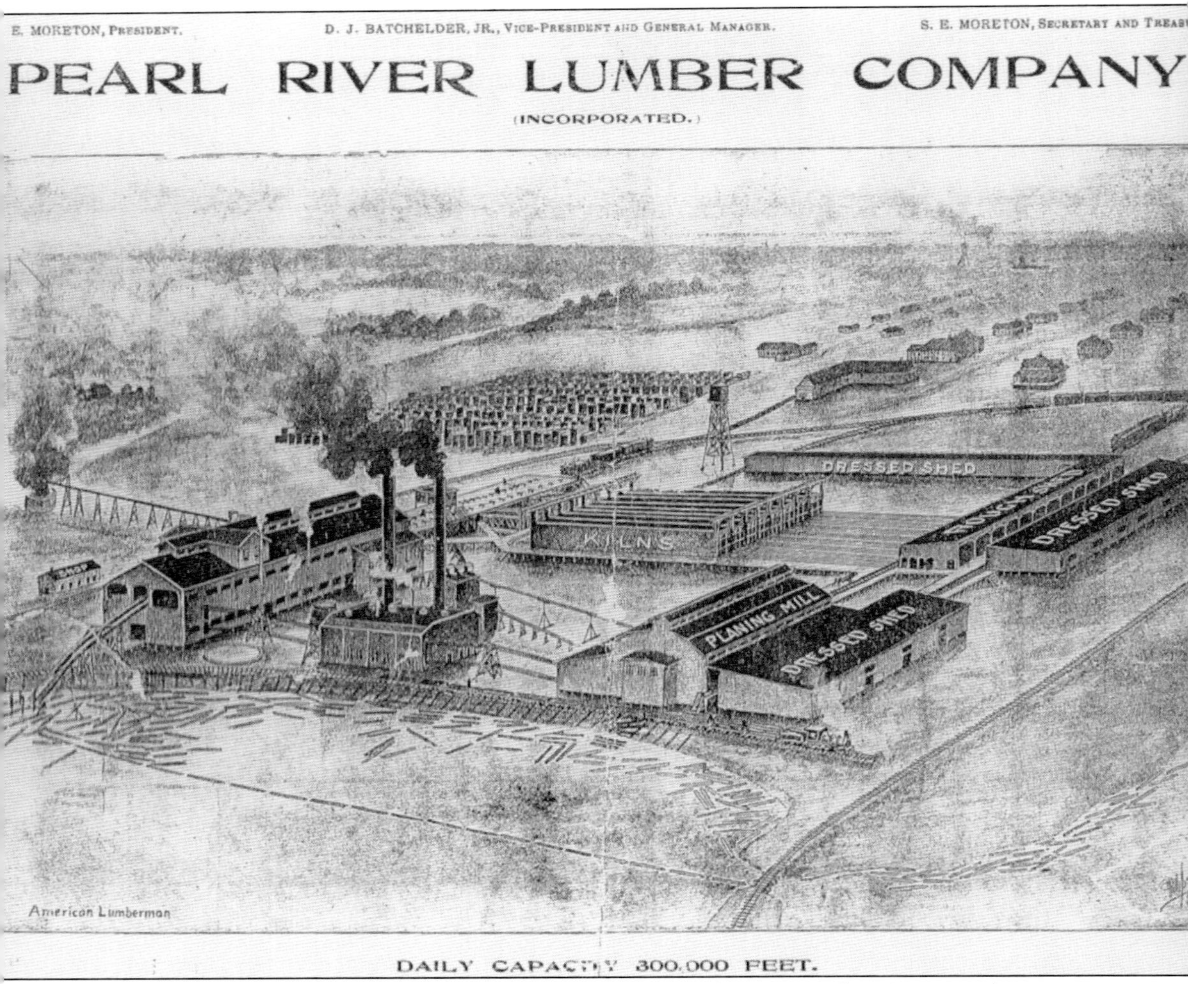

Pearlhaven started as a lumber community built by Pearl River Lumber Company beginning in 1899. According to the Mississippi Department of Archives and History, Pearlhaven was chartered as a village on August 7, 1901, with 310 people, stores, a hotel, a hospital, boardinghouses, a school, and churches. (Sue Dorman.)

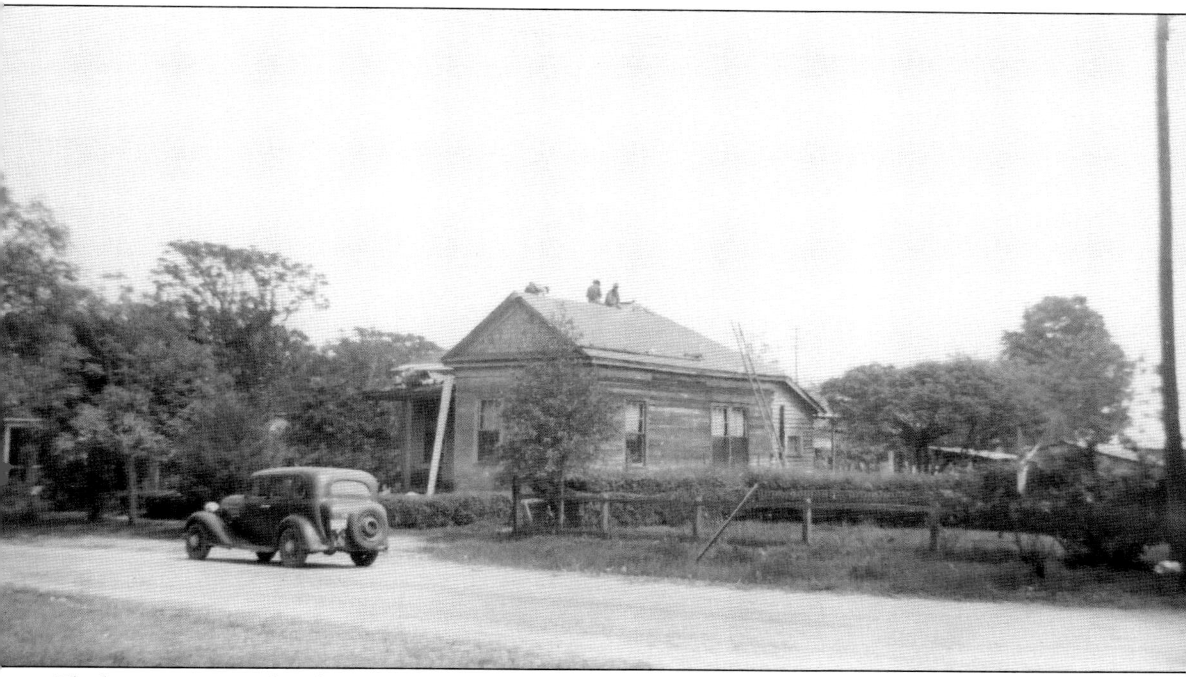

The house at 306 Railroad Street, shown here in 1940, is one of many mill homes built for supervisors of Pearl River Lumber Company. It still stands today. The lumber company was eventually sold, and the homes were auctioned off to individuals between 1912 and 1917. Brookhaven annexed Pearlhaven as a subdivision in 1912. (Tammie Santos Brewer.)

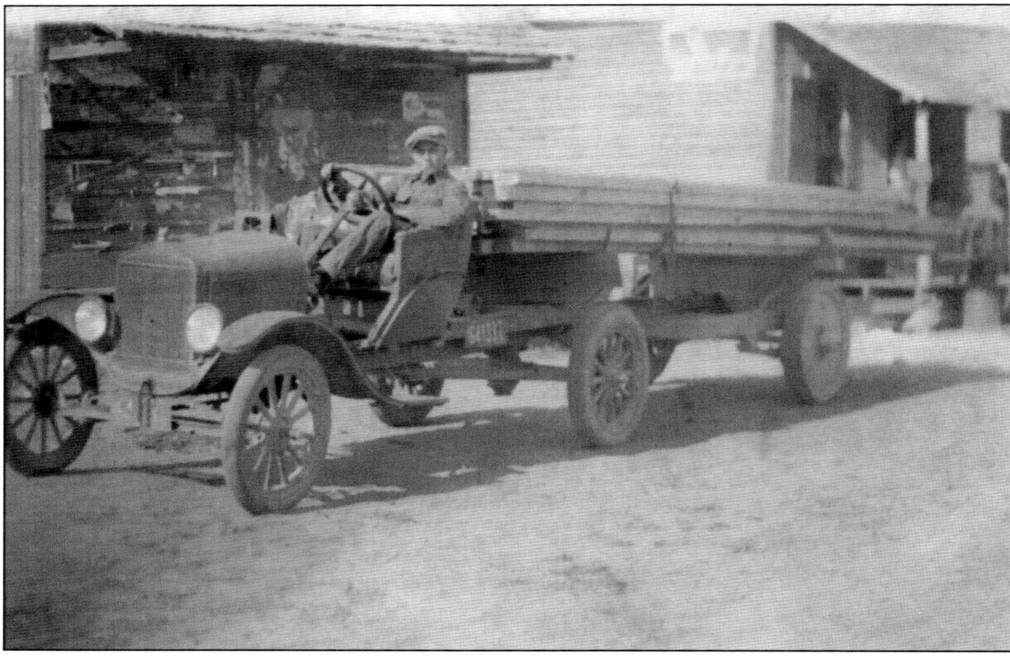

Wroten Godwin, at the intersection of Jackson-Liberty Drive and St. Stephens (now Zetus) Road, hauls a load of milled lumber. The old Vaughan grocery can be seen in the background. (Elliott Smith.)

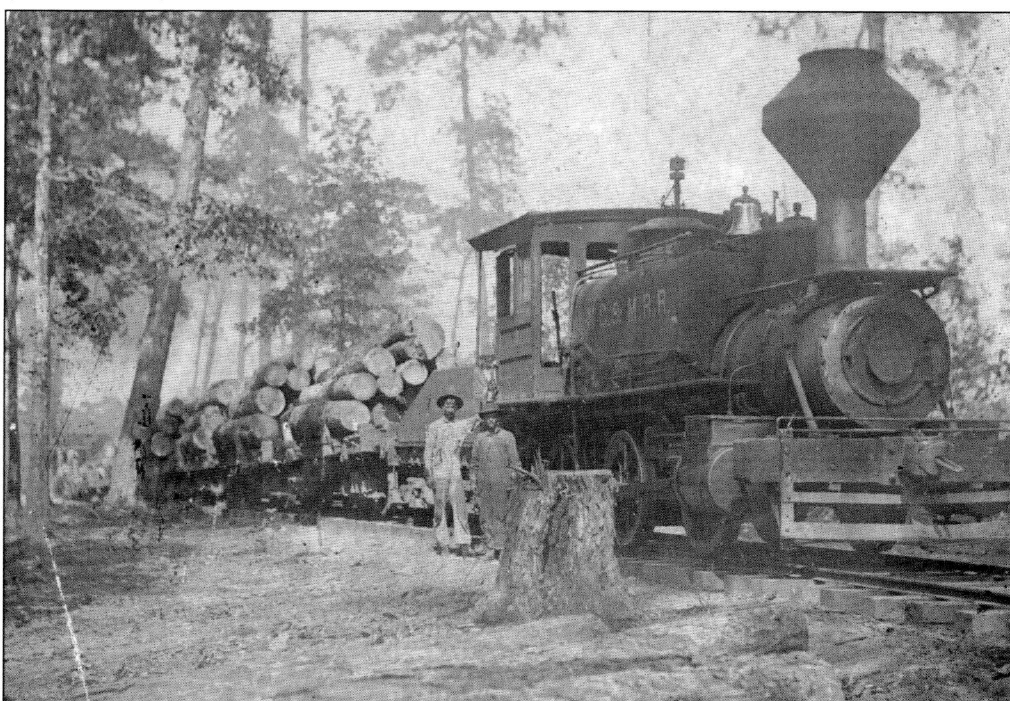

Ira Moak (left) ran a locomotive engine in the logging industry for Norwood & Butterfield Company, shown here around 1903. Moak was from the Ruth community. The person on the right is unidentified. (Martha Sinclair.)

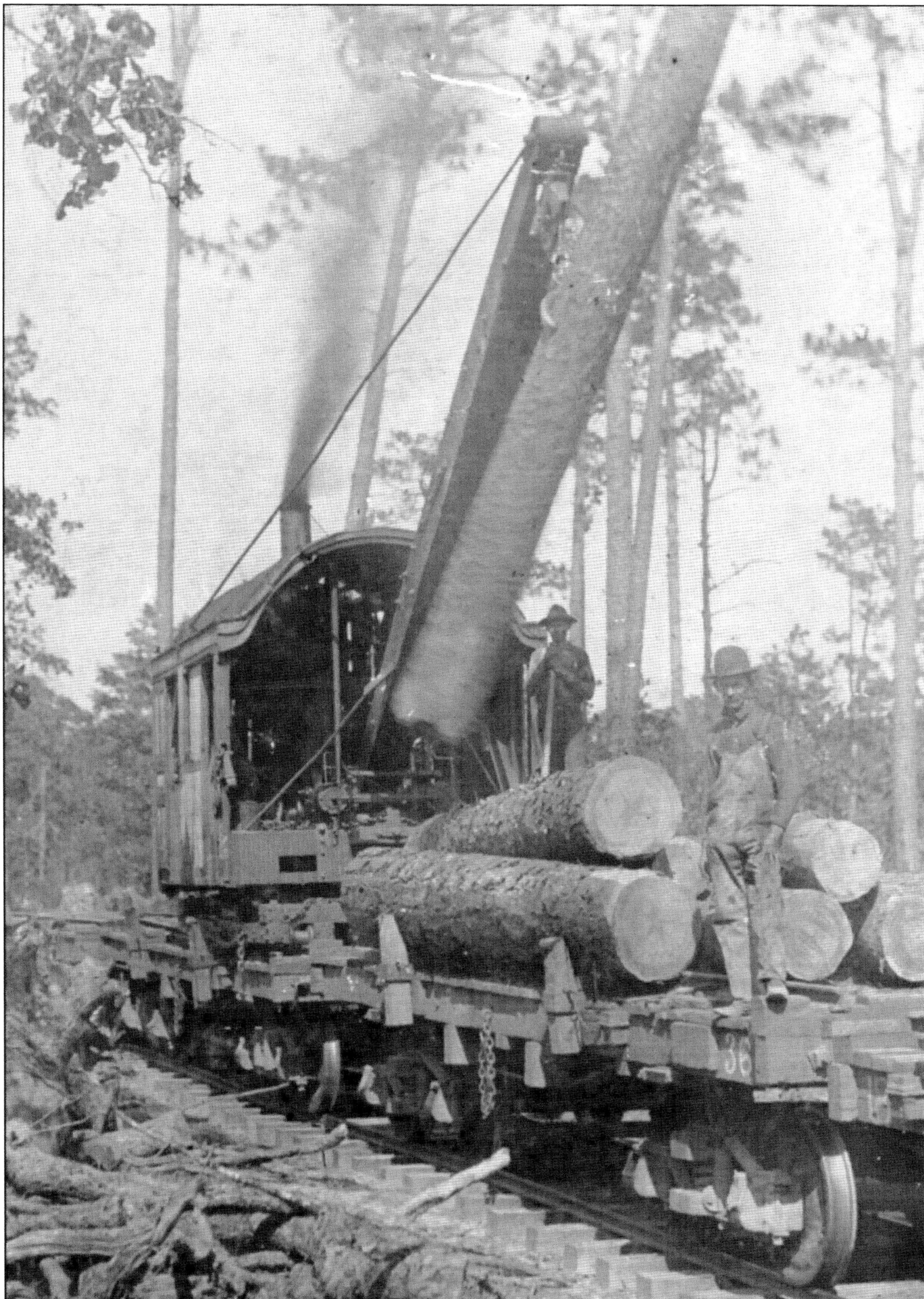

Sam Moak (in derby hat) is one of the workers identified in this 1903 photograph of early logging efforts. The machine was used to lift logs onto railway cars to take to lumber mills. (Martha Sinclair.)

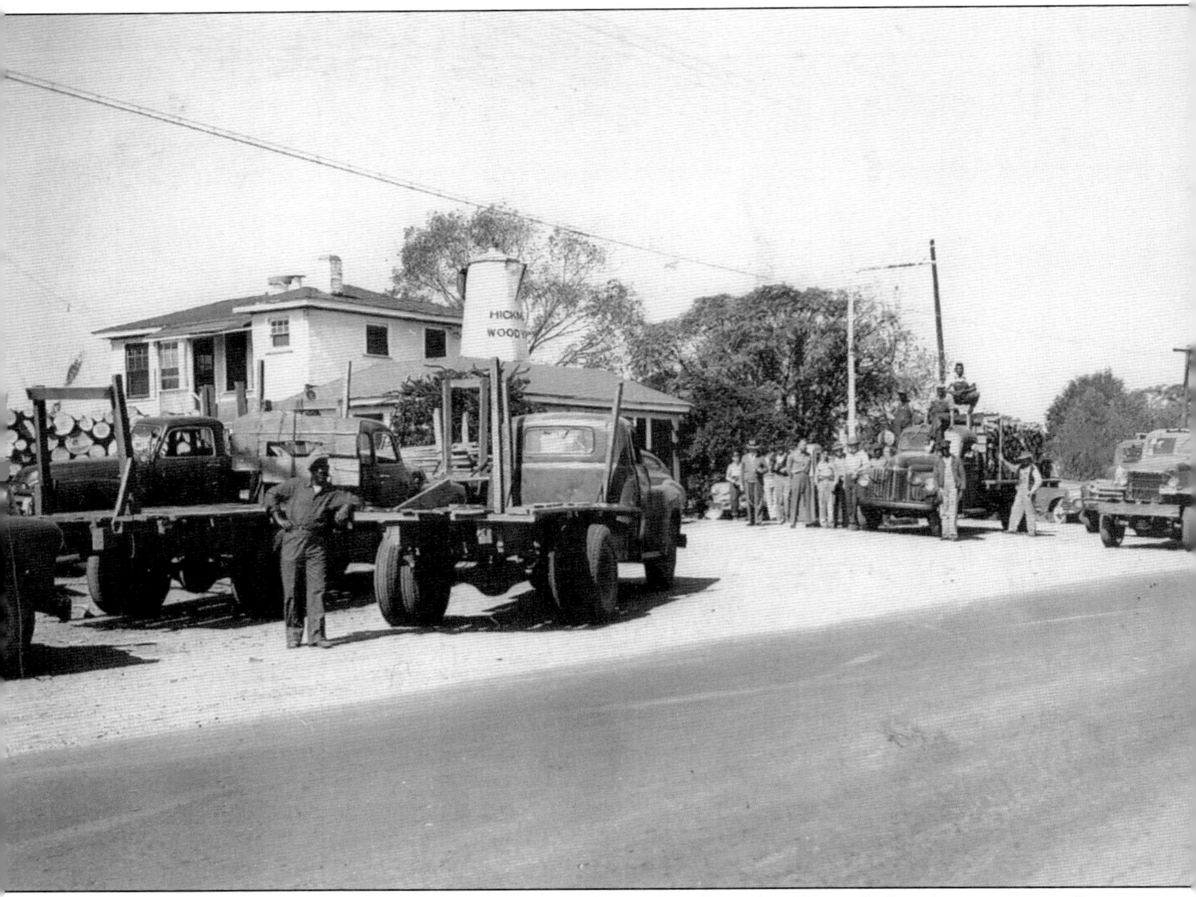

The Coffee Pot was a main attraction on Highway 51 when the Carruth family constructed it in 1931 as a café. It was touted as the first fast-food restaurant in the South. Operating one of the largest Masonite dealerships in Mississippi and Louisiana, Tom Hickman purchased the property in 1946. Hickman kept his office there until he died in 1975. The property was sold several years later. According to his grandson Bill Hickman, this was a "happening" part of town in the 1940s and 1950s. An icehouse and a canning factory were located nearby. (Bill Hickman.)

Two

Real Pioneers

The rich, fertile soils of south Mississippi lured pioneering families to the area. Tales of vast acres of uncut timber to build homes, farmlands that could be cleared for crops and pastures, plus an abundant water supply appealed to those looking for a place to call home.

Hardships were common in those days. Indian attacks, like the one at Fort Mims, Alabama, in 1813, did not deter early settlers. Forging roads from Indian trails, hunting for food, sleeping on the ground, and leaving personal possessions behind were just a few of the adversities endured. But, still the people came, and they continued to come into the raw Mississippi Territory. Thomas Maxwell Jr. and others moved from Franklin County, Georgia, around 1810 and made a home in the Fair River community of what is now Lincoln County. The Lewis, Dickerson, and Hollingsworth families traveled with the Maxwells.

Many others, including John Gill of South Carolina, obtained passports through the Indian Nations in 1812. Gill settled in the Cold Springs area near Bogue Chitto. Isham Smith and his large family made their homes from Fair River north across the area to the southern edge of Copiah County. Samuel Jayne established a trading post just south of present-day Brookhaven. Others came to the area via St. Stephens Road.

In the 1780s, a group of Presbyterians left Scotland for South Carolina. By 1825, the families of McLaurin, Buie, Magee, Watson, Brown, Gilchrist, Anding, and Applewhite, to mention only a few, reached the area now known as Caseyville.

With the opening of the railroad, the town moved slightly northwest. Others began arriving, including the Cohns and Heucks of Prussia; Schercks of Germany; Beckers of France; and D'Antonis of Italy.

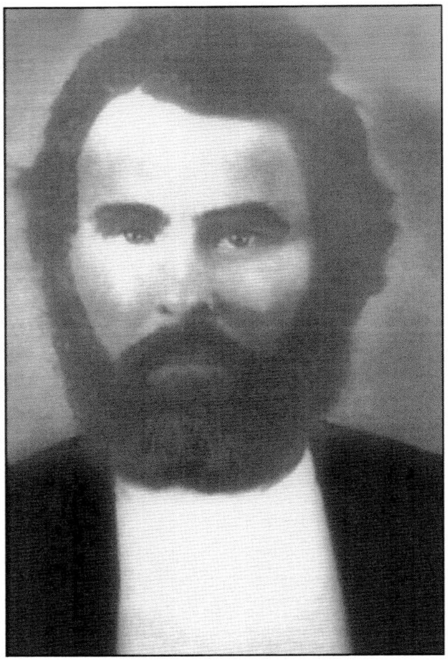

Samuel Jayne arrived in Lawrence County with his two brothers, Anslem and Brewster, about 1818 and settled in the Monticello area. In the early 1830s, he started selling his land and moved 20 miles west, purchasing 395 acres from James H. and Lovey Bull on the east fork of the Bogue Chitto River. There, he opened a store, gristmill, and tannery and was named postmaster. He named Brookhaven after his hometown in New York. Jayne married Mary Johnson Burns on October 5, 1848. They had no children. He died on July 28, 1861, at age 66. (Vicki Cooper.)

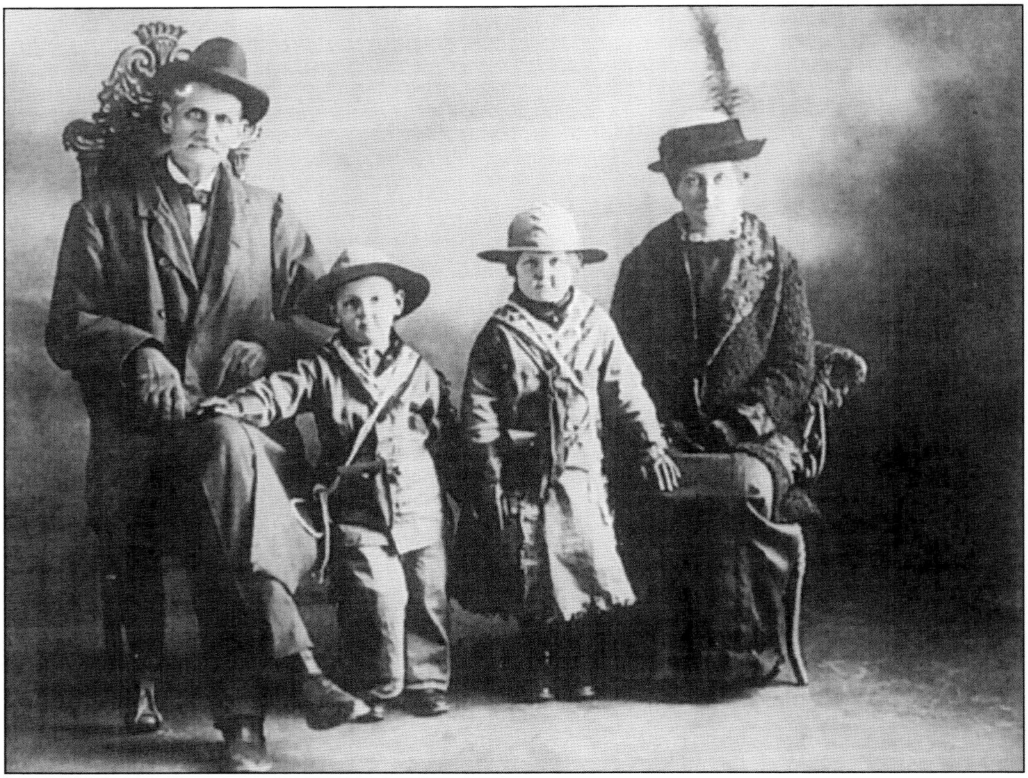

William Abshagen came to America as a small boy from Germany. He settled near Fair River and married Theresia Heuck, sister of Charles Heuck Sr. Abshagen opened a shoe store in Brookhaven that he operated until 1930, when he retired. He also built Abshagen's Bakery for his sons. Shown here are, from left to right, William, grandson and namesake William III, granddaughter Theresia Anne, and wife, Mary Theresia. William III died at the age of 16, and Theresia Anne became one of the most loved English teachers at Brookhaven High School. (LCHGS.)

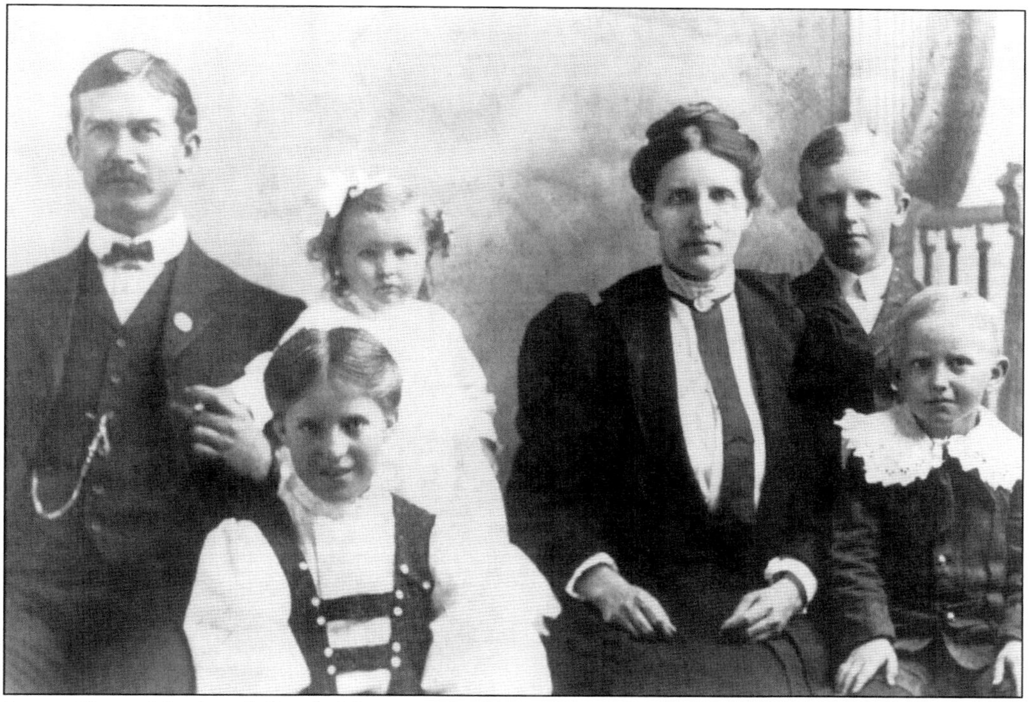

James Owen Neal and Sarah Minerva Rials Neal pose with their children around 1905 in Brookhaven. The children are, from left to right, Edna, Ivy, Jessie, and Eugene. Daughter Edith and son Fulton were born later. James (1868–1933) of the East Lincoln community was known for his singing and musical abilities. He was the son of Samuel Neal (1811–1895) and Sabrina Burnett Neal (1811–1900), who made their home in northern Pike County in 1840, which later became part of Lincoln County. (Tammie Santos Brewer.)

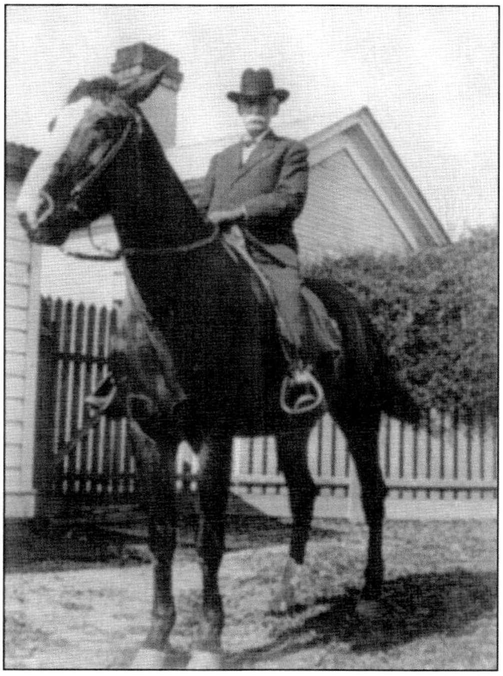

Capt. Alfred E. Moreton, born in Carroll County, Maryland, on August 9, 1835, came to Brookhaven in the late 1850s to help erect the buildings of Whitworth College. He also constructed the Storm Building, the old courthouses, and several other buildings in town. Moreton was a leader in the industrial, civic, fraternal, and church life in this area. He married Laura Decell, and they raised eight children. Captain Moreton died on November 24, 1925, and was buried in Rosehill Cemetery. His obituary stated, "His presence graced the city whose history he helped to make." Here, he sits atop his prized horse, Fred. (Phyllis Spearman.)

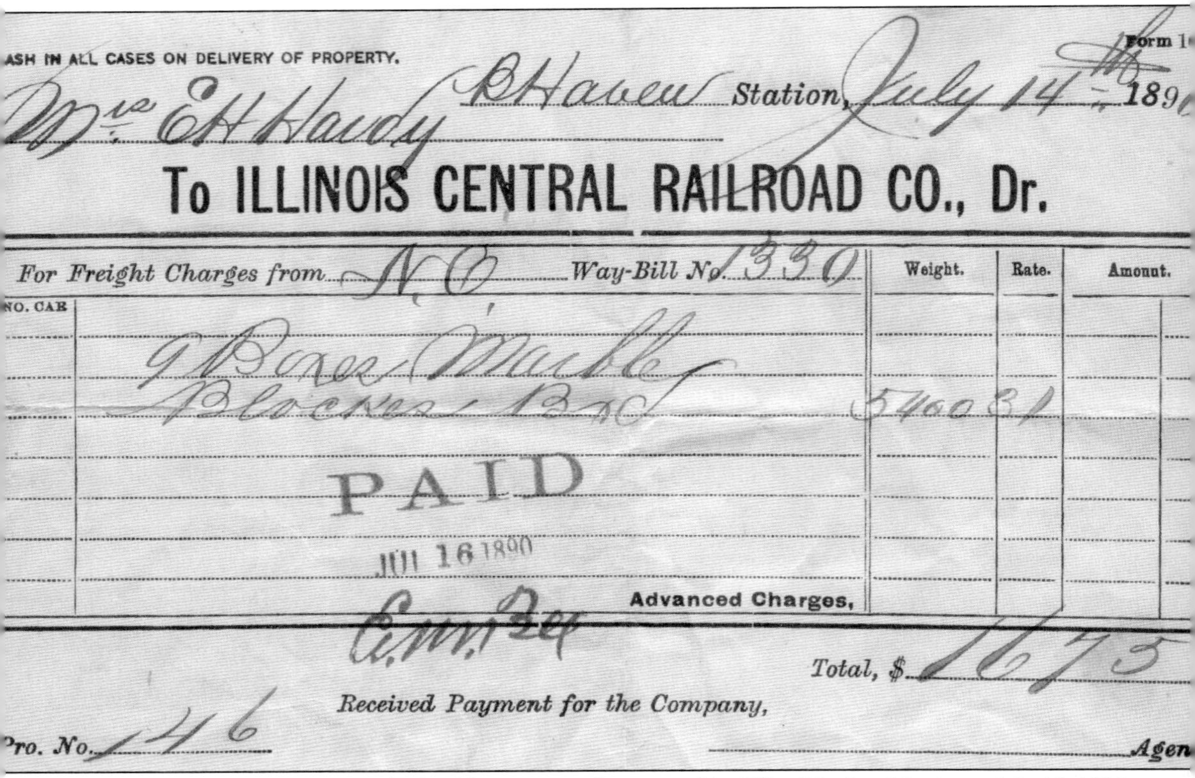

ASH IN ALL CASES ON DELIVERY OF PROPERTY. Form 1

Mrs. E H Hardy B Haven Station, July 14th 1890

To ILLINOIS CENTRAL RAILROAD CO., Dr.

For Freight Charges from N.O. Way-Bill No. 1330

NO. CAR		Weight.	Rate.	Amount.
	9 Boxes Marble Blocks B.O.	5400	31	
	PAID JUL 16 1890			
	Advanced Charges,			

Total, $ 16 75

Received Payment for the Company,

Pro. No. 146 Agen

This is a copy of a receipt for building materials received by Ellen Hooker Hardy on July 16, 1890, at the Brookhaven Railroad Station. The need for nine boxes of marble at a weight of 5,400 pounds with a total cost of $1,675 is unknown. (Marti Parker.)

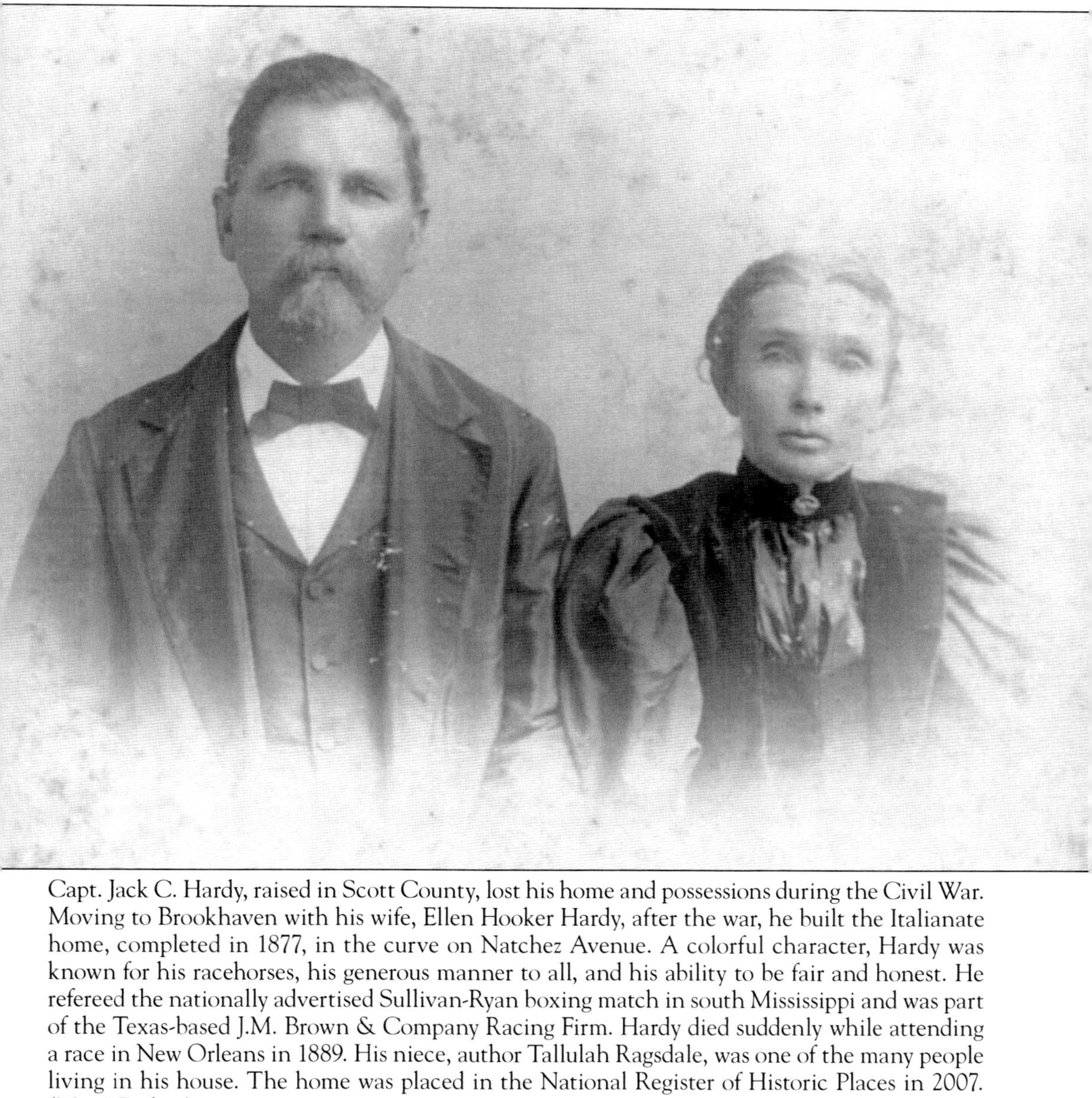

Capt. Jack C. Hardy, raised in Scott County, lost his home and possessions during the Civil War. Moving to Brookhaven with his wife, Ellen Hooker Hardy, after the war, he built the Italianate home, completed in 1877, in the curve on Natchez Avenue. A colorful character, Hardy was known for his racehorses, his generous manner to all, and his ability to be fair and honest. He refereed the nationally advertised Sullivan-Ryan boxing match in south Mississippi and was part of the Texas-based J.M. Brown & Company Racing Firm. Hardy died suddenly while attending a race in New Orleans in 1889. His niece, author Tallulah Ragsdale, was one of the many people living in his house. The home was placed in the National Register of Historic Places in 2007. (Marti Parker.)

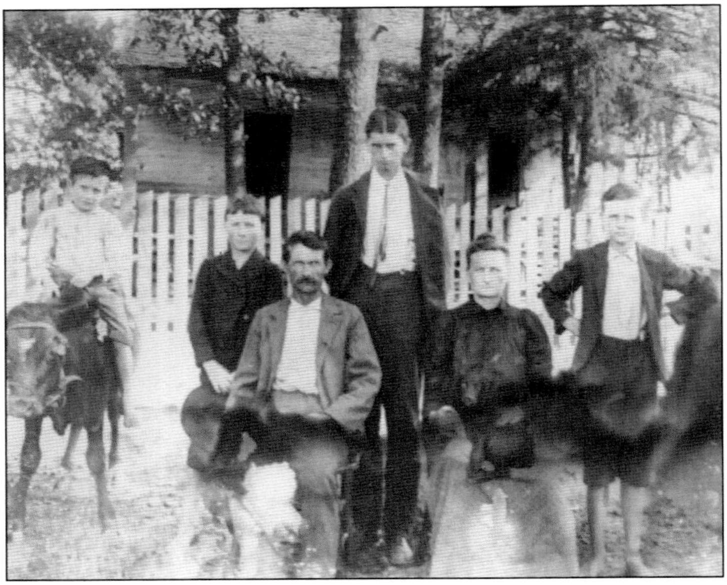

This photograph was identified as the family of Andrew "Babe" Maxwell (1854–1939). He was the son of Augustus Maxwell and Clara Adkins and was married to Ann Prestridge. Babe remembered the first schools he attended as a young boy and when Yankee troops were mustered out under Harry Tibbs. Babe was a carpenter and built some of the first houses in Brookhaven. He and Ann are buried in Union Hall Cemetery. (LLF.)

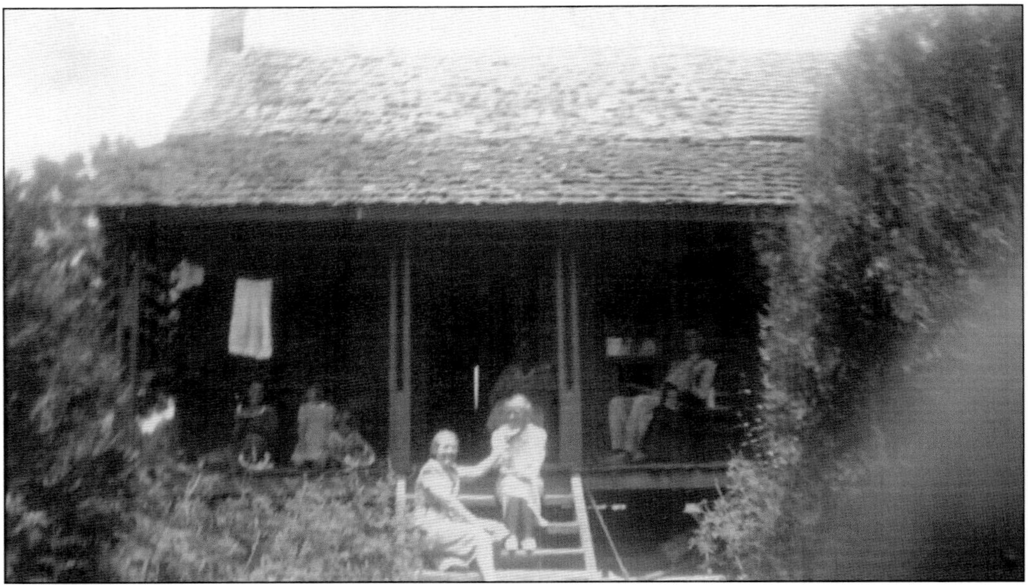

This house was probably built by William M. Burt Sr. (1822–1893) on land he purchased from the government in 1853 and 1859. It was located one and a half miles east of the West Lincoln community, near the Burt-Tarver Family Cemetery, where he, his wife, Mary Ann Lofton, and some of his 11 children are buried. The Burts' son Trisvan also lived in this home with his family. Sitting on the steps are Etive B. Lofton (left) and Effie B. Jordan. (Roffie Burt.)

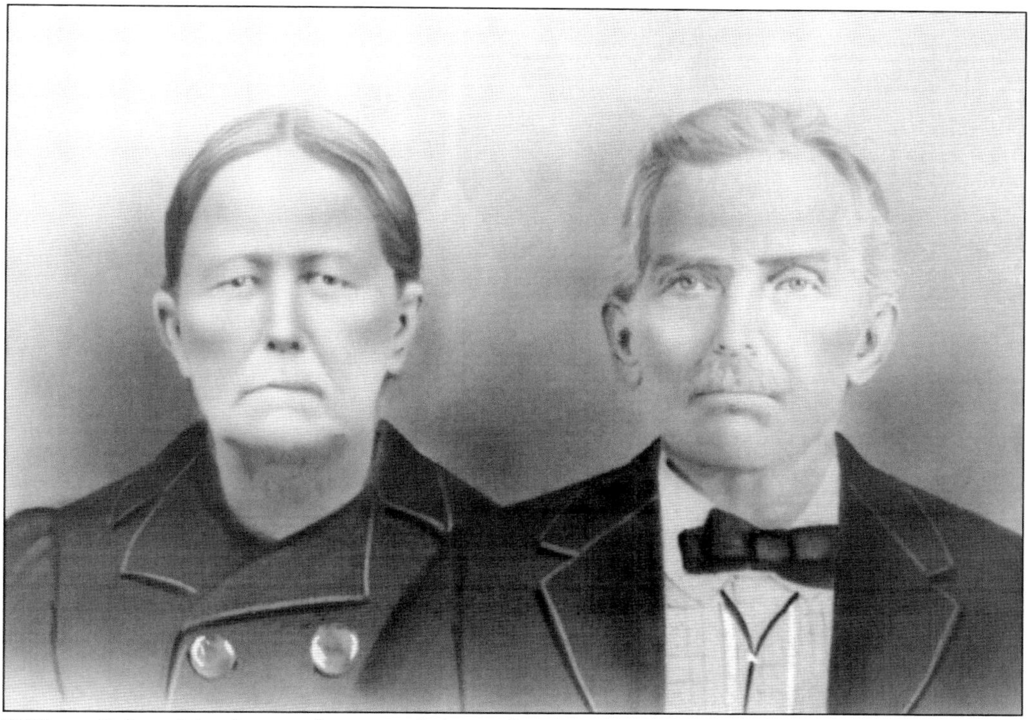

William Sidney Vaughan is shown with his wife, Margaret East Vaughan. William Sidney was born on November 2, 1831, in Yazoo City, Mississippi. He died on May 29, 1920, and is interred at Friendship Baptist Church Cemetery. Margaret was born in Franklin County on February 3, 1840. She died on November 16, 1898, and is also buried at Friendship Baptist Church. The couple was married on May 29, 1856, in Franklin County. (Mary Jane Russell.)

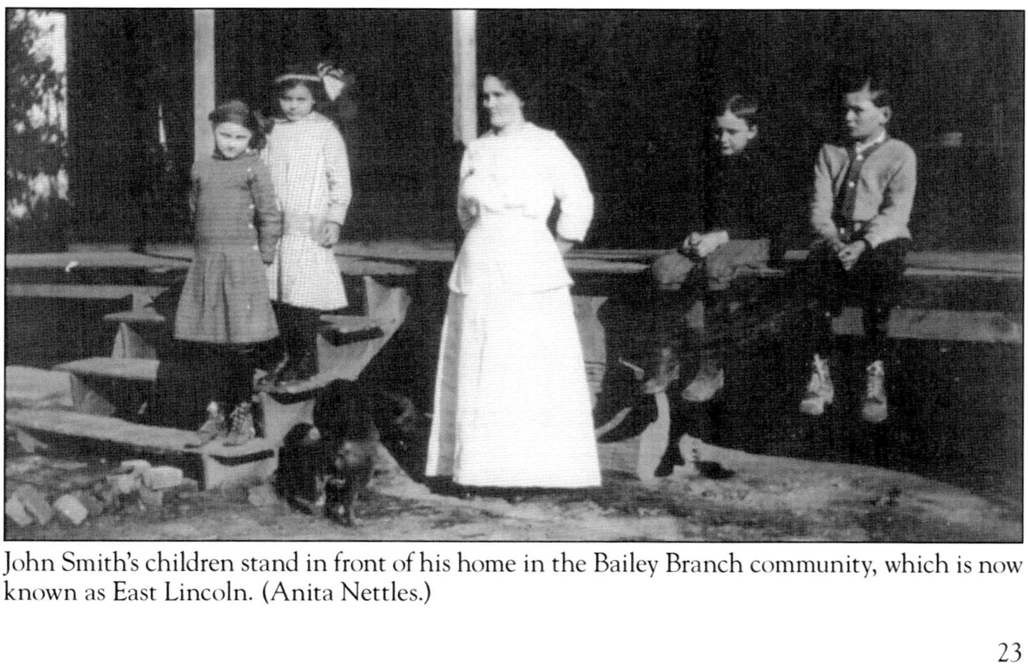

John Smith's children stand in front of his home in the Bailey Branch community, which is now known as East Lincoln. (Anita Nettles.)

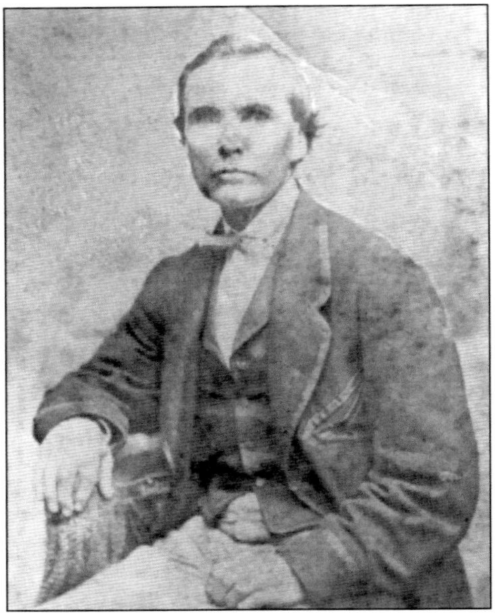

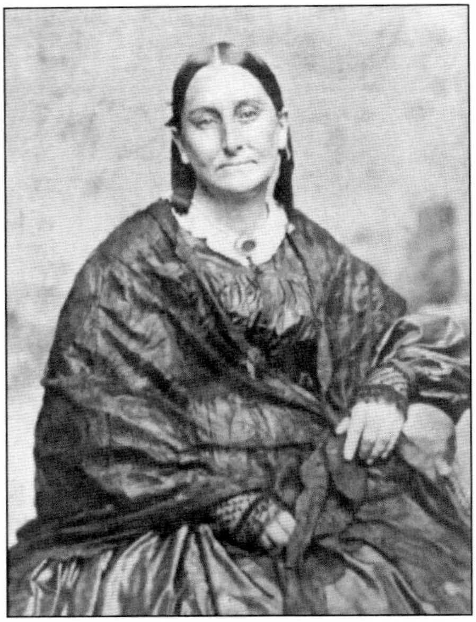

One of the youngest first settlers in Caseyville, David Denon McRee was born in Georgia on March 18, 1814, to William McRee and Mary McCorkins on their move from South Carolina to Mississippi. He is shown here with his "gypsy" wife, Epsy Mariah Leach, born on March 30, 1822, near Gallatin, Copiah County. Some other settlers in the vicinity were the Buies, Godbolds, McLaurins, Millsaps, Woolleys, and Decells. (Hattie Woolley Posey Collection.)

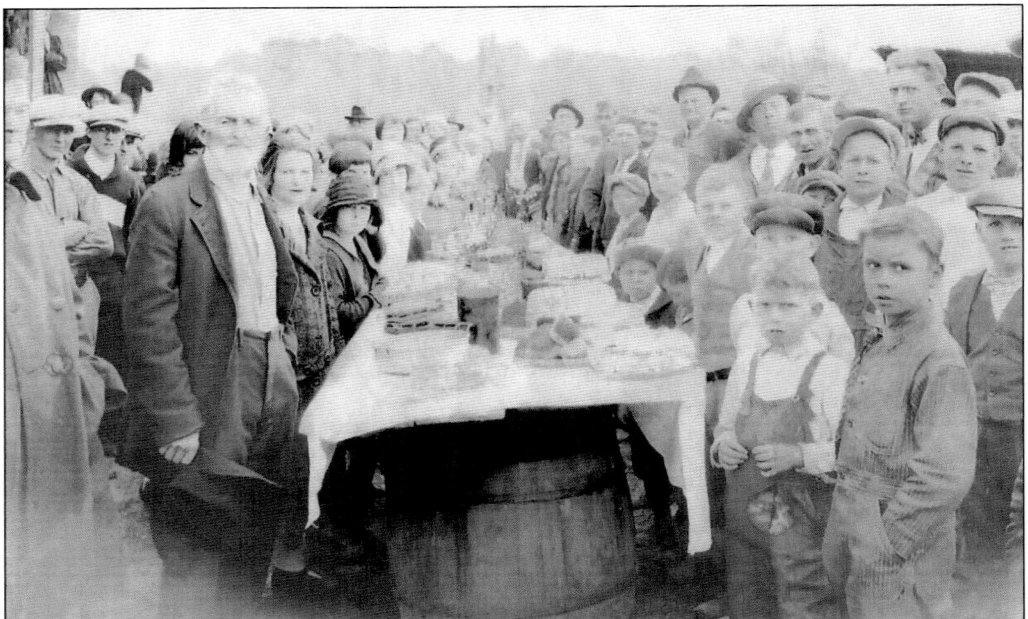

James Jackson Foster (standing to the left of the table) celebrated his birthday with his many children, grandchildren, and other family members around 1927. Foster was a Civil War prisoner of war and helped build Fort Massachusetts, on Ship Island, 12 miles off the Mississippi Coast. Standing next to Foster is his third wife, Letha Minton. Foster's previous wives had died. Foster, father to 32 children, lived and farmed in the Nola community of Lincoln County. He was born on February 19, 1843, and died of skin cancer on September 5, 1937. (Phyllis Sanders.)

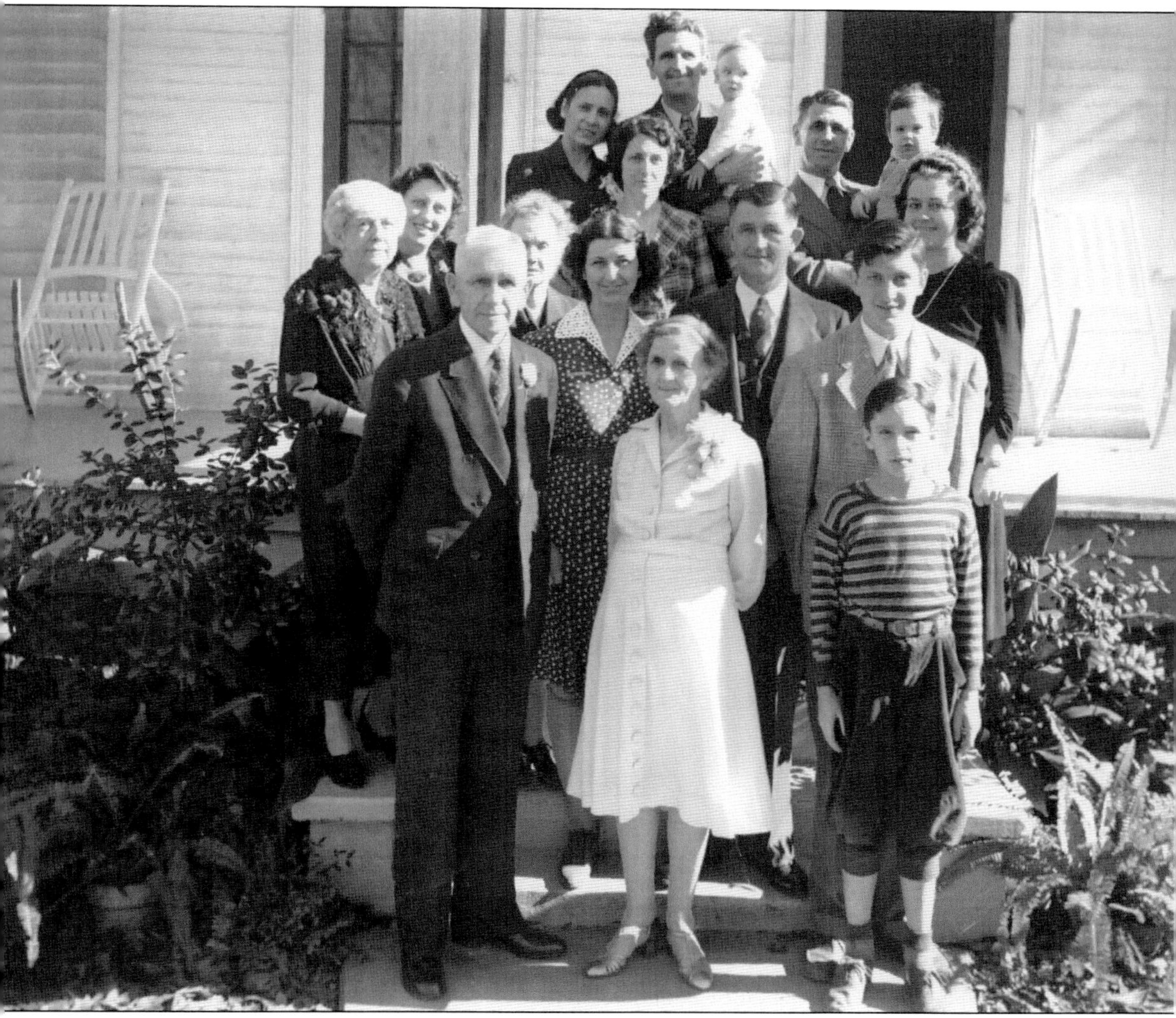

Members and friends of the Felder family gathered for a photograph in January 1946. They are, from left to right, (first row) F.S. Swalm, Wessie Martin Swalm, and Peter F. Swalm; (second row) Mary Matthews Baggett, Mamie Martin, Dolly Swalm Marchette, Frank Swalm, and W. Terry Swalm; (third row) Anelle Gordy Decell, Marjorie (Mamarge) Gordy Swalm, and Anabelle Swalm; (fourth row) Kathryn Felder Swalm, Terry S. Swalm, Terry "Steve" Swalm Jr., Sherman Swalm, and Sherman W. Swalm Jr. Mamie Martin was a beloved elementary teacher in Brookhaven. Mamie Martin Elementary School is named in her honor. (Martha Sinclair.)

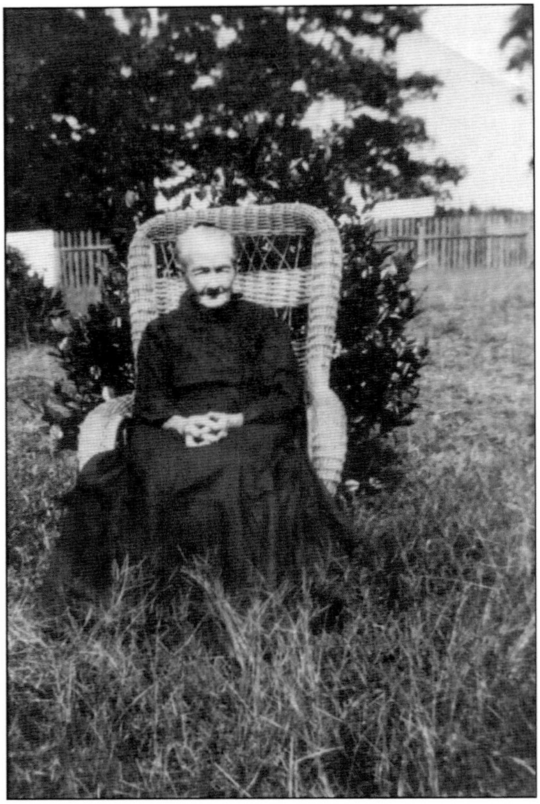

Rebecca East Smith, born on March 4, 1845, is pictured in the backyard of her daughter Catherine Smith Posey's and husband Nola's home in 1939. Rebecca was the daughter of James East and granddaughter of two early settlers, Joel East and William Lofton. (Hattie Woolley Posey Collection.)

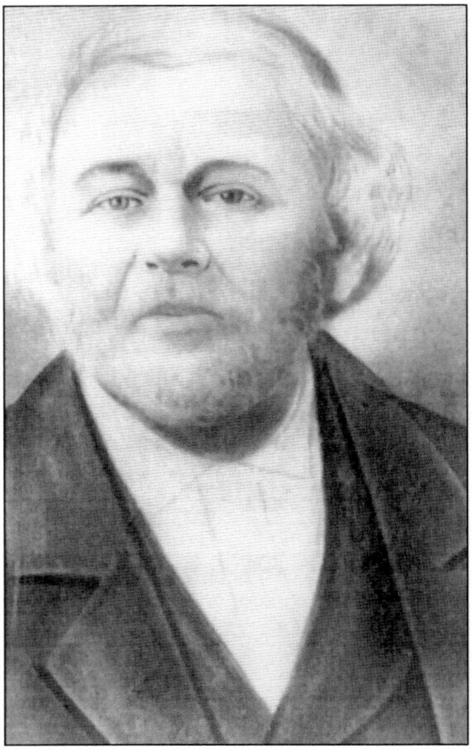

Reason W. Woolley was born on May 10, 1824, in North Carolina. He came to Copiah County to marry Elizabeth Buie on October 22, 1849. They settled at Caseyville and reared 14 children. He built the small Woolley School (later called Leake Creek School) for his and neighboring children. For many years, gypsies camped near Caseyville on their treks from New Orleans to Meridian. Local children were warned to stay close to home when gypsies were there. (Hattie Woolley Posey Collection.)

Bettie Price Dunn was born on December 20, 1847, to one of the largest landowning families in Lincoln County. Her father's land included part of the Whitworth College campus. She married Confederate veteran Samuel Dunn, and they had six sons and three daughters. She died in September 1937 and is interred next to the tomb of her husband in the Dunn Cemetery. (Barbara Todd.)

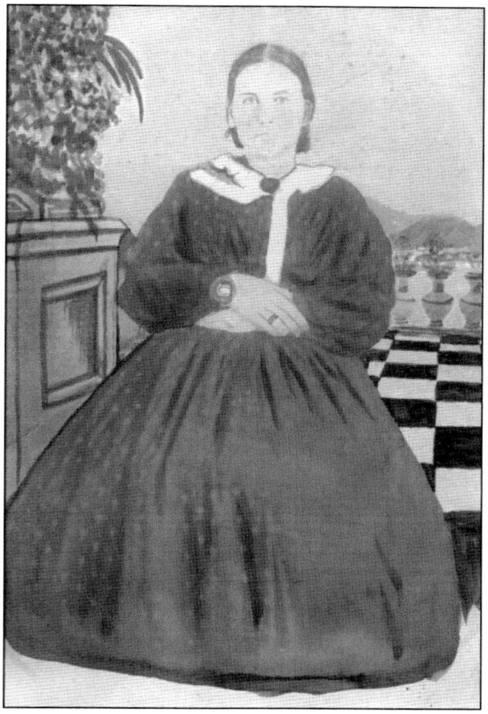

The John Jasper Smith family was photographed around 1915. Pictured are, from left to right, (first row) Smith (1851–1915) and his wife, Catherine Cupit Smith (1852–1927); (second row) children Pearl Smith, Rebecca Smith Vaughn, and Nicholas Smith. At far right is Louiza Cain, an unknown relation. The Smiths lived in the Vaughan community of Lincoln County. (Mary Jane Russell.)

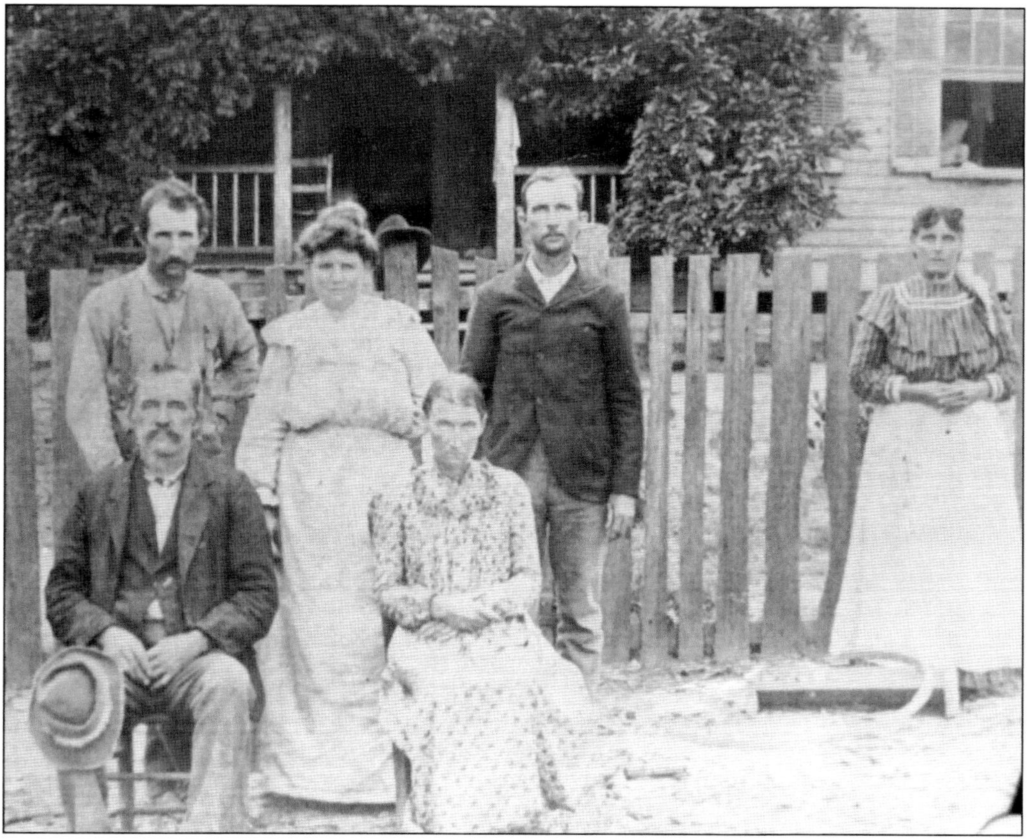

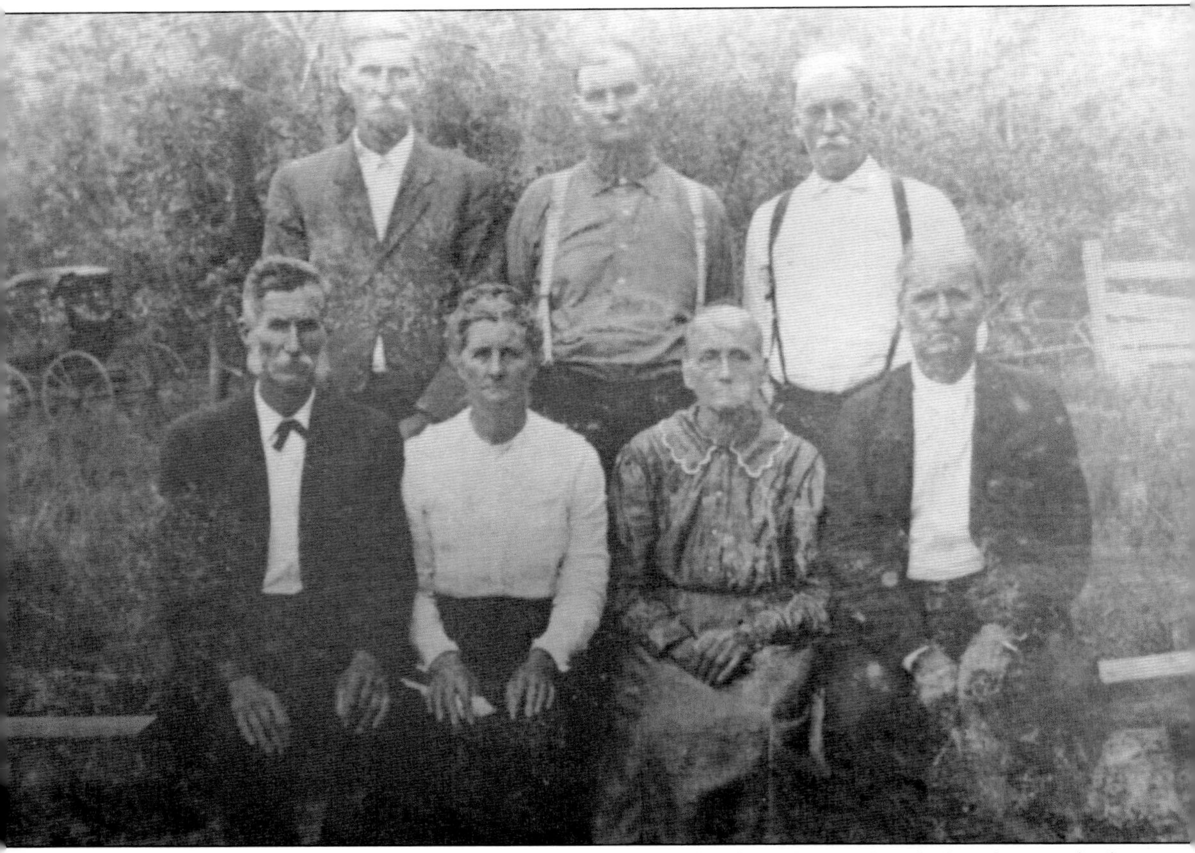

Indentured servant Andrew Moak came from Switzerland in 1740 to South Carolina with the original name Mog, which sounded like "Moak." He was the grandfather of Andrew Moak, who settled in 1811 on a tributary of the Bogue Chitto River, now called Moak's Creek. The settlement, according to a historic marker erected in 1968, claims to be the oldest in Lincoln County. The first three generations were farmers, while the last three generations have had interests in education, business, and medicine. Shown here are, from left to right, (first row) Henry Franklin Moak, Sarah M. Williams, Catherine M. Rawls, and William Moak; (second row) Owen Moak, Thaddeus Moak, and David Moak. (Martha Sinclair.)

T. Hugh Smith, born in the Mount Zion community of Lincoln County in 1870, was a lifelong resident. The son of John Everett Smith and Adeline Womack, he married Nettie McGee in 1895. Hugh was a farmer and served as Lincoln County tax assessor in 1915. He was a descendant of several generations of Smiths who migrated from North Carolina and Georgia between 1810 and 1820 and settled near the present-day Fair River Baptist Church east of Brookhaven. Later, the Hugh Smiths moved to the Mount Zion Baptist Church area in western Lincoln County. He and his wife are buried in the Macedonia Baptist Church Cemetery. (Jubal Smith.)

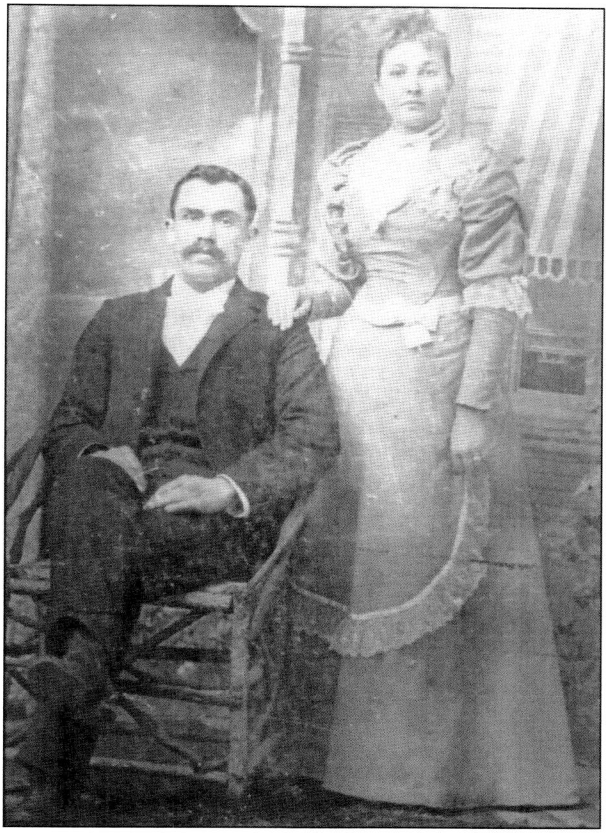

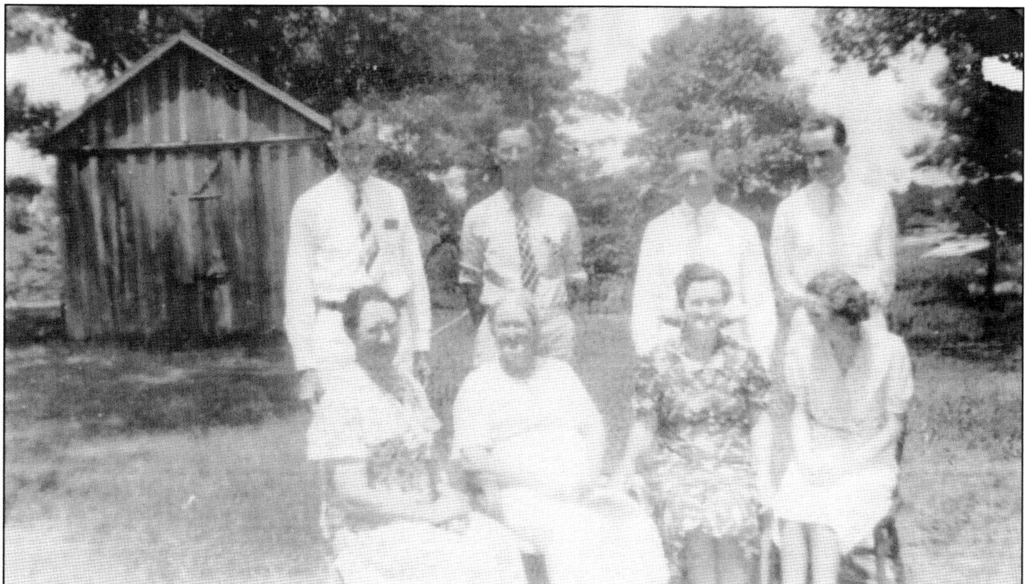

Mollie Clark is pictured with seven of her children. Shown are, from left to right, (first row) Jessie C. Roberts, Mollie, Mattie C. Kyzar, and Josie Clark Ritchie; (second row) Teunison Cary Clark, Clifton C. Clark, Clyde F. Clark, and Floyd Venable Clark. The Clarks lived in the McClendon community of Lincoln County. (Martha Sinclair.)

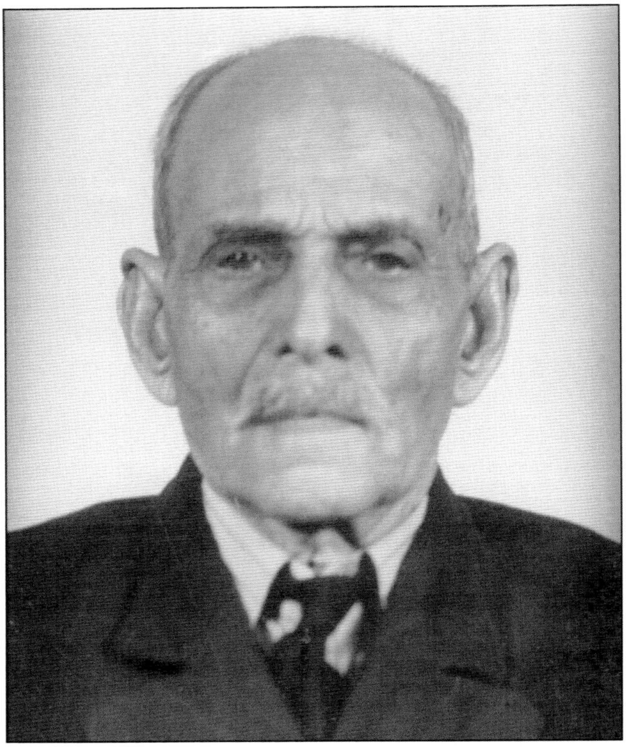

Frank D'Antoni was one of the first Italians to arrive in Lincoln County. He emigrated from Cefalu, Sicily, in 1882, first settling in California and working there as a net fisherman. In 1898, he came to Lincoln County in a wagon with only the horse and a dog as companions. He met and married Rosa Fertitta in 1901. Together, they operated a small grocery story. D'Antoni died in 1952 at the age of 97. It was said that he was a quiet man who loved God, family, and his adopted country. (Robbie Arnold.)

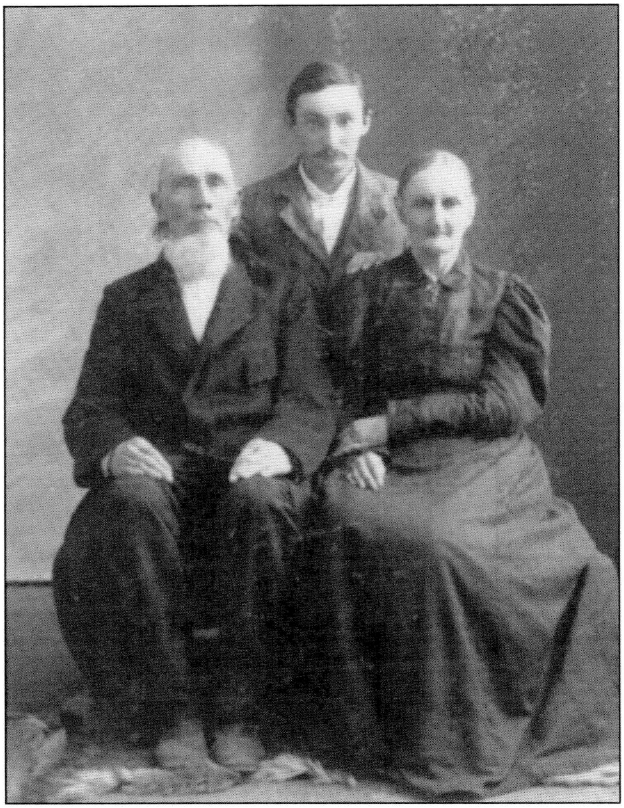

Shown here are Lorenzo Dow Posey, his wife, Lucinda Matilda Lofton, and son Rufus, who was one of six children. Lorenzo was born in 1826 in Alabama. Around 1834, he was bound out to Dudley Lofton, father of Gwinn Lofton. Lorenzo married on July 26, 1853. A sergeant during the Civil War, he was captured in Salisbury, North Carolina, on April 12, 1865, and was a prisoner of war at Camp Chase, Ohio. He never talked about his life, sending his descendants on years of detective work. (Hattie Woolley Posey Collection.)

Three

Diversity in Industry, Agriculture, and Business

Although the lumber industry was initially the main moneymaking business in the county, it was not long before things changed. The tall, yellow longleaf pine trees disappeared, and the lumber companies moved on.

The railroad was still there, and people were encouraged to farm. The rich soil would grow almost any crop that was planted. Early settlers became farmers and dairymen, paving the way for two local creameries, one of them shipping butter as far as New York. Bogue Chitto, New Sight, and East Lincoln were locations of large community hatcheries. Chickens and eggs were shipped by train.

Cotton may not have been king, but it was a major crop, along with sweet potatoes, corn, and peas. Soon, a canning factory was needed, and a new industry was started. These farmers needed seeds to plant and other supplies for their home; those who could not farm opened stores that sold these supplies.

The largest gravel pit in the United States was located in the county, with shipments made as far as Memphis, Tennessee. At one time, the roads between Jackson and Memphis were covered with gravel from Lincoln County. Growing gladioli became a big business in the county; entire families participated in picking and packing the gladioli, which were then shipped by train to customers.

As soon as automobiles became popular, dealerships and repair shops opened. An Auto Laundry opened for business, guaranteeing that it would "absolutely clean your car." If there was a need, someone stepped up and started a business that fulfilled that need, thus creating a new industry.

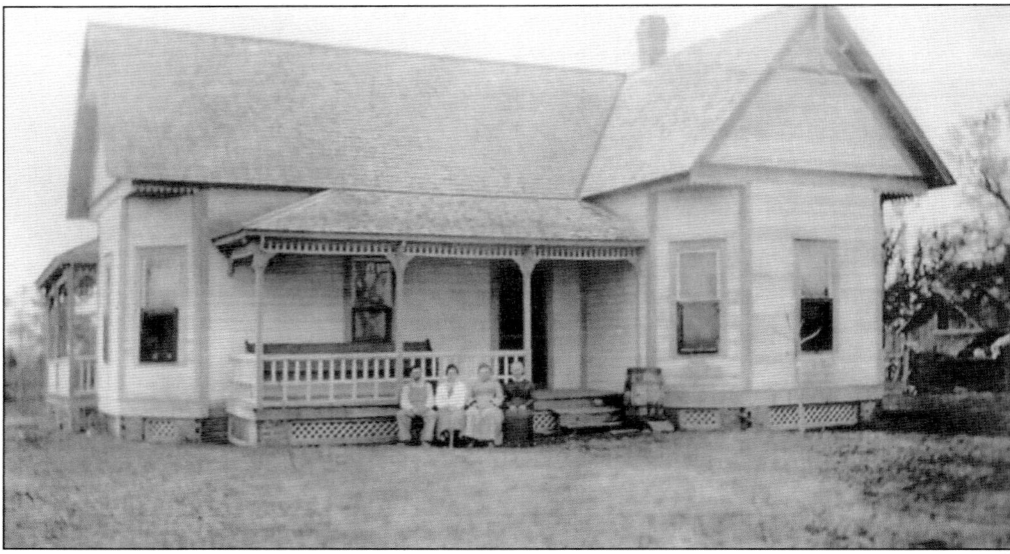

The Freine family, originally from France, is believed to have operated the first Lincoln County dairy, which bottled milk and delivered to homes. Eugene Freine (left) immigrated to the United States on July 25, 1892, on the ship *La Gascogne* from the Port of Le Havre, France. Freine family graves can be found in the St. Francis of Assisi Catholic Church Cemetery. (LCHGS.)

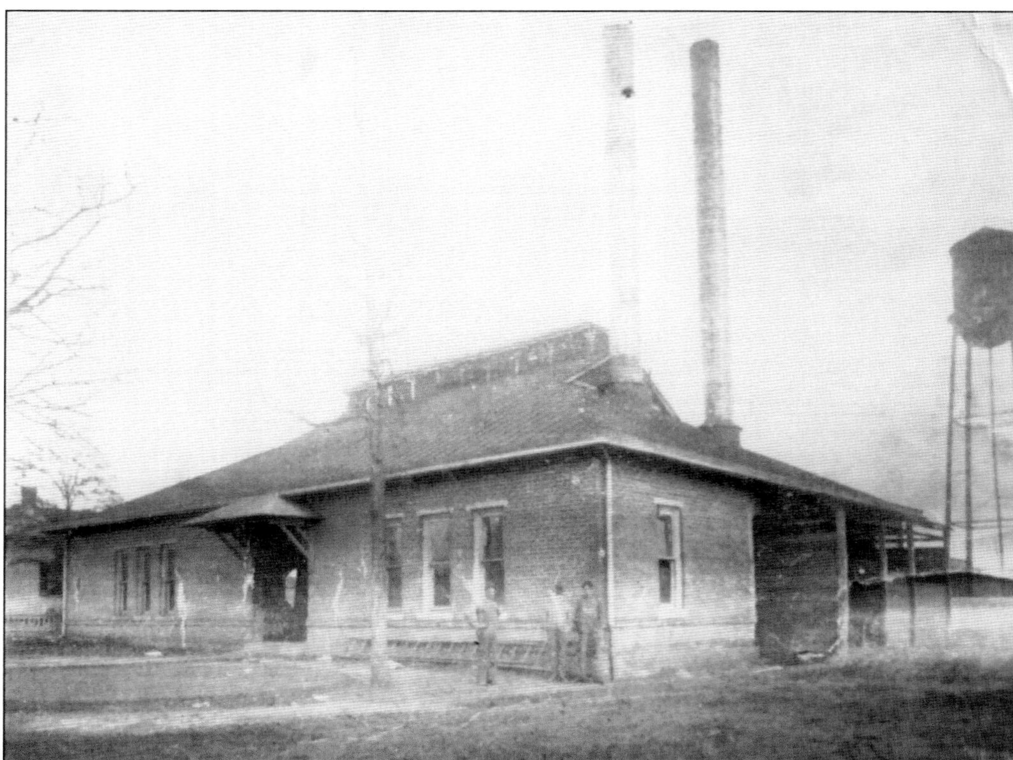

Brookhaven's first electrical power and water plant was erected around 1898 north of downtown. Its unique dual smokestacks could be seen from passing trains. A 90,000-gallon water tower was also constructed near the site. One smokestack still remains today. (LLF.)

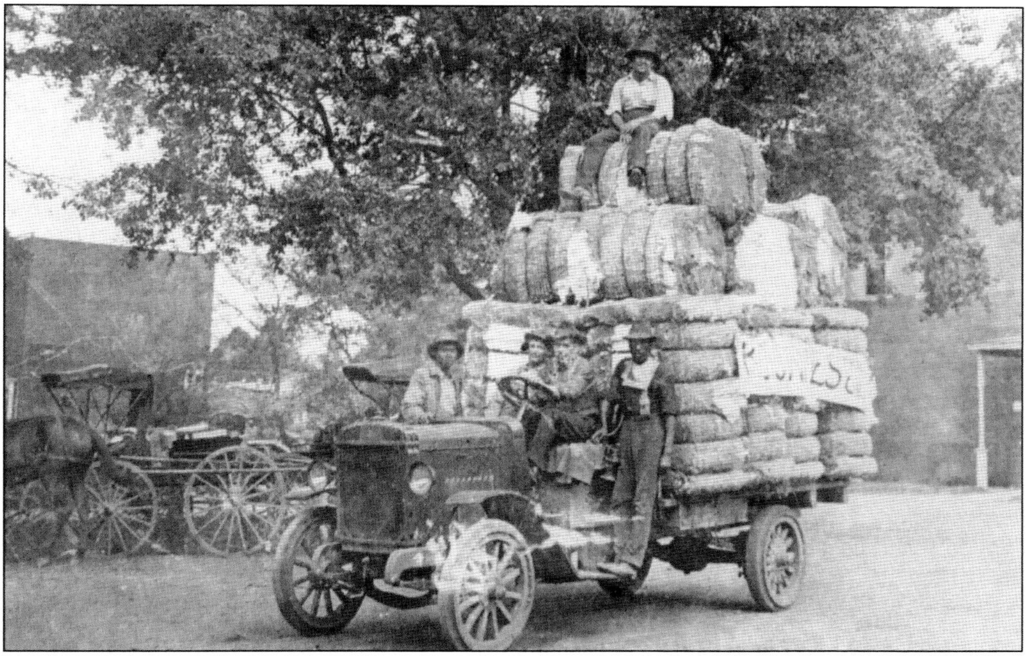

Bartley Eugene "Gene" James (1879–1948) sits on top of cotton bales as his younger brother, Med Davidson James, drives them to Brookhaven. Gene was the fourth child of John Quincy James, who moved his family from Copiah County to Lincoln County around 1900. Gene was active in local politics, serving as an alderman for 18 years, and was instrumental in building Brookhaven Elementary School on South Church Street. (Edna James Kinchloe Collection.)

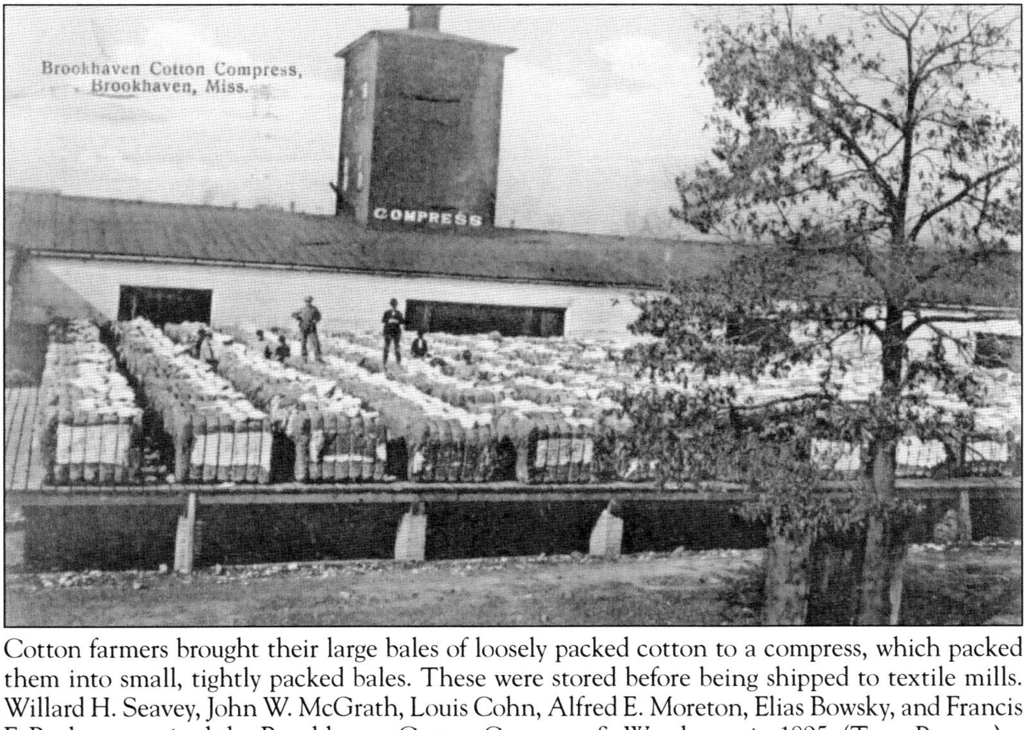

Cotton farmers brought their large bales of loosely packed cotton to a compress, which packed them into small, tightly packed bales. These were stored before being shipped to textile mills. Willard H. Seavey, John W. McGrath, Louis Cohn, Alfred E. Moreton, Elias Bowsky, and Francis F. Becker organized the Brookhaven Cotton Compress & Warehouse in 1895. (Terry Pappas.)

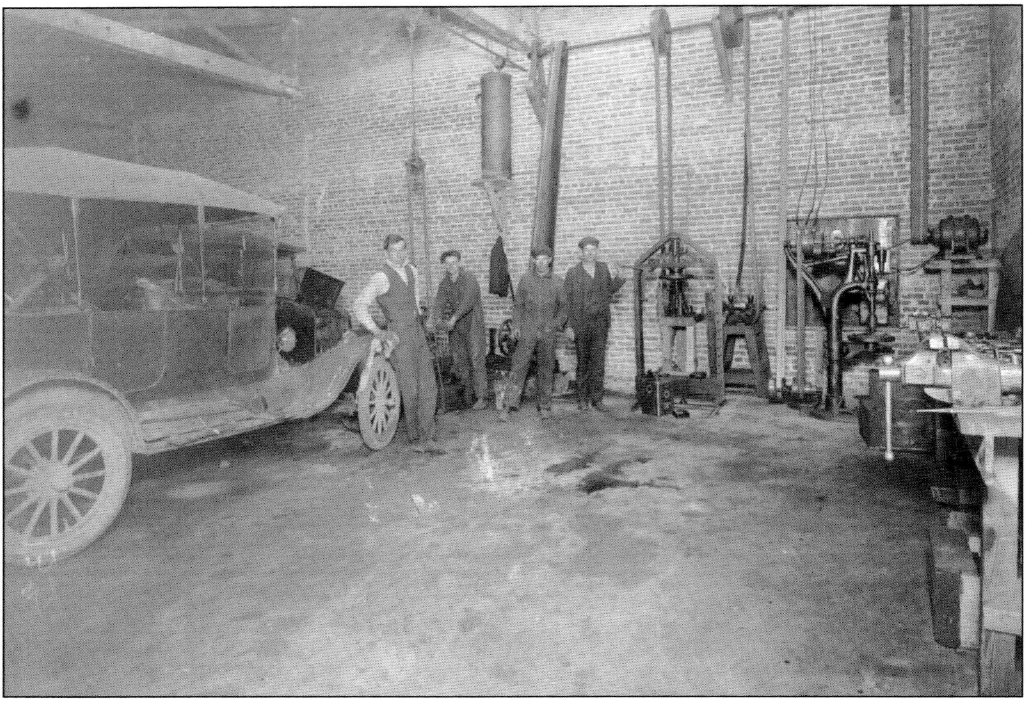

Med James (far left) visits the Laird garage in downtown Brookhaven. James, fascinated by motors and cars, later became a mechanic. At this time, Laird's garage was probably the most progressive in town and was open on South First Street for many years. The other men are not identified, but one is said to be Laird. A few years after this photograph was made, Laird purchased the Ford dealership in Lincoln County. (LLF.)

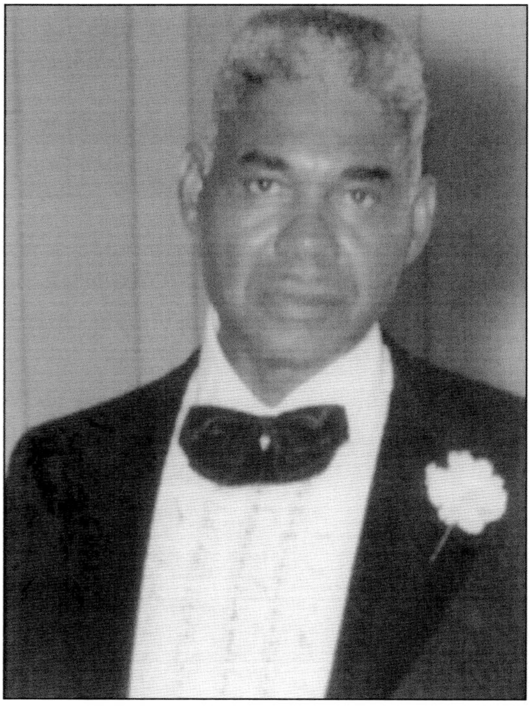

In the late 1930s, Robert Smith, born in 1917, was the first black male to own a cleaners (Smith Cleaners) and a motel (later Smith Apartments) in Brookhaven. Through the years, his businesses expanded into White Castles Café, a barbershop, and Robert Smith Logging. He was a member of the NAACP, Masons, and Elks. He was married to Alberta Newman and, later, Mary Emma Diggs. He died on November 22, 1998. (Maxine Allen.)

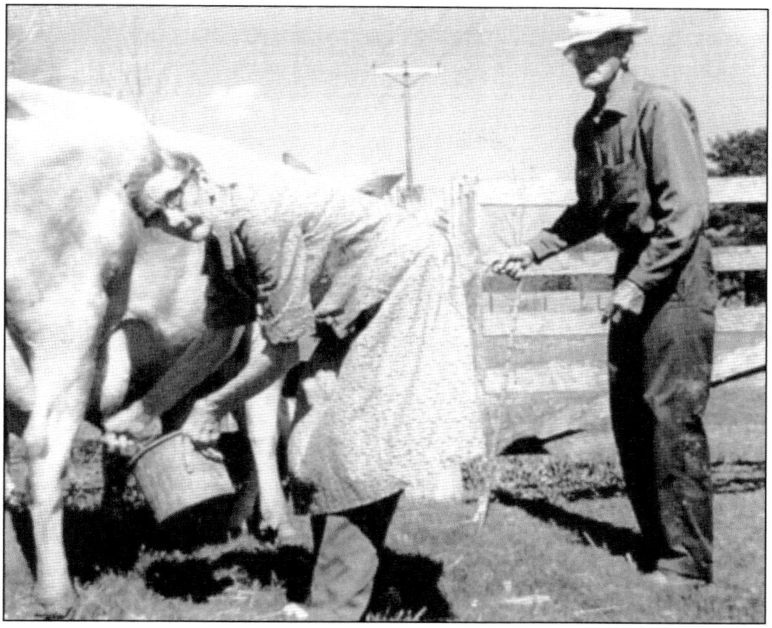

Wylie Allen and his wife, Lela, milked cows by hand at least once per day. Fresh milk was poured from the bucket into cans, and Wylie loaded the cans onto his truck and drove them from the Loyd Star community to a dairy in Brookhaven. Between milking, he grew cotton, until the government began paying farmers not to grow cotton. (Seth Allen.)

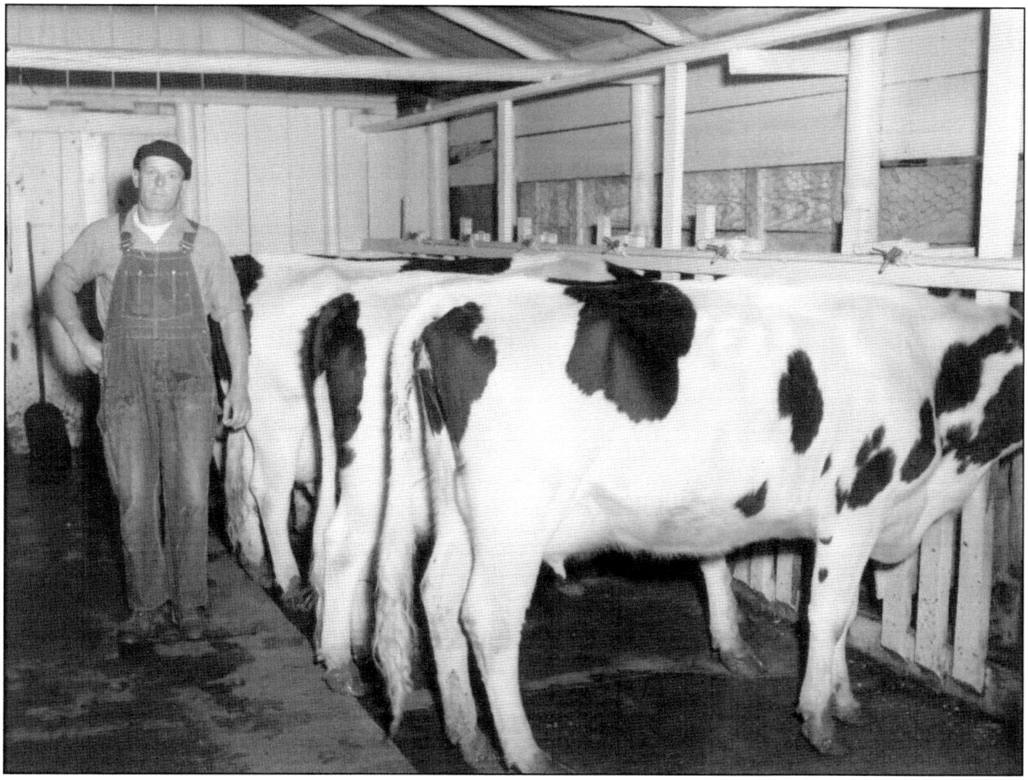

This unidentified dairy farmer was photographed by a member of the Mississippi Farm Bureau between 1940 and 1960 as he toured and visited agricultural facilities throughout the state. Note the cleanliness of the barn, the cattle feeders used as the cows were being milked, and the man's clothing, which was typical for a dairy farmer at that time. (MDAH.)

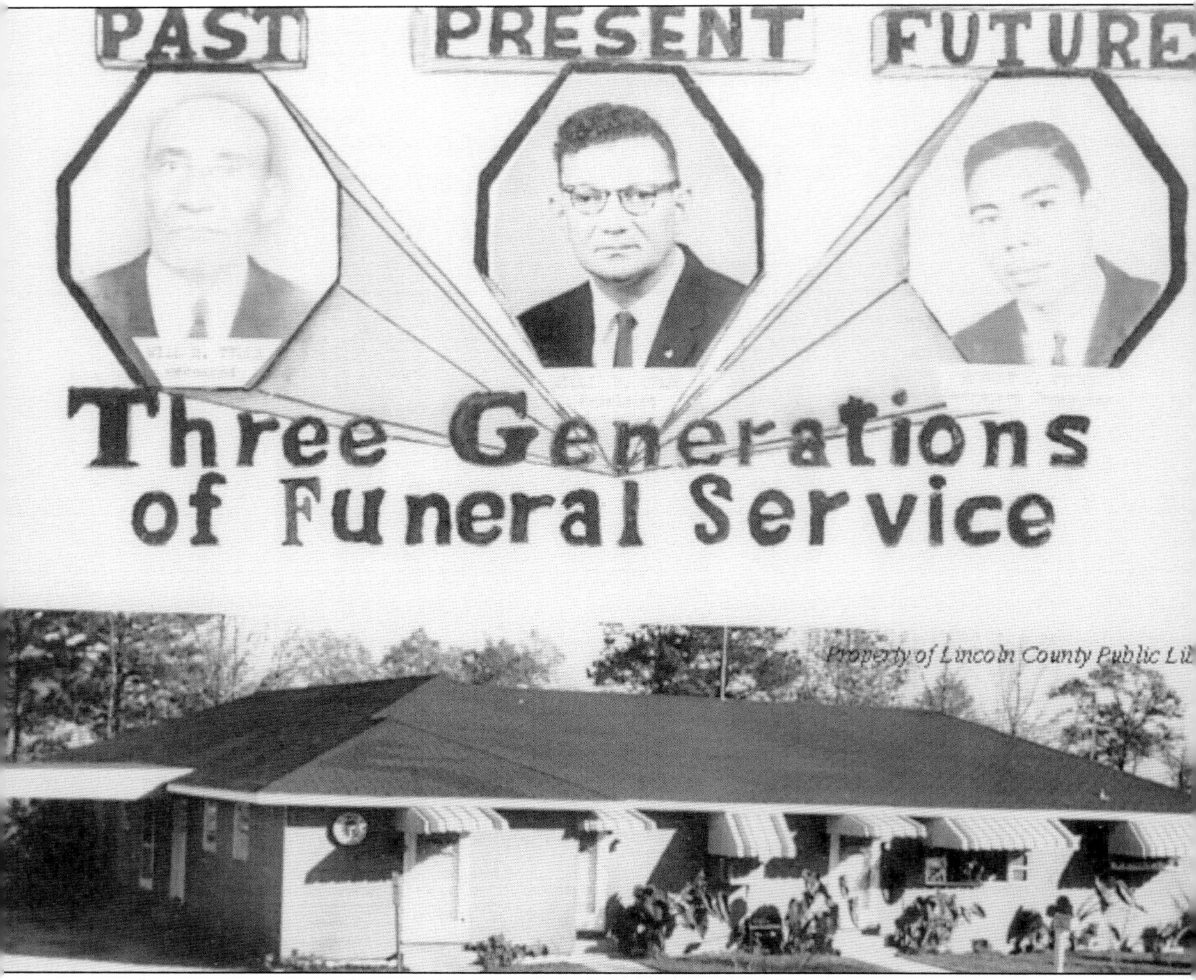

"Three Generations of Funeral Service" reads the text in an advertisement for the Tyler Funeral Home, which shows the building and its past, present, and future leaders. The men shown are Will R. Tyler (left), Willie R. Tyler, president (center), and Robert Tyler, secretary-treasurer. The funeral home was founded in February 1960 and is still serving families in 2015 under the leadership of Robert, his wife, Ruby, and their daughter Robin Tyler Faust. (LLF.)

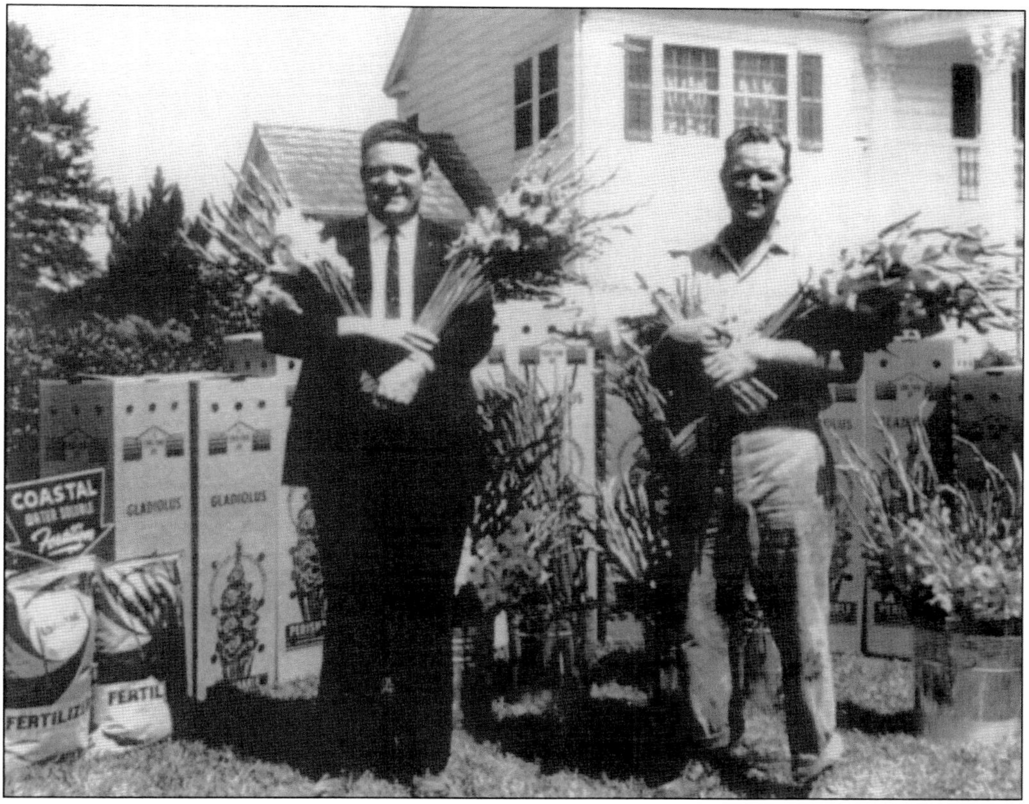

Several families living in Lincoln County grew gladioli and shipped them by train to wholesale florists in Chicago. Pictured are future country comedian Jerry Clower (left), at that time a salesman for the Yazoo Chemical Company, and Frank Burns, a local gladioli grower. Burns had about 50 acres planted with these beautiful flowers. (Carroll Montgomery.)

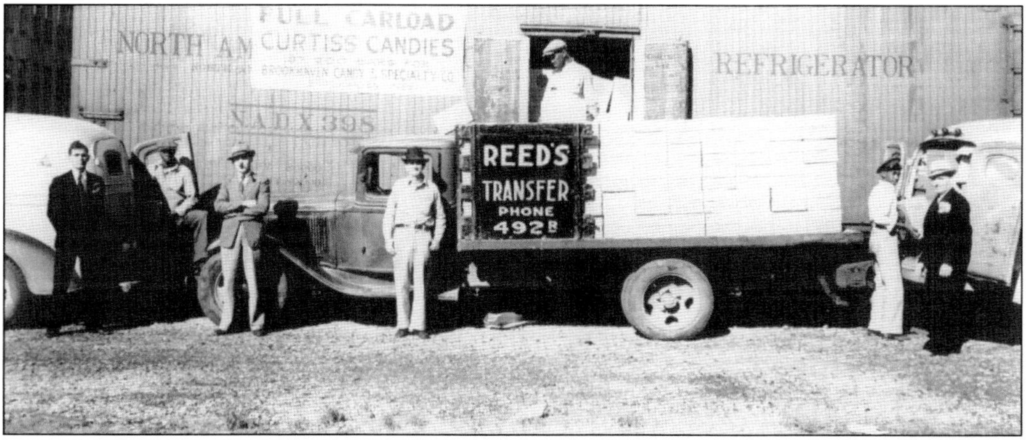

Unloading 187,200 Curtis Candy Bars for the Brookhaven Candy & Specialty Company are P.L. Douglas, Herbert Douglas, Lonnie P. Reed and E.E. Thompson. Their positions in the photograph are not known. (Barbara Todd.)

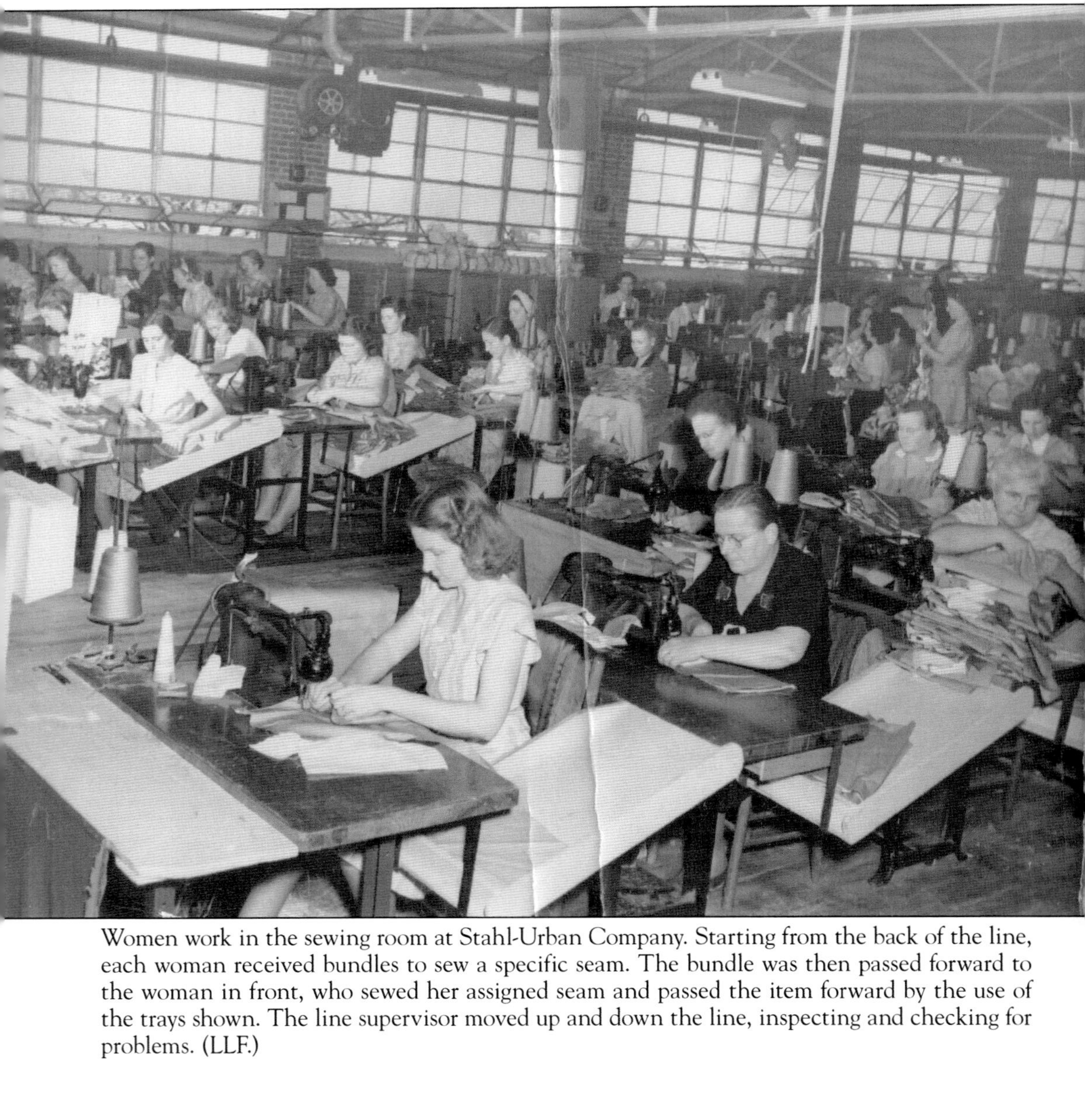

Women work in the sewing room at Stahl-Urban Company. Starting from the back of the line, each woman received bundles to sew a specific seam. The bundle was then passed forward to the woman in front, who sewed her assigned seam and passed the item forward by the use of the trays shown. The line supervisor moved up and down the line, inspecting and checking for problems. (LLF.)

Stella West (right) and her sister Louise West moved from Staunton, Indiana, to Brookhaven in February 1936 as part of the work crew with Stahl-Urban Company. Stella would later meet J.P. Reeves, marry, and have a son, Keith. Keith said his mother was 25 or 26 when she moved to Brookhaven and his aunt was three years her senior. (Keith Reeves.)

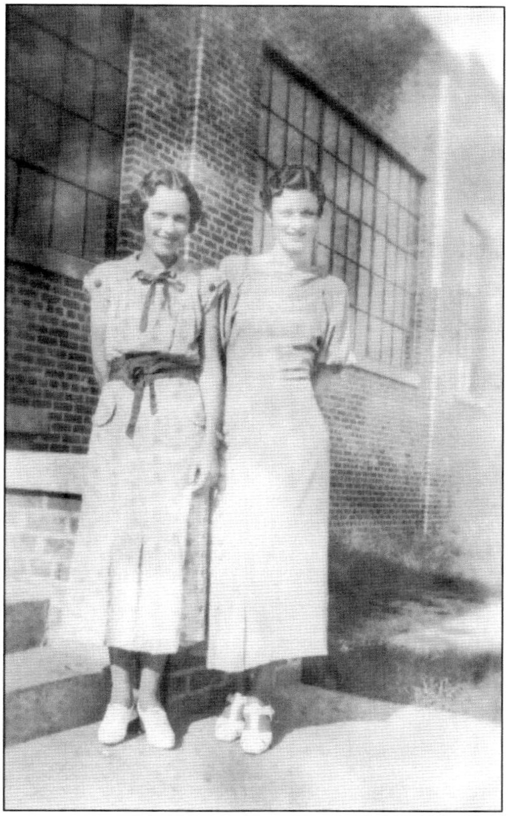

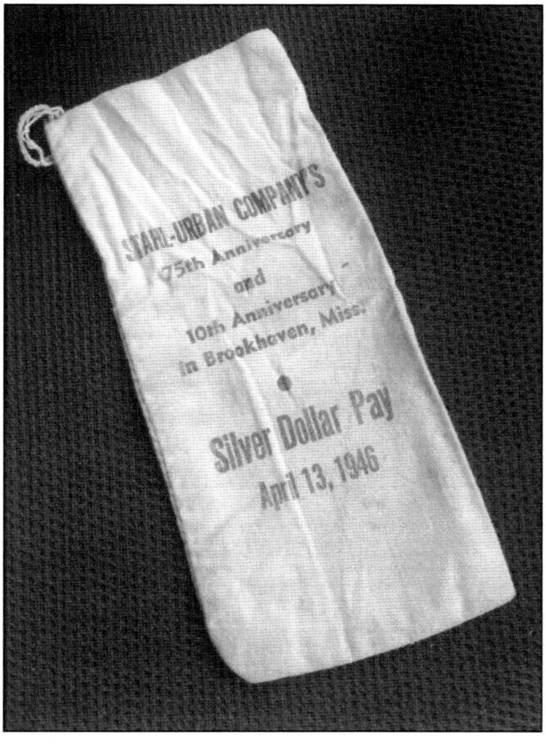

Stahl-Urban Company presented employees' wages in silver dollars once a year, to show merchants where employees spent their money and how the factory impacted the local economy. This particular canvas bag, dated April 13, 1946, was made in honor of the company's 75th anniversary and its 10th anniversary in Brookhaven. (Tammie Santos Brewer.)

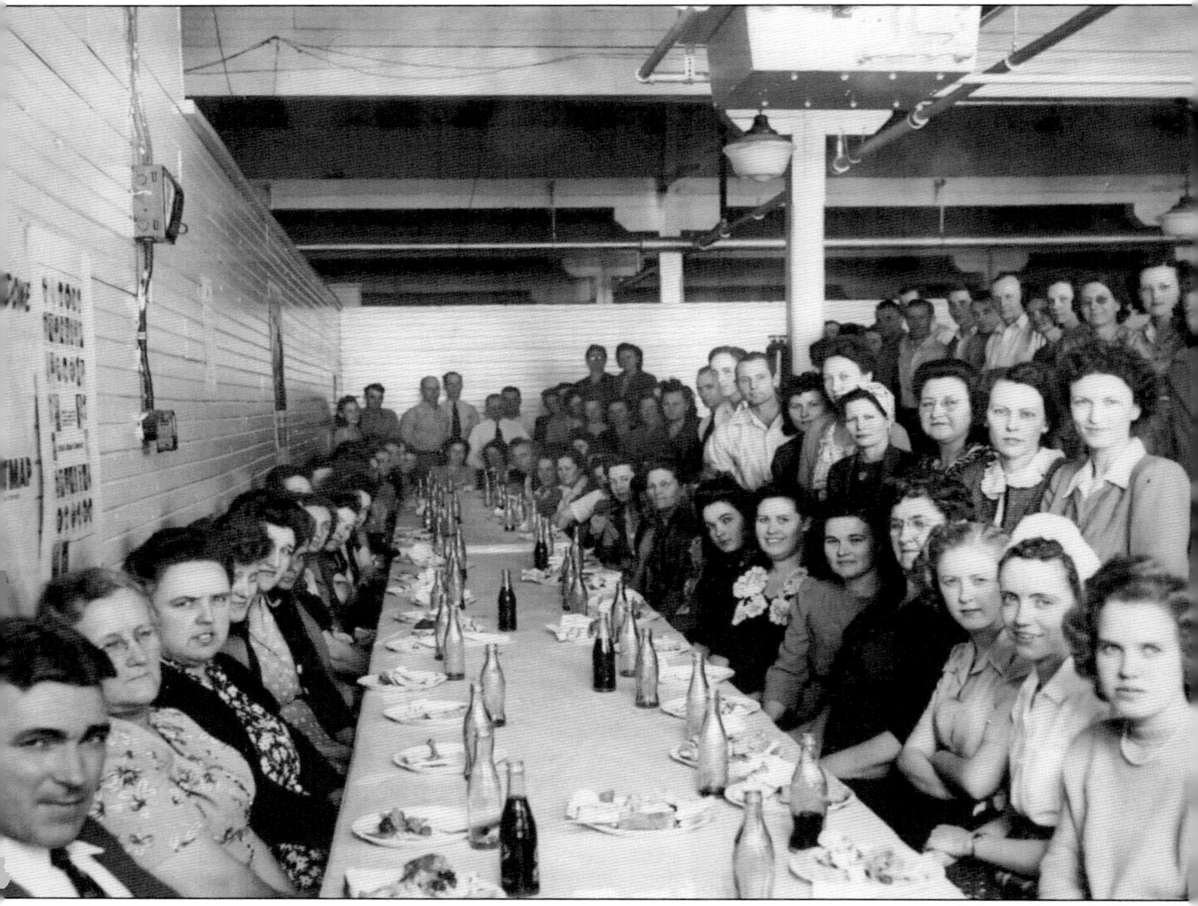

Stahl-Urban Company employees are shown at an annual Christmas dinner around 1950. Each employee was provided a meal and a bottled Coca-Cola. Identified are John A. Garrigan Jr. (far left), vice president of production, who moved to Brookhaven from Indiana with the company; Hazel Allen (seated, second from right); and Helen Montgomery (seated, third from right). (LLF.)

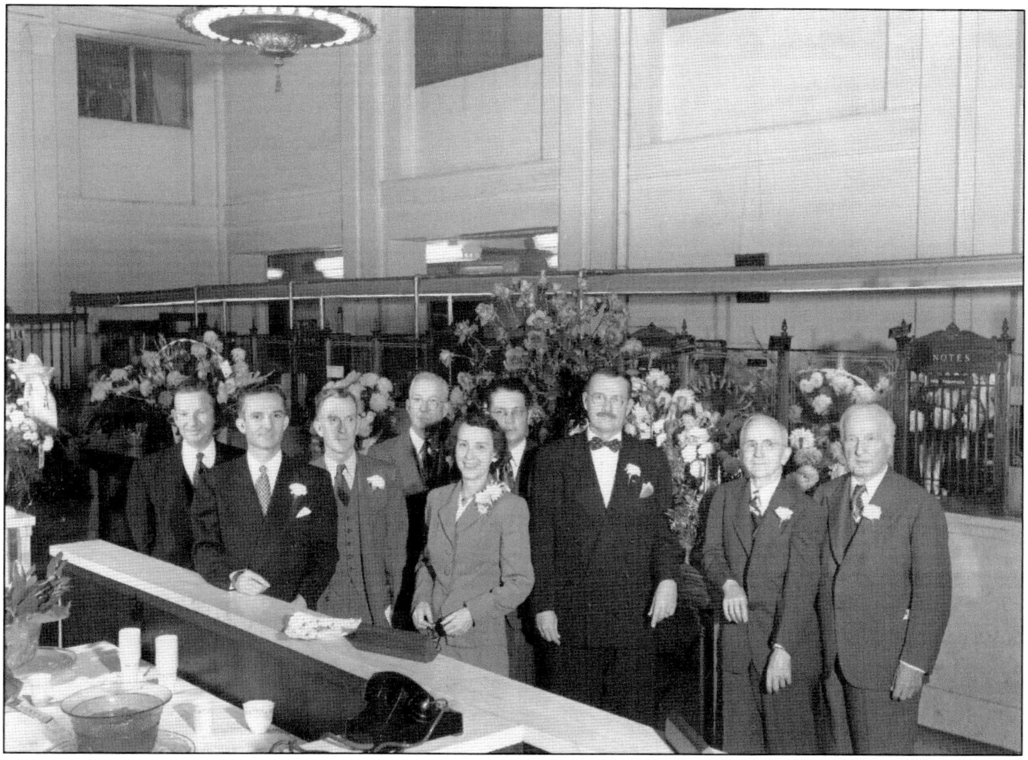

Brookhaven Bank & Trust observed its 50th anniversary with a celebration at its main office on Whitworth Avenue. Shown here are, from left to right, Elisha Washington Brien, Francis Ferdinand Becker, S.E. Moreton Jr., Virgil D. Youngblood, Stella T. Harper, T.E. Applewhite, Judge Tom Brady, Charles Marion Higdon, and Samuel Evans Moreton Sr. The bank was originally incorporated in December 1900 as Bank of Brookhaven, but was chartered as Brookhaven Bank & Trust in 1907. (LLF.)

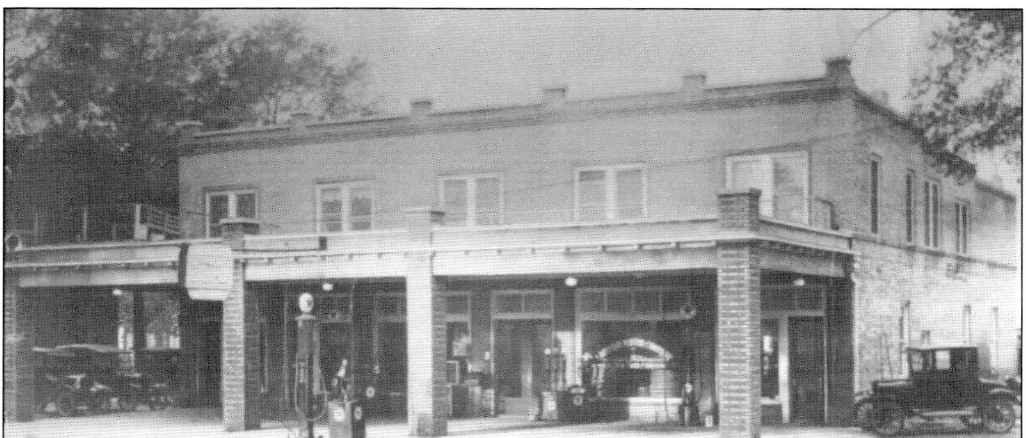

The Laird-Day Motor Company was founded in 1924 by L.J. Laird and Clyde Day. It was the local dealership for Ford, Mercury, and Lincoln automobiles. The partnership was dissolved when Day became postmaster. In January 1940, the dealership was sold to Chester Clark and R.M. Ayers. This building is located across from the present-day Lincoln County/Brookhaven Government Complex. (LLF.)

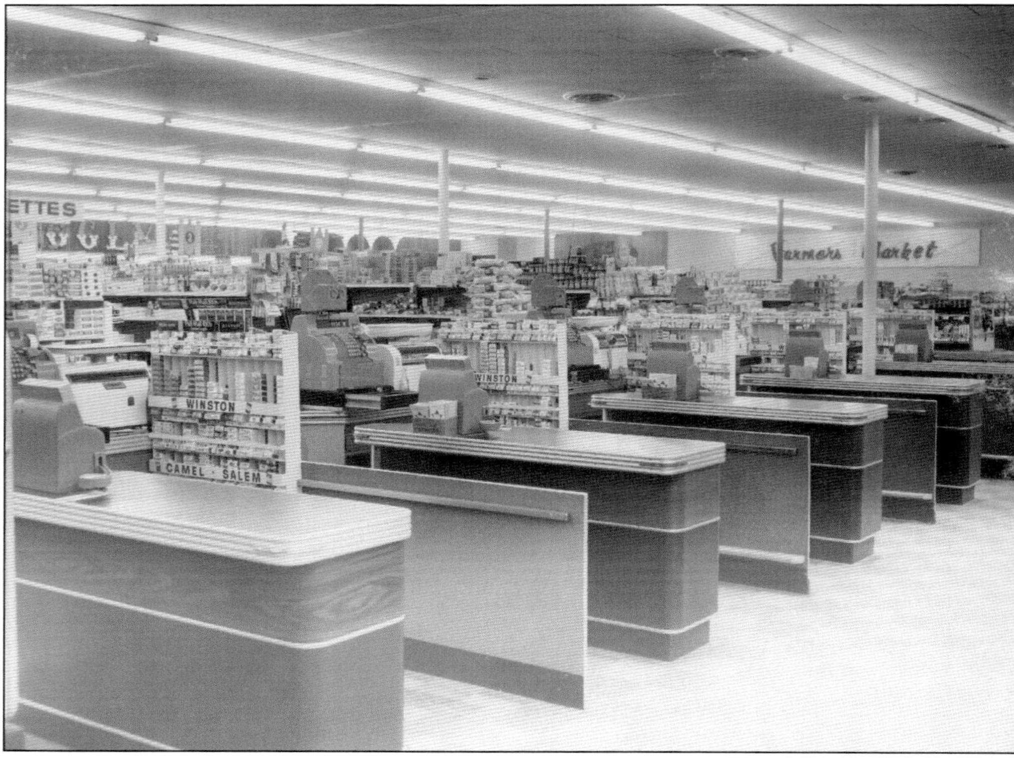

Roy Malta was granted a franchise to operate a Piggly Wiggly grocery store in Brookhaven, and construction on the new store began in November 1951 at the corner of Court and South Jackson Streets. The brick building was to be 100 feet by 46 feet, with all-new fixtures and merchandise. Malta was the owner of Malta Grocery Store and the Rex Theatre. (Both, LLF.)

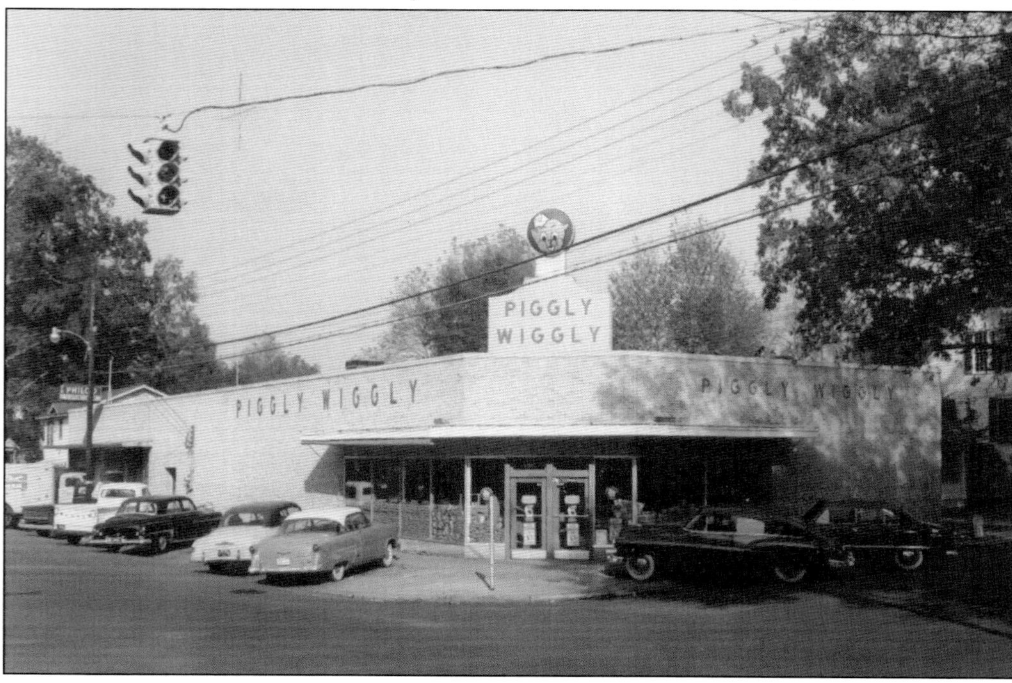

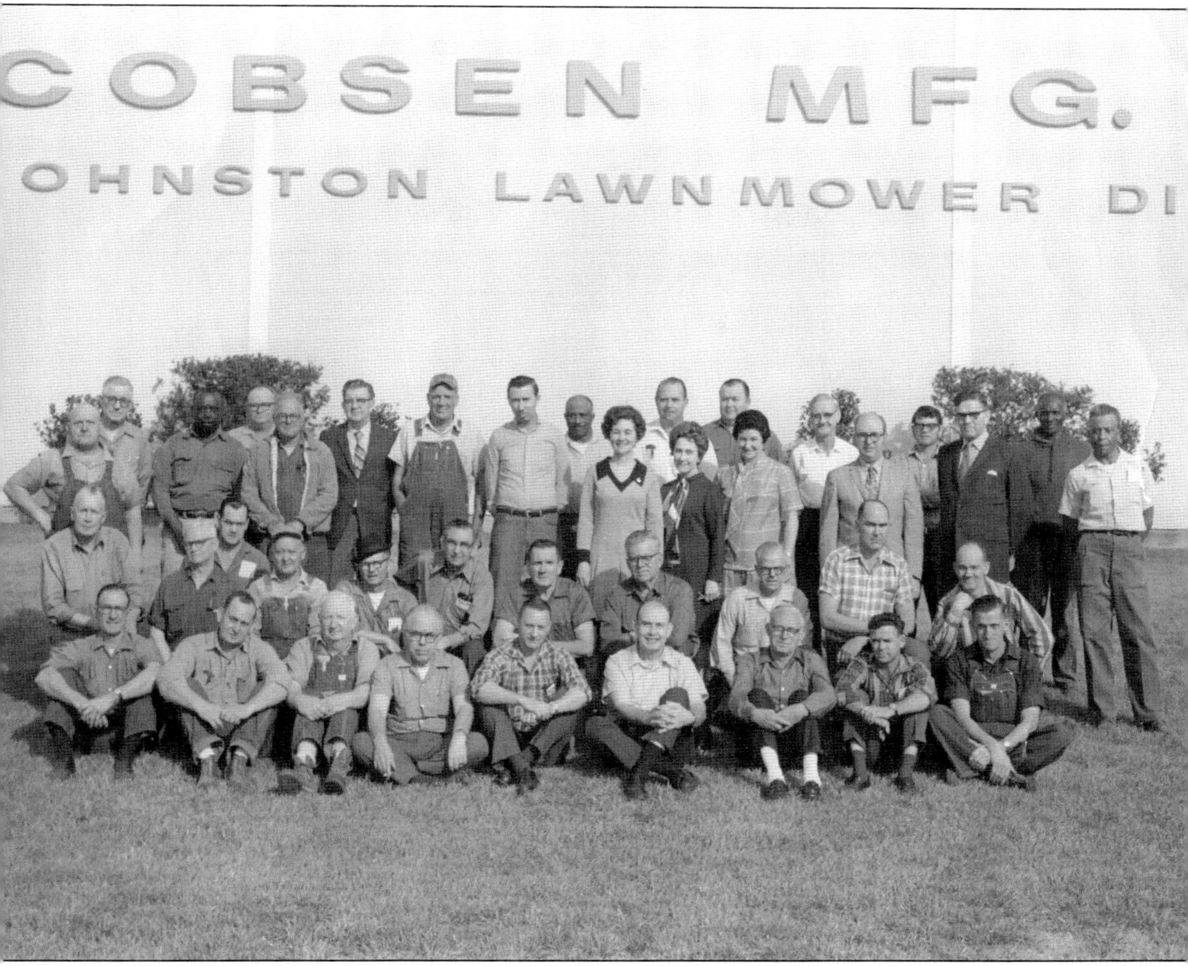

Employees of Jacobsen Manufacturing Company, Johnston Lawnmower Division, in Brookhaven gather below the building's sign. The plant was located in Brookhaven's Industrial Park. Johnston Lawn Mower selected Brookhaven as a new plant site in 1952, and a 237,175-square-foot building was constructed on the 21-acre lot. After standing vacant for many years, the building and site were sold to a developer in 2008, and the original building was torn down. (Carroll Montgomery.)

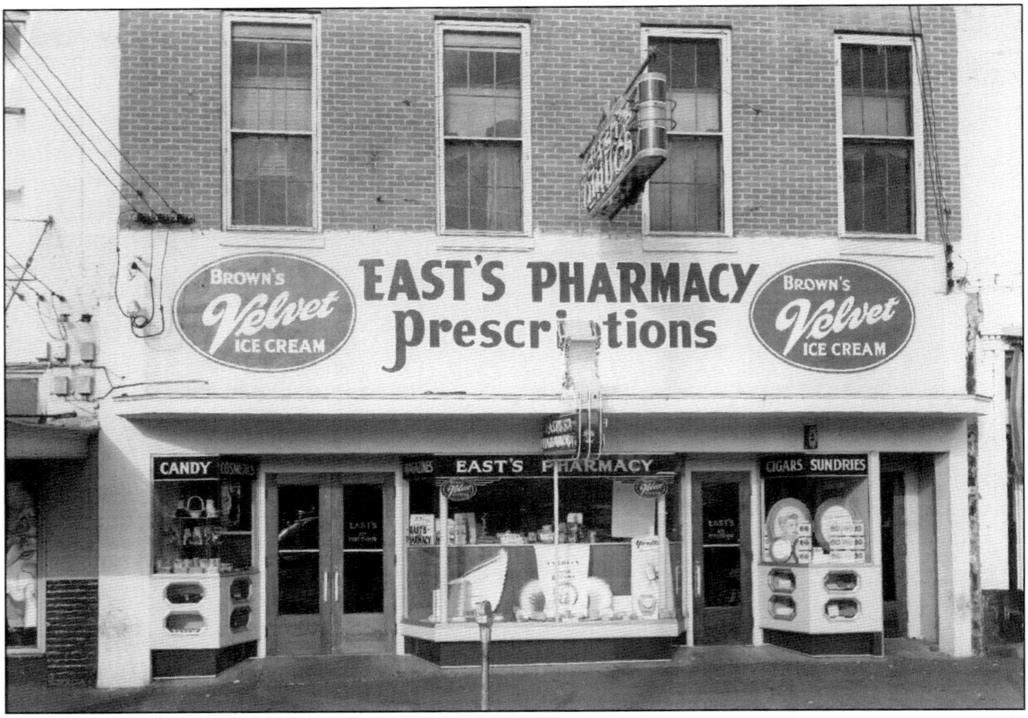

In 1943, Floyd C. East, a well-known local pharmacist, decided to open his own drugstore. He decided he would carry everything a drugstore sold, but would specialize in prescription medicine. It became one of the 10 largest and best-equipped drugstores in the state. Floyd's sons Billy East and Floyd East Jr. ran the store after his death. Today, it is remembered for the good service given and the fresh-roasted cashew nuts sold there. (LLF.)

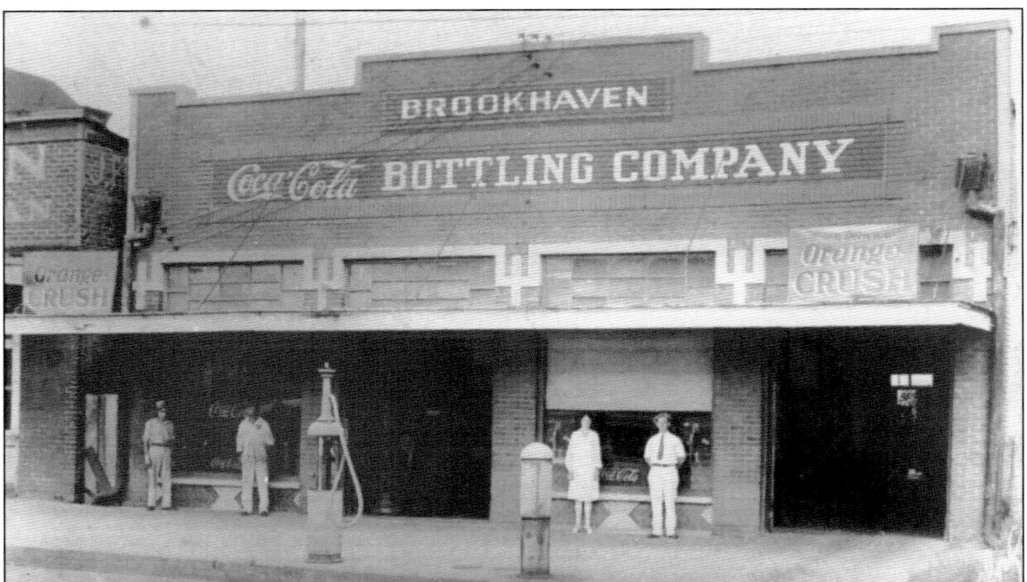

The Brookhaven Coca-Cola Bottling Company, located on South Railroad Avenue, was legally chartered by the State of Mississippi on February 17, 1923, with William B. Elrod, registered agent. A new building was constructed later at the intersection of Highways 51 and Old 84. (LLF.)

The Brookhaven Locker Plant was located on First Street. Families having livestock butchered, or with more vegetables on hand than storage capacity at home, could pay for freezer use. (LLF.)

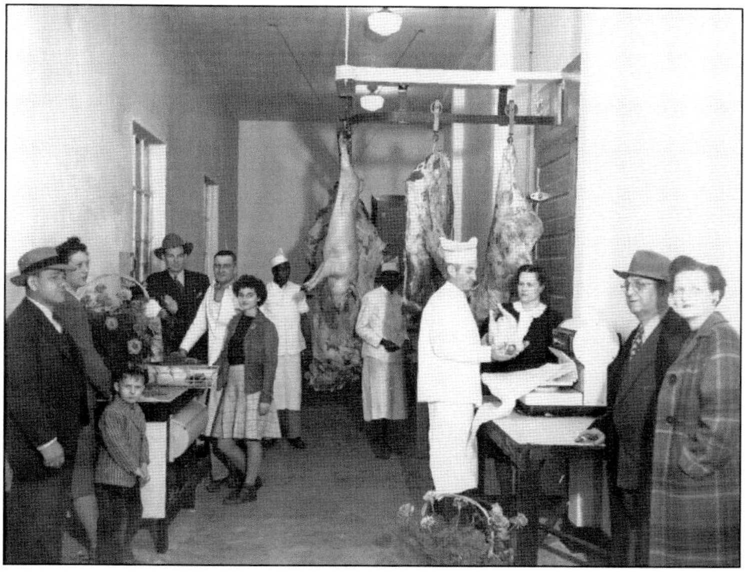

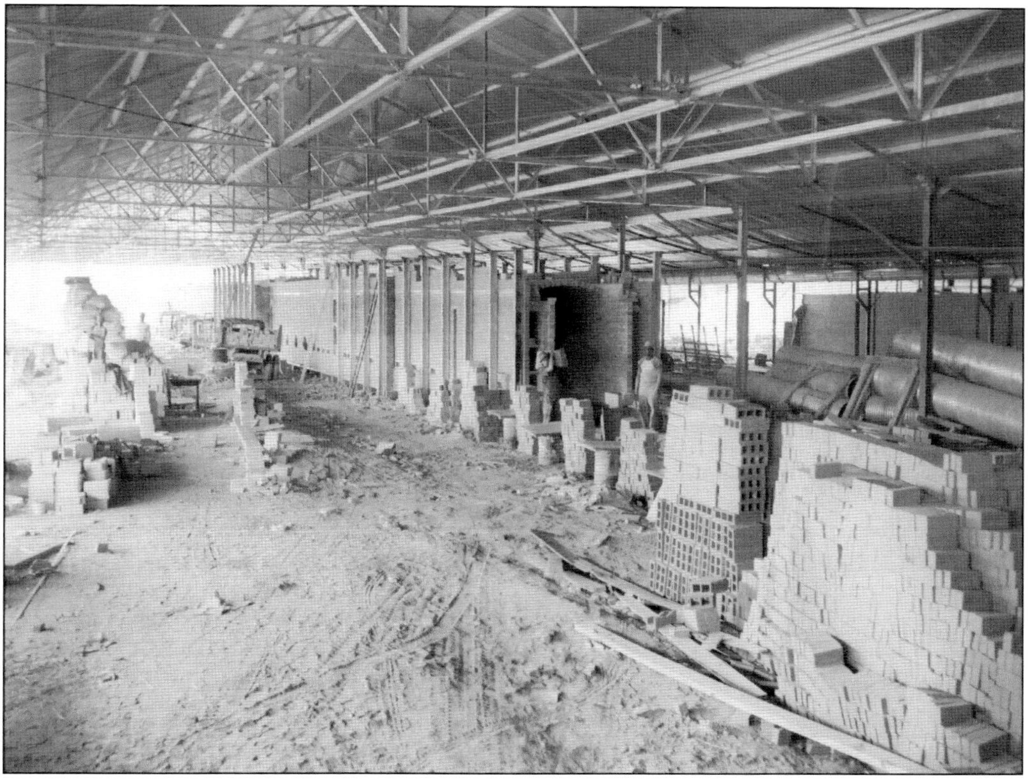

Incorporated in July 1906 by J.J. Phillips and his associates, Brookhaven Pressed Brick & Manufacturing produced brick from deposits of clay in Lincoln County. All the brick used locally had been handmade until the Brookhaven plant began producing machine-made bricks. It shipped brick all over Mississippi and to adjoining states. Most of the new buildings in town, including First Baptist Church and the post office, were built with brick made by this company. Officers in the company were Felix May, A.C. McNair, Hyman Zwirn, Hiram Cassedy, and Martin D. McGrath. (LLF.)

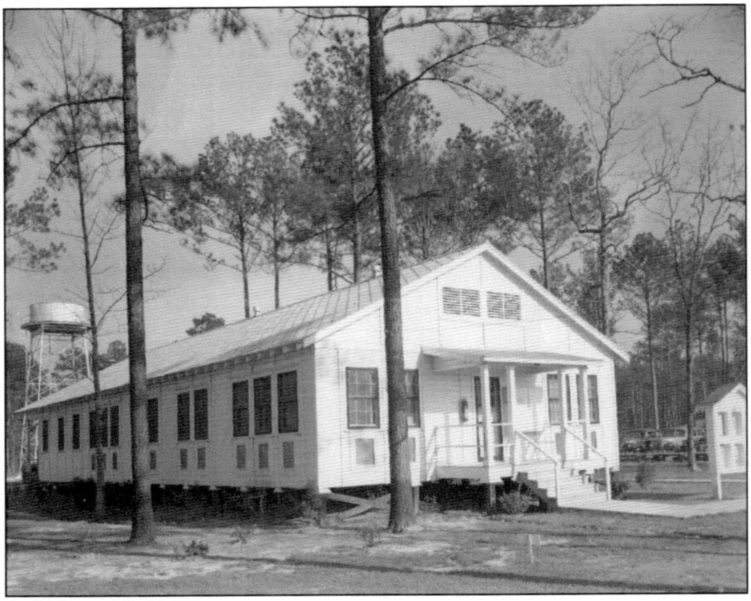

This building was identified as belonging to Humble Oil Company in the 1940s. Humble & California Oil Company built three styles of similar white, wood-frame buildings: an office, a barracks for single male workers, and small houses for workers with families. When the oil business moved to other areas, most of the buildings were sold to local people and moved to their property. (LLF.)

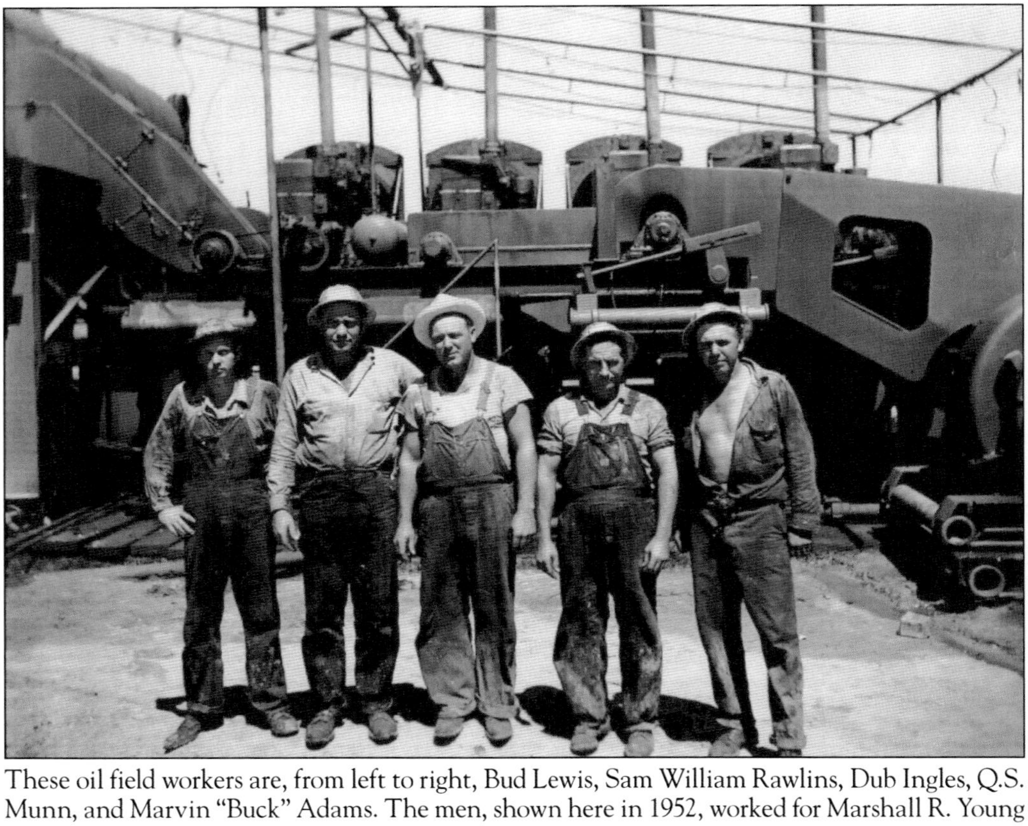

These oil field workers are, from left to right, Bud Lewis, Sam William Rawlins, Dub Ingles, Q.S. Munn, and Marvin "Buck" Adams. The men, shown here in 1952, worked for Marshall R. Young Drilling Company. (LLF.)

J.W. Fore's store was located diagonally across the street from Brookhaven's post office. The store burned down in April 1928. Fore had stores in Bastrop, Louisiana, and Monroe, Louisiana. The receipt shows the costs of goods in 1922. (Anita Nettles.)

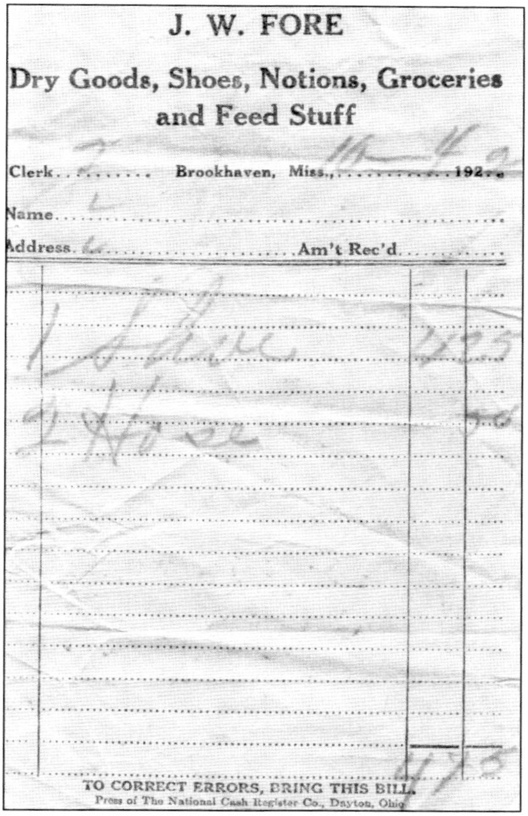
J. W. FORE

Dry Goods, Shoes, Notions, Groceries and Feed Stuff

Clerk........ Brookhaven, Miss.,.............192..

Name..

Address........................Am't Rec'd...........

TO CORRECT ERRORS, BRING THIS BILL

Press of The National Cash Register Co., Dayton, Ohio

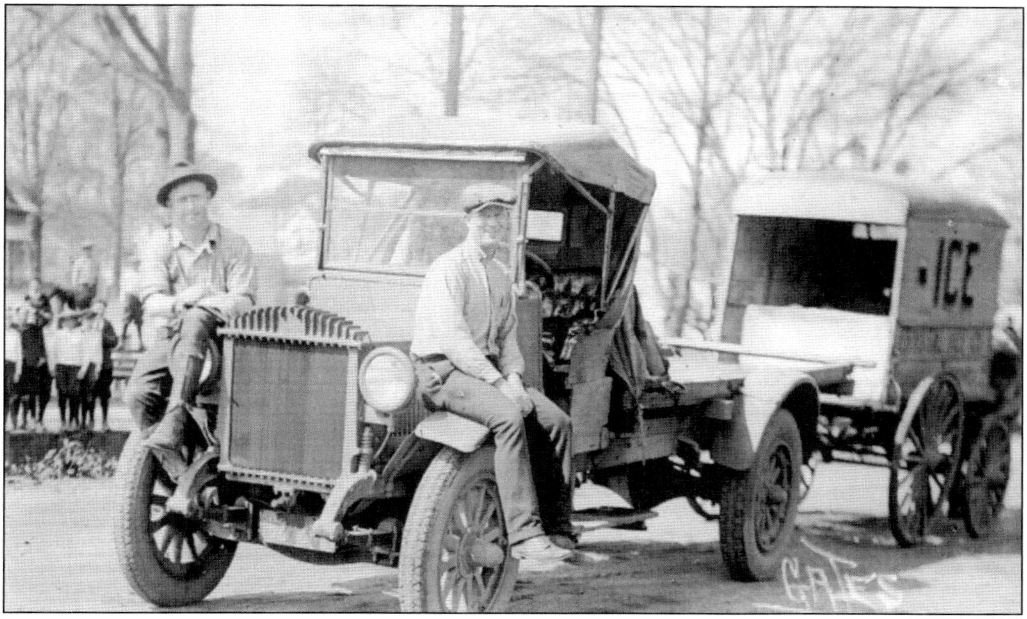

Joe Tanner (left) made deliveries for Crystal Ice Company in Brookhaven in the 1920s. John Bernard Nalty and C.A.C. Steinweg incorporated the ice company on December 10, 1906. Nalty was known for the lumber business, but later expanded into the ice and dairy industries. (Mary Ann Smith.)

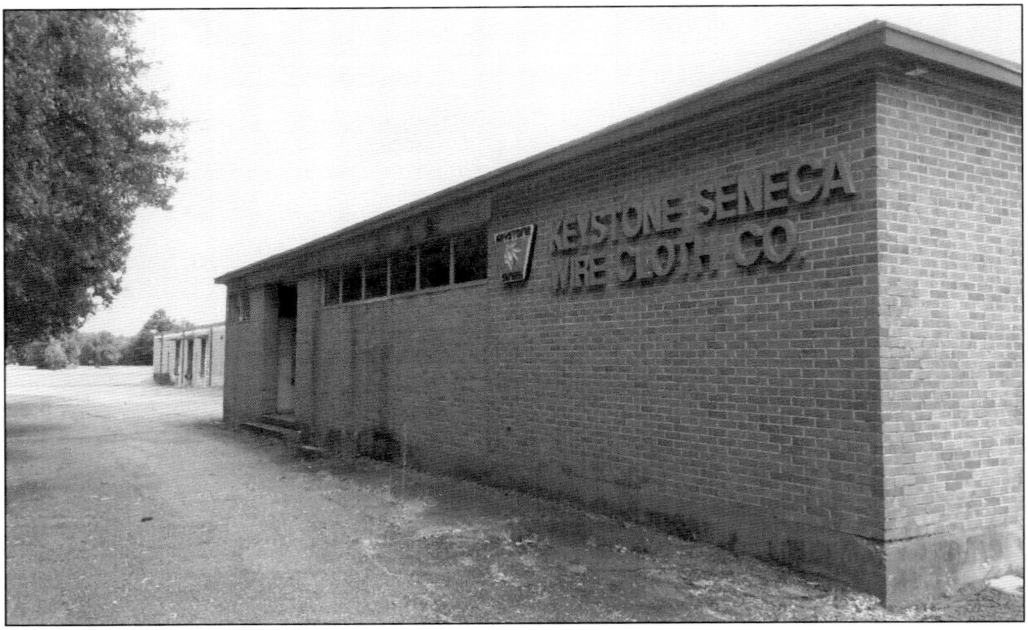

The Standard Wire Cloth & Screen Company, later Keystone Senecca, opened in Brookhaven's industrial park the summer of 1956. Moving to the area with the company were Benjamin F. Bahn, his wife, Marold Bupp, and daughter, Brenda—all from York, Pennsylvania. Mr. Ben, as he was known to employees, passed away in 1992; his wife died in 2002. His daughter, Brenda Bahn Bowman Simmons, has two daughters, several grandchildren, and currently lives in Brookhaven. The factory is now empty, but the building still stands. (Tammie Santos Brewer.)

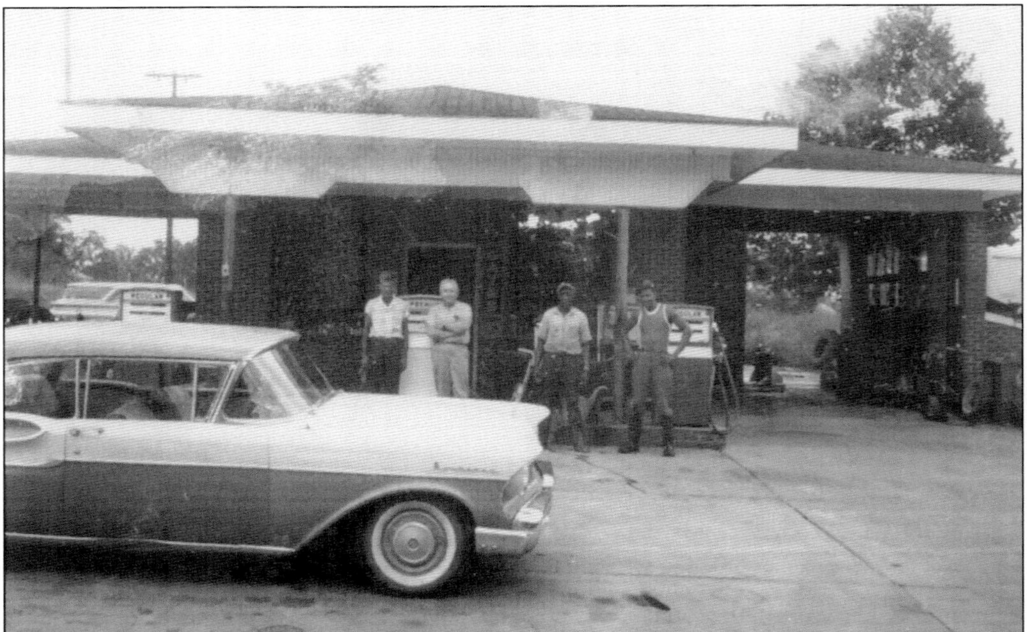

Reeves Service Station, located on Old Highway 51, opened on November 9, 1945, next door to its present location. Station workers shown here in 1958 are, from left to right, Charles Lee, J.P. Reeves (owner), W.C. Pittman, and an unidentified worker. (Keith Reeves.)

Annie Bell Richardson Lewis (b. 1918) and her husband, James, were the first blacks in Lincoln County to build a housing development in Brookhaven. Called Peco Village, it was located between Mullins School and the old site of Eva Harris School. Lewis was multitalented—a teacher, a skilled seamstress, an interior/exterior designer, and partner with her husband in design and construction. (Maxine Allen.)

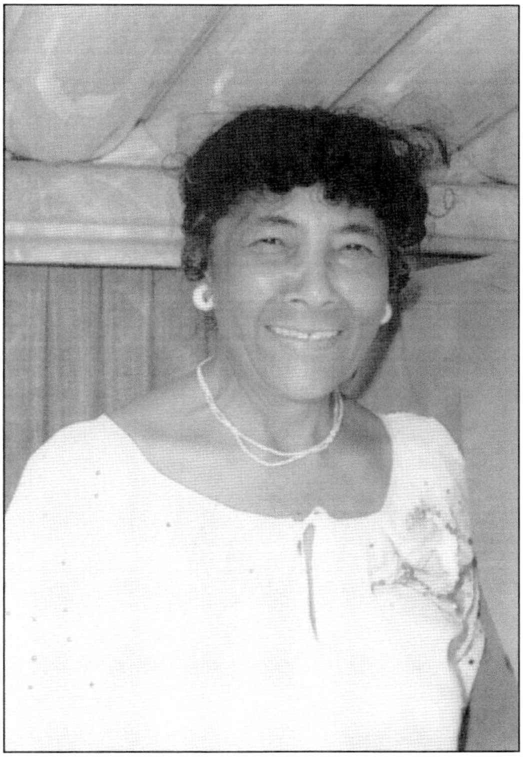

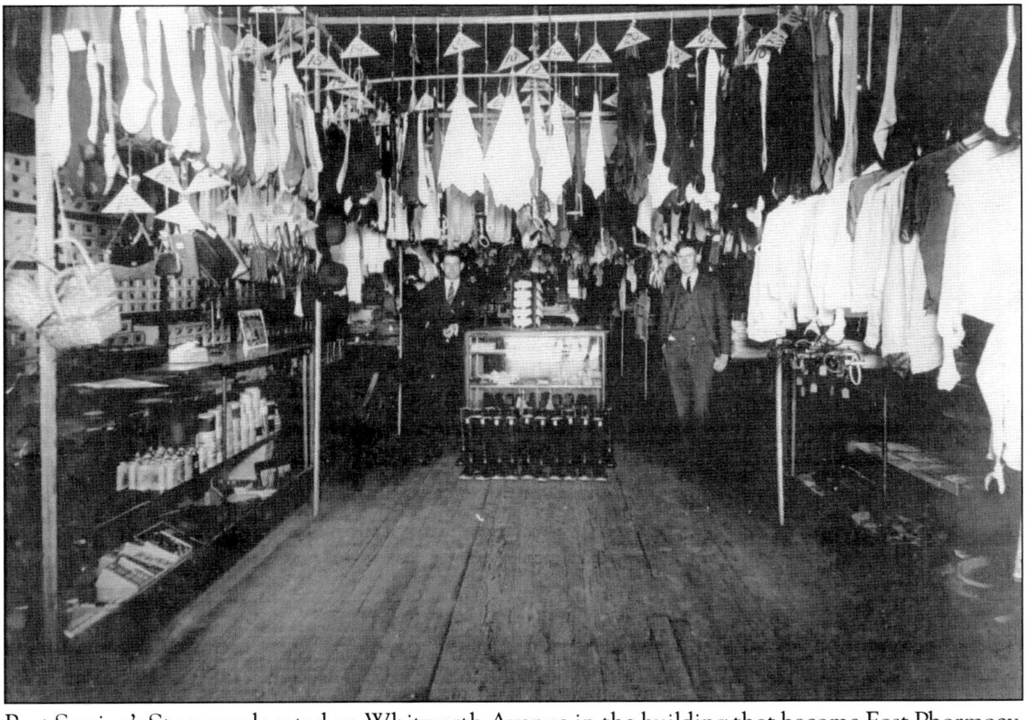

Bert Session's Store was located on Whitworth Avenue in the building that became East Pharmacy. Session sold the building to Floyd C. East and relocated his business to Highway 51. Employee John W. Beacham (left) was originally from the Caseyville area. (Anita Nettles.)

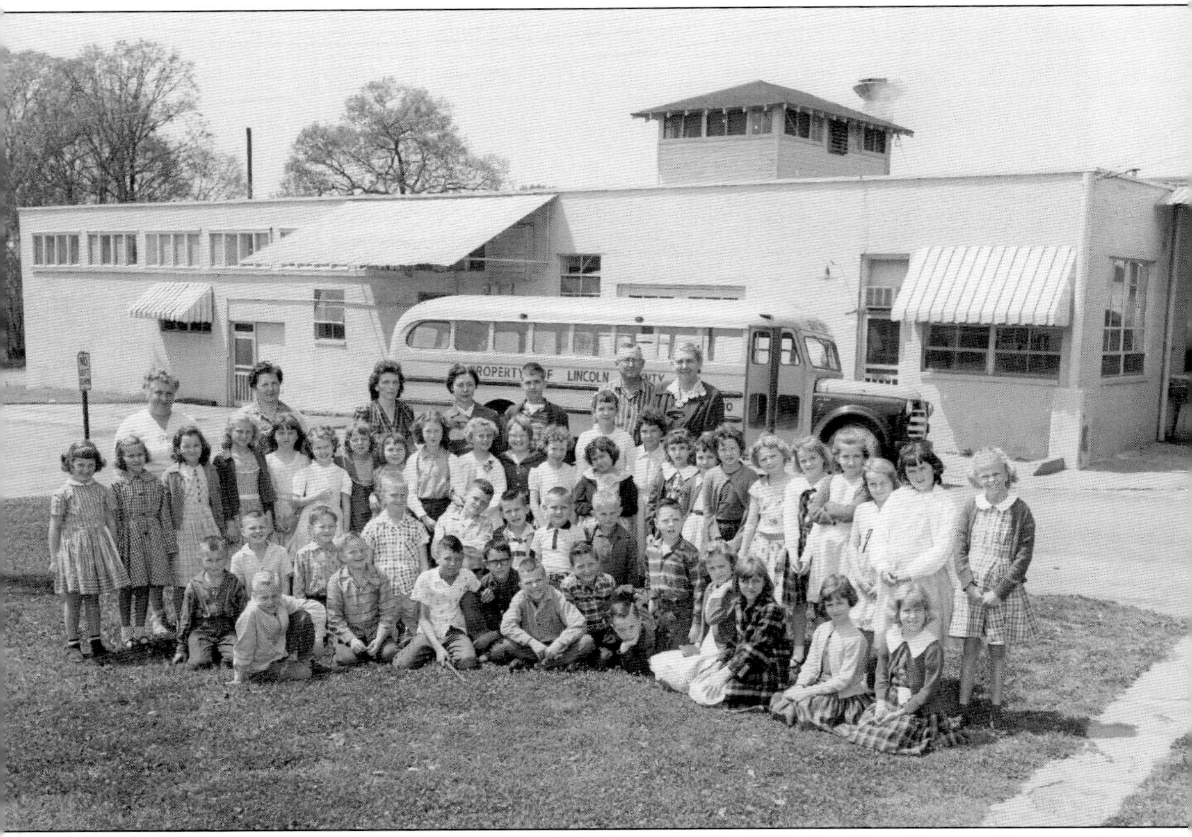

Brookhaven had three creameries in the early 1900s. In 1911, the Brookhaven Cooperative Creamery Association opened; it encouraged farmers to enter the dairy business by lending them $50 to purchase a cow. The farmer either brought the milk to town or left the can beside the road for the cooperative to pick up. This milk was mainly used for butter. Ferdinand Becker opened the Brookhaven Creamery Company in 1913; John B. Nalty opened the Dixie Creamery Company in 1915, and he later began the Purity Ice Cream Company. While Nalty's main business had been logging, he complemented the creamery by also opening Crystal Ice Company. (LLF.)

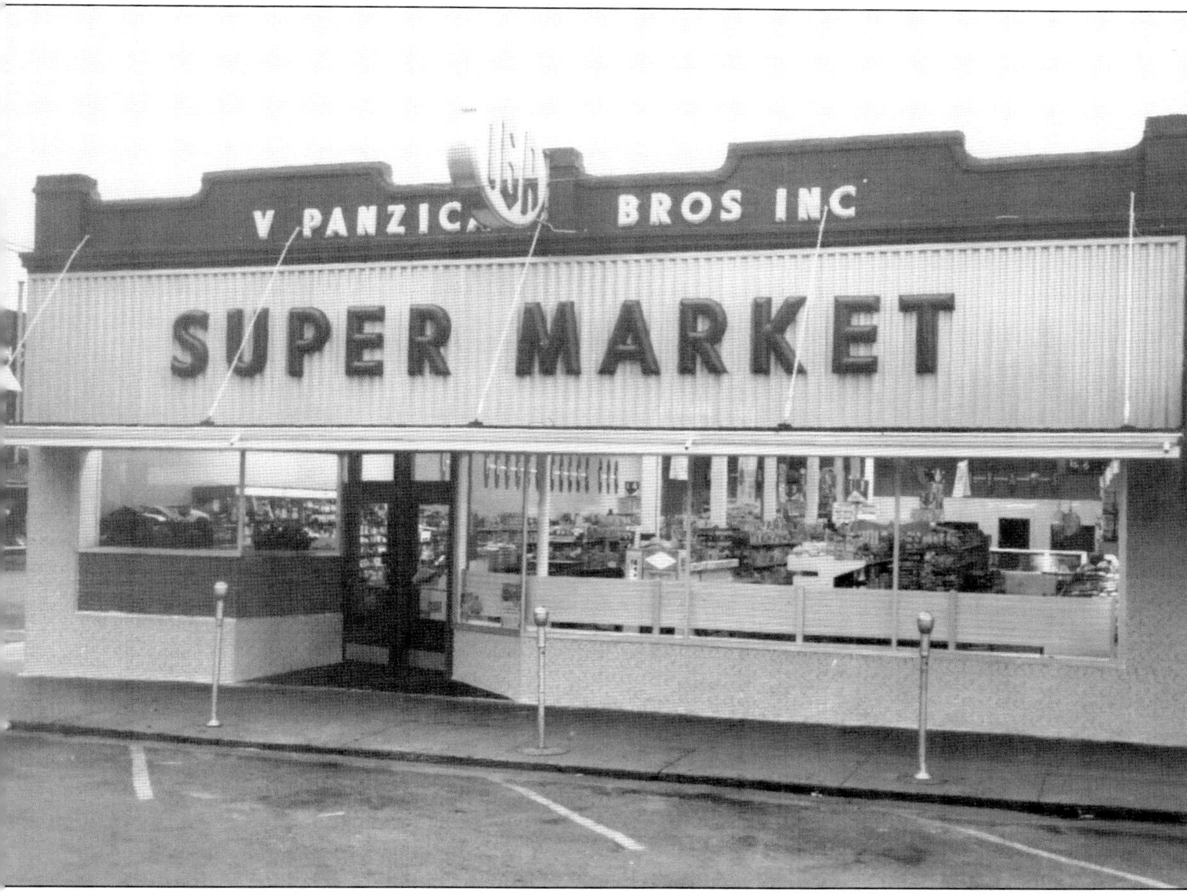

Anthony "Tony" and Rosa Panzica are listed on the federal census as being born in Italy. Documents state that three of the men in the family were naturalized citizens and indicate that they entered the country through Ellis Island and made their way to Lincoln County between 1890 and 1910. They ran the grocery on the corner of Monticello and First Streets in an older building for many years, before this one was remodeled. (LLF.)

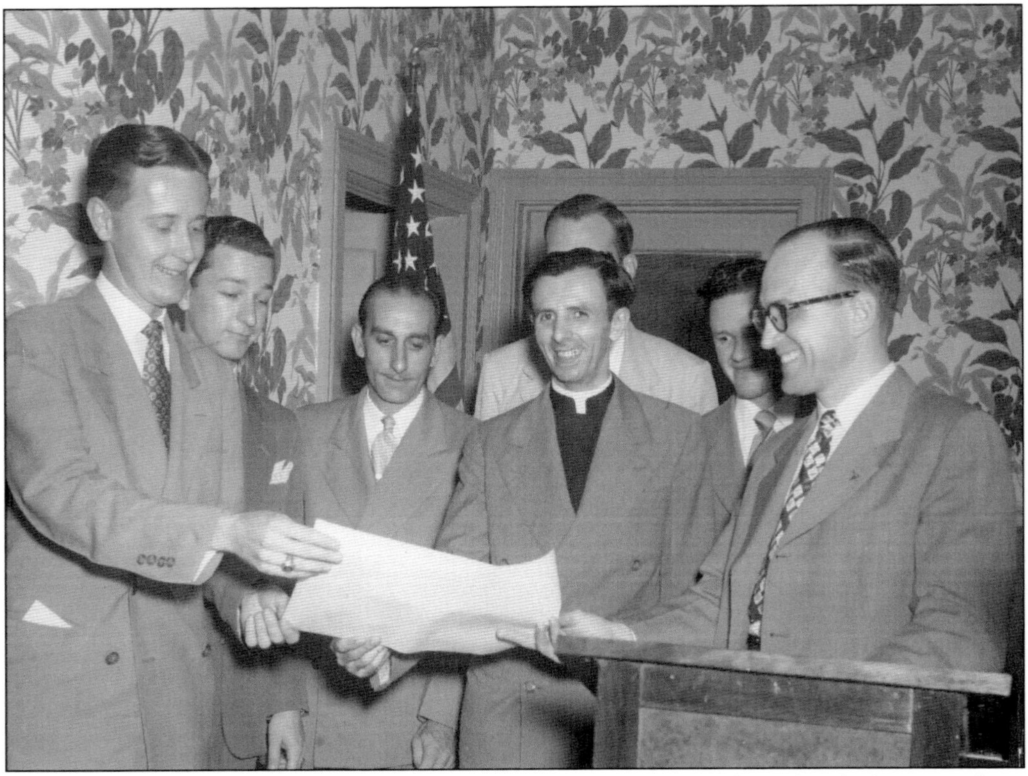

The officers of the Brookhaven Junior Chamber of Commerce are pleased with their president, Thomas H. Perkins III (far left), who is accepting the charter presented by state president Harry Clark (far right). Shown here are, from left to right, Perkins, James F. Noble Jr., Phillip Panzica, Fr. William V. Albert, Henry Ware Hobbs Jr., Owen Roberts, and Clark. (LLF.)

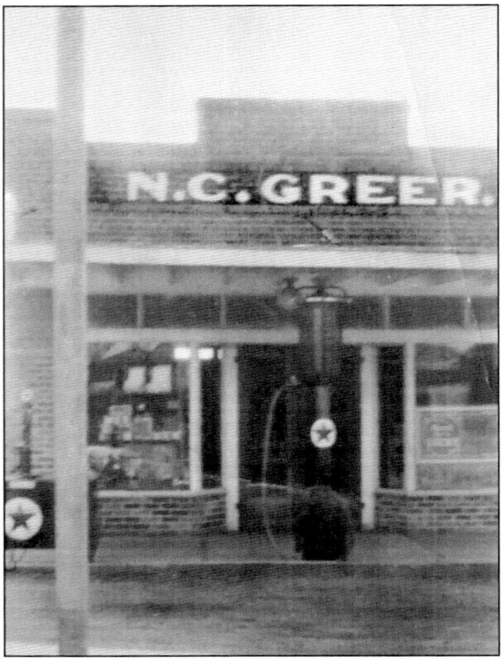

Corrie Greer pinched pennies until she had enough money to build the N.C. Greer Grocery Store in Pearlhaven to help support her family. Her husband, Noah Clifton Greer, held various jobs and was justice of the peace for Pearlhaven. Later, their daughter Gussie Greer Griffin was elected justice of the peace. After the death of her parents, she operated the store for several years. (Jimmy Griffin.)

Four

The Way They Traveled

Travel in Lincoln County in the late 1800s could be slow and frustrating. Most modes of travel within the county included horses, oxen, wagons, and a person's own two feet.

Most early settlers came to the area via the St. Stephens Trail, which ran from Mobile, Alabama, to Natchez, Mississippi. The early Indian trail was a common path for stagecoaches traveling east and west by the mid to late 1800s. Several small towns and communities sprang up along the way as way stations or stopping points for coaches.

By 1857, travel took on a faster mode with the coming of the railroad. Journeys north and south could be made in a matter of days. With the construction of the railroad came communities and towns, such as Brookhaven. The railroads brought people and assisted in the growth of each community's economy. Shipping goods to other parts of the country and to ports of call were now within reach via the railroad.

One of the first automobiles to be made available to the public was the Ford Motor Company's Model T in 1908. B. Frank "Buddy" Roberts Sr. was one of the first Lincoln Countians to own an automobile. It was purchased in Brookhaven at Jess Day Auto Agency in 1912. Highways and byways were constructed to accommodate the new automobile. Major roadways were Highway 51 and Highway 84, which facilitated commerce.

Many roadside cafés were built to serve weary travelers, including the Coffee Pot on Highway 51. This café, which was built in 1931, was touted as the first "fast-food" restaurant in the South. Although no longer a café, the iconic Coffee Pot building can still be seen today.

Soon, a bus terminal was erected downtown, and an airport was built to serve small airplanes north of Brookhaven.

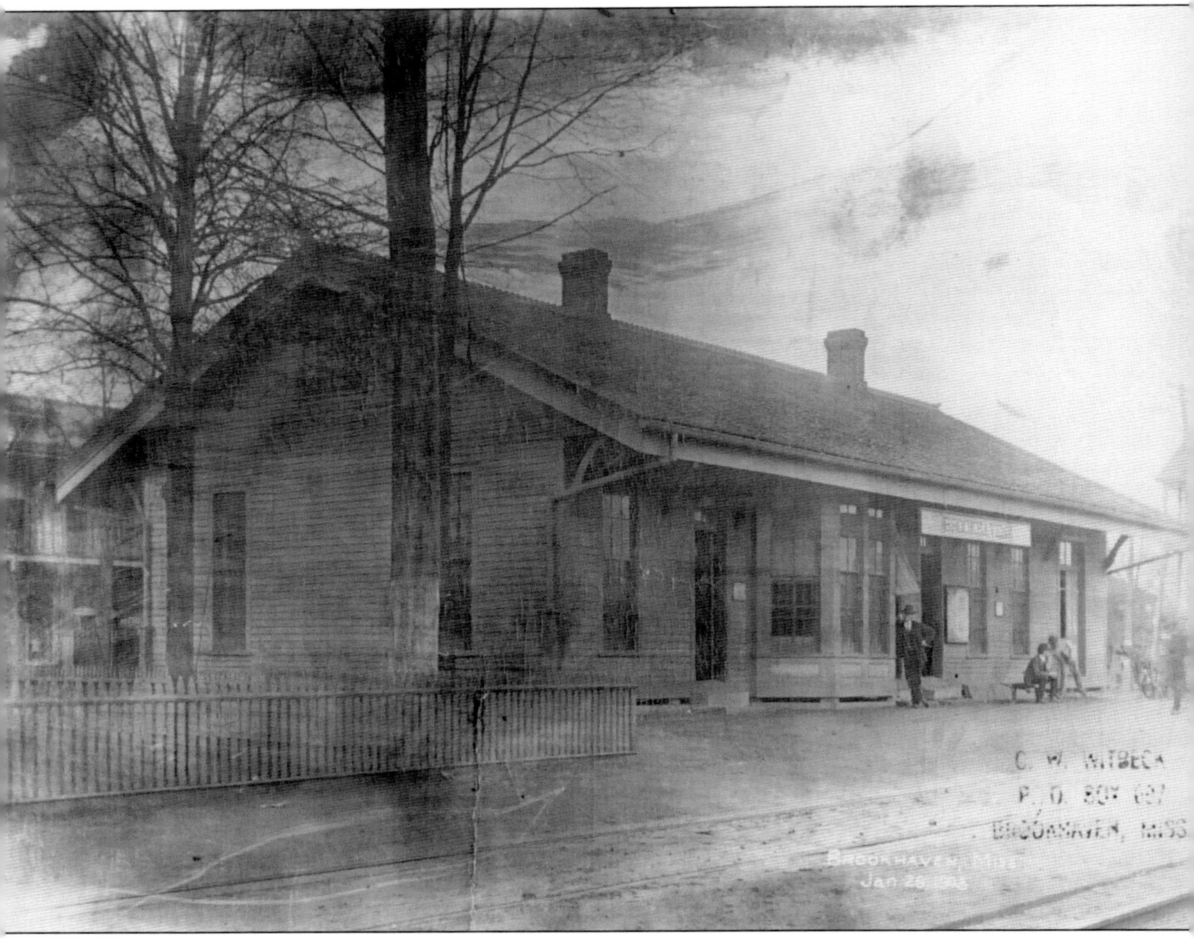

This Witbeck photograph, dated January 28, 1903, may depict Brookhaven's first wooden depot. The sign with the depot's location, Brookhaven, also gives the distances to Chicago (783 miles away) and New Orleans (129 miles). In 1907, the Illinois Central Railroad constructed a depot and freight house downtown. Designed by F.D. Chase, the brick buildings were of the Tudor Revival style. In 1980, the current depot was placed in the National Register of Historic Places. (LLF.)

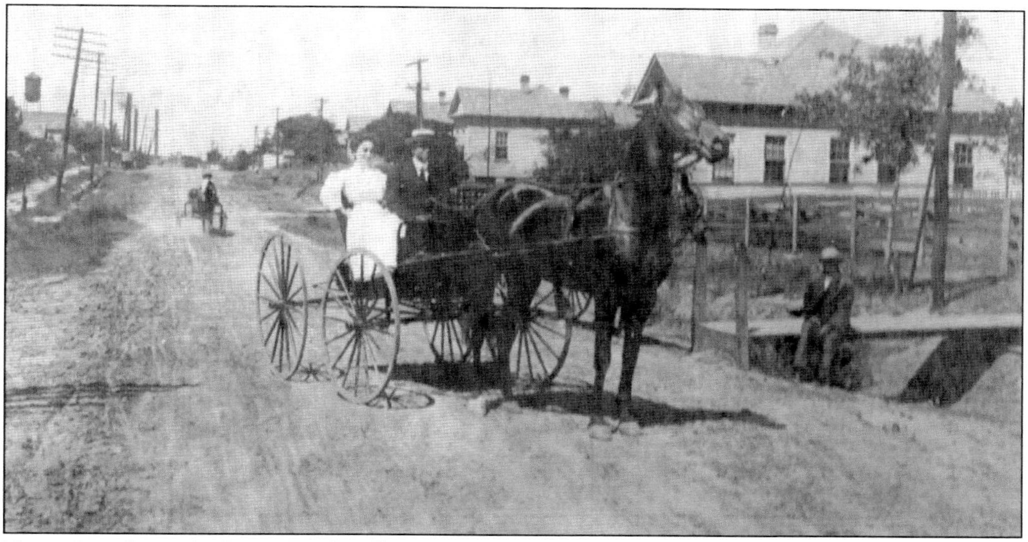

Nurse Josephine A. "Josie" Eitel Gilliam (left) rides in a horse and buggy with a local doctor. Her career was first noted as one of the incorporators, with E.L. Summers and S.G. Wilson, of the Wilson Infirmary Training School for Nurses. The original purpose of the Domestic Business Corporation was to offer a hospital for employees of Pearl River Lumber Company, located in the village of Pearlhaven, later part of Brookhaven. Soon after the last filing date for the corporation—November 20, 1908—Dr. Wilson moved to New Orleans. Gilliam (1878–1969) is buried in Rosehill Cemetery in Brookhaven. (LCHGS.)

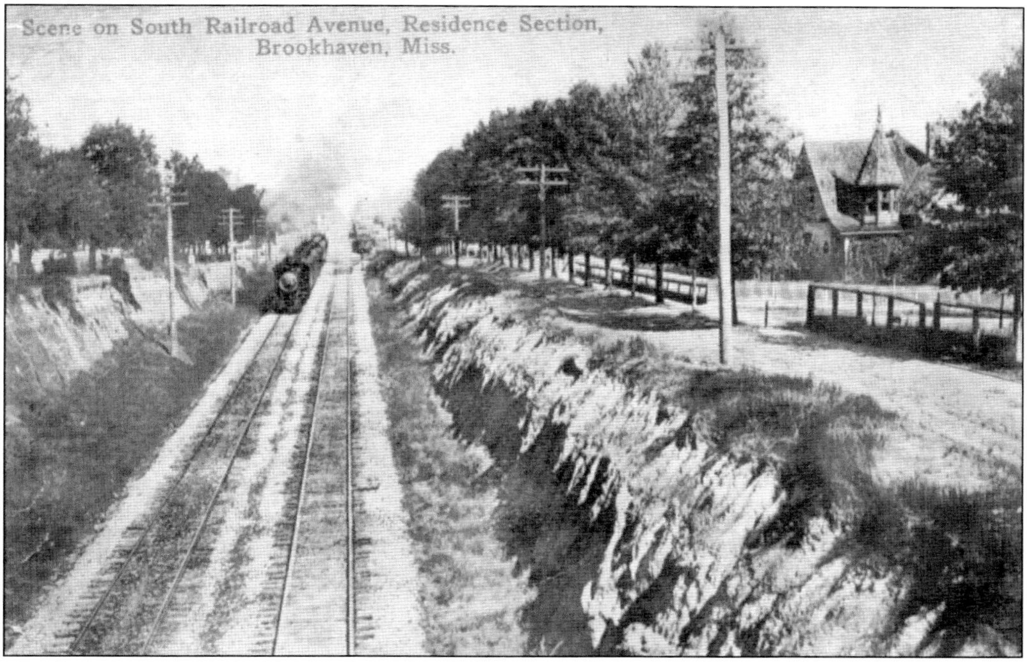

The first train to come through Brookhaven was a freight train, but it was not long before several passenger trains were passing through on their way north or south, making travel faster, easier, and more comfortable. This postcard shows a train traveling south through Brookhaven in the early 20th century. (Carroll Montgomery.)

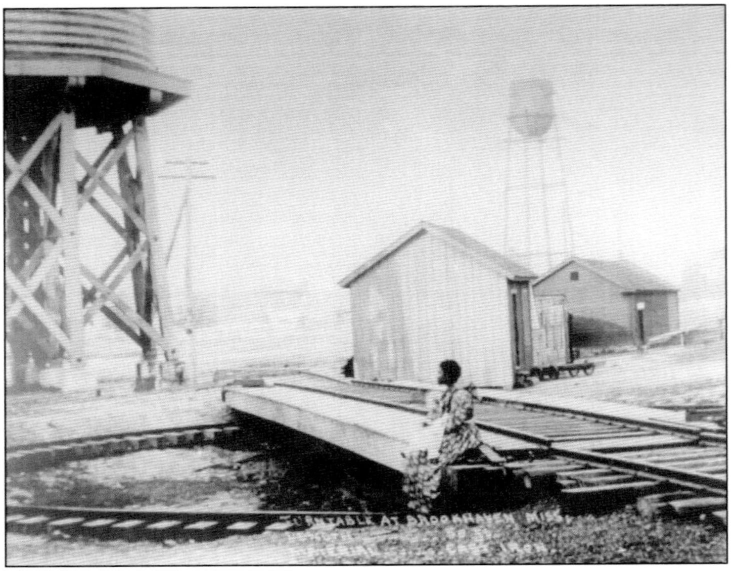

A railroad turntable is depicted in this 1898 photograph, made in Brookhaven. Turntables or wheelhouses were often used for turning locomotives around for return trips. Information at the bottom of the photograph indicates the material used (cast iron) and the length (50 feet). (Carroll Montgomery.)

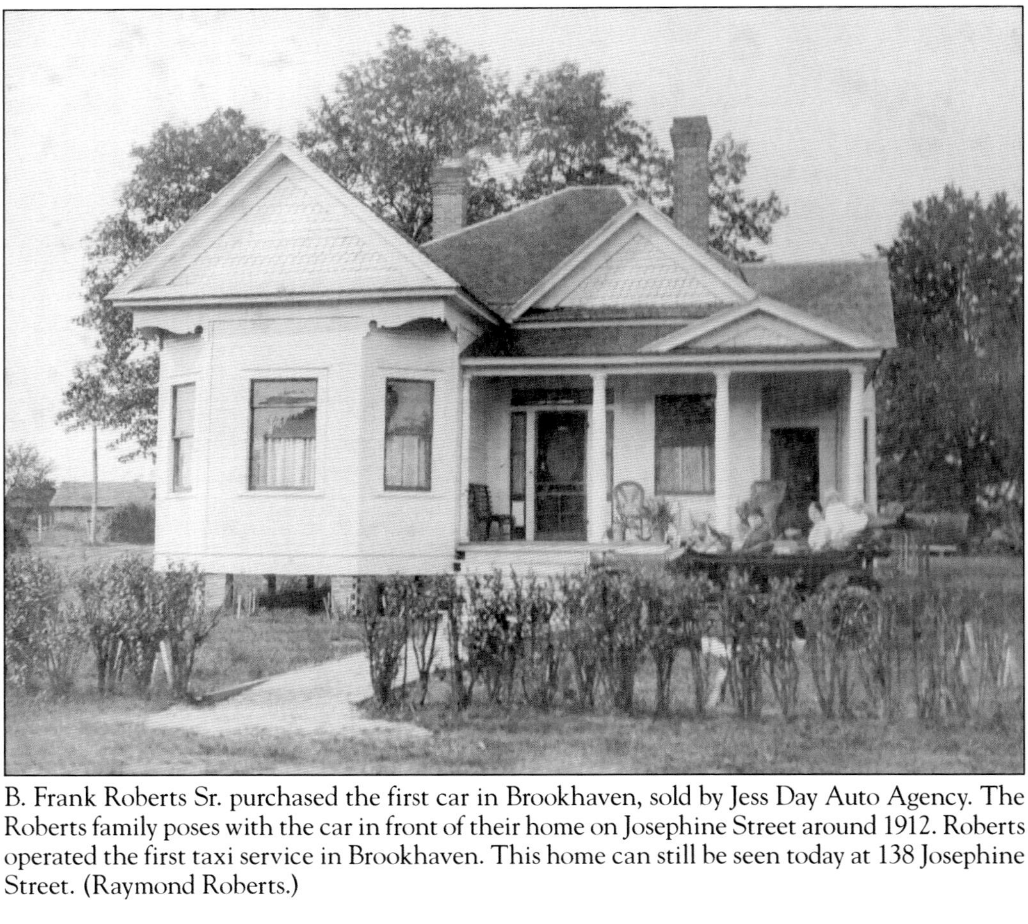

B. Frank Roberts Sr. purchased the first car in Brookhaven, sold by Jess Day Auto Agency. The Roberts family poses with the car in front of their home on Josephine Street around 1912. Roberts operated the first taxi service in Brookhaven. This home can still be seen today at 138 Josephine Street. (Raymond Roberts.)

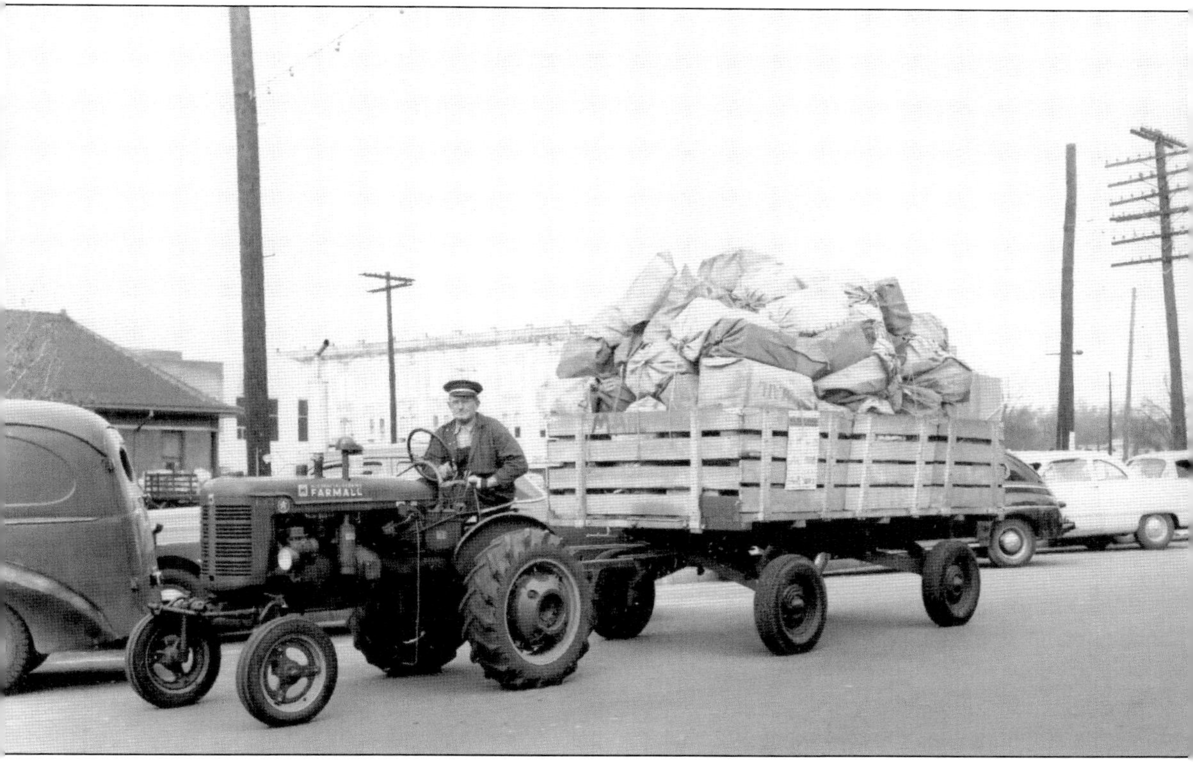

Often, US Post Office mail sacks were pulled by tractor from the railroad depot to the post office, located a block away. This practice was common at the time; today, it is illegal to handle mail in this way. The driver is not identified. (LLF.)

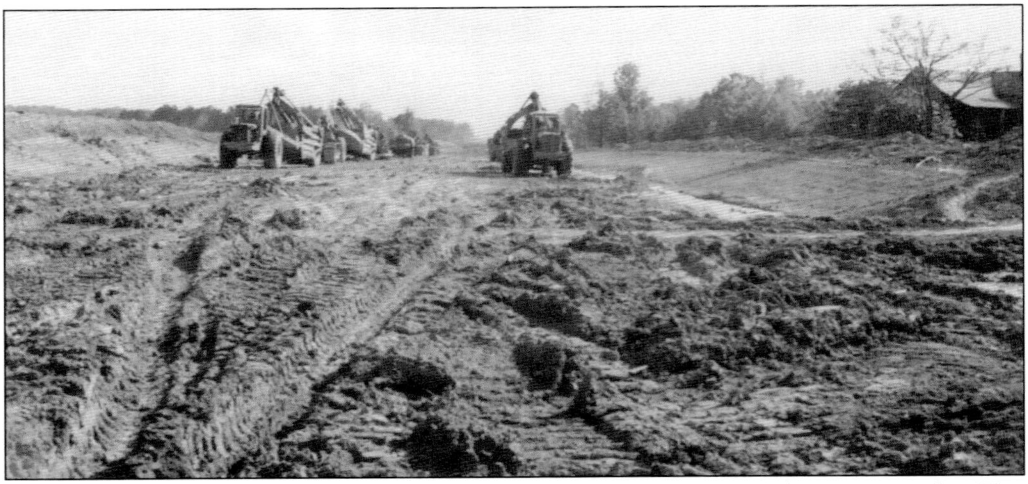

Construction began in the 1940s on a major two-lane highway from New Orleans to Memphis. This highway moved the transportation lanes from the center of small towns along the railroad to west of the towns. Highway 51 eased traffic problems and caused permanent changes to the downtown business areas as strip malls and stores were developed along the new road. (MDAH.)

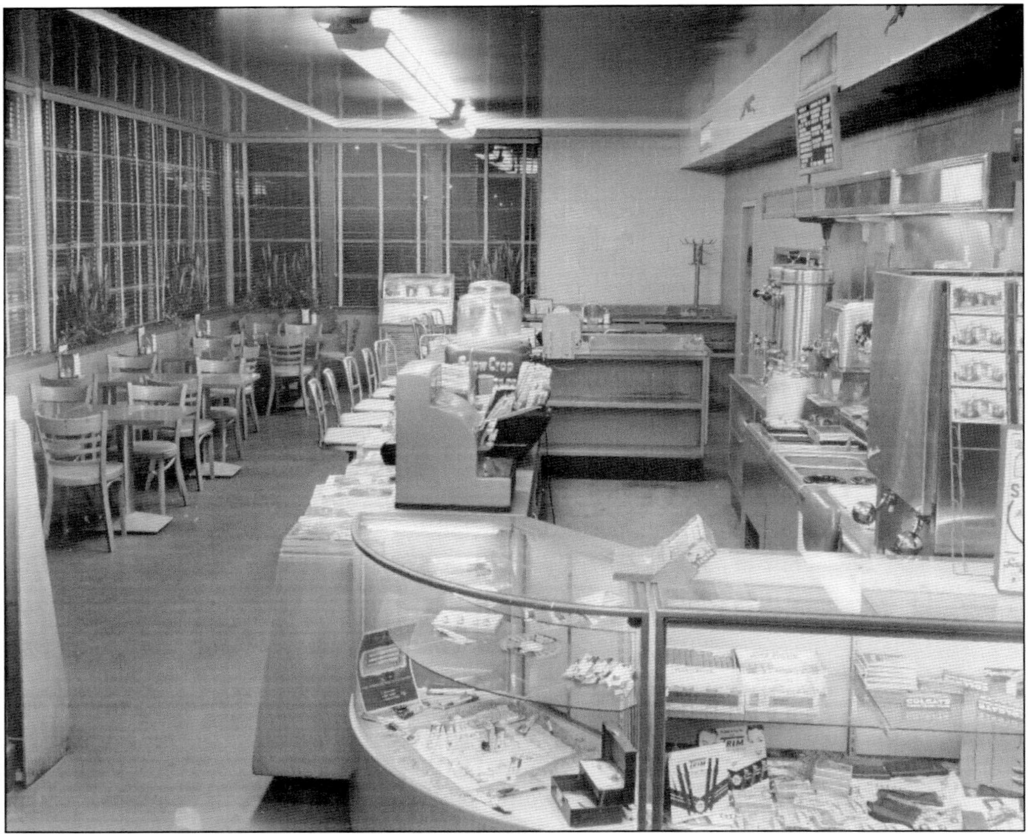

The Greyhound Bus Station, located on North Jackson Street, was a busy place. There were six buses daily to New Orleans and seven to Memphis. Built by the Greyhound Corporation in 1950 at a cost of $65,000, the facility had a lunch counter for hungry travelers, who usually had no more than 30 minutes to grab a bite before their bus left. (LLF.)

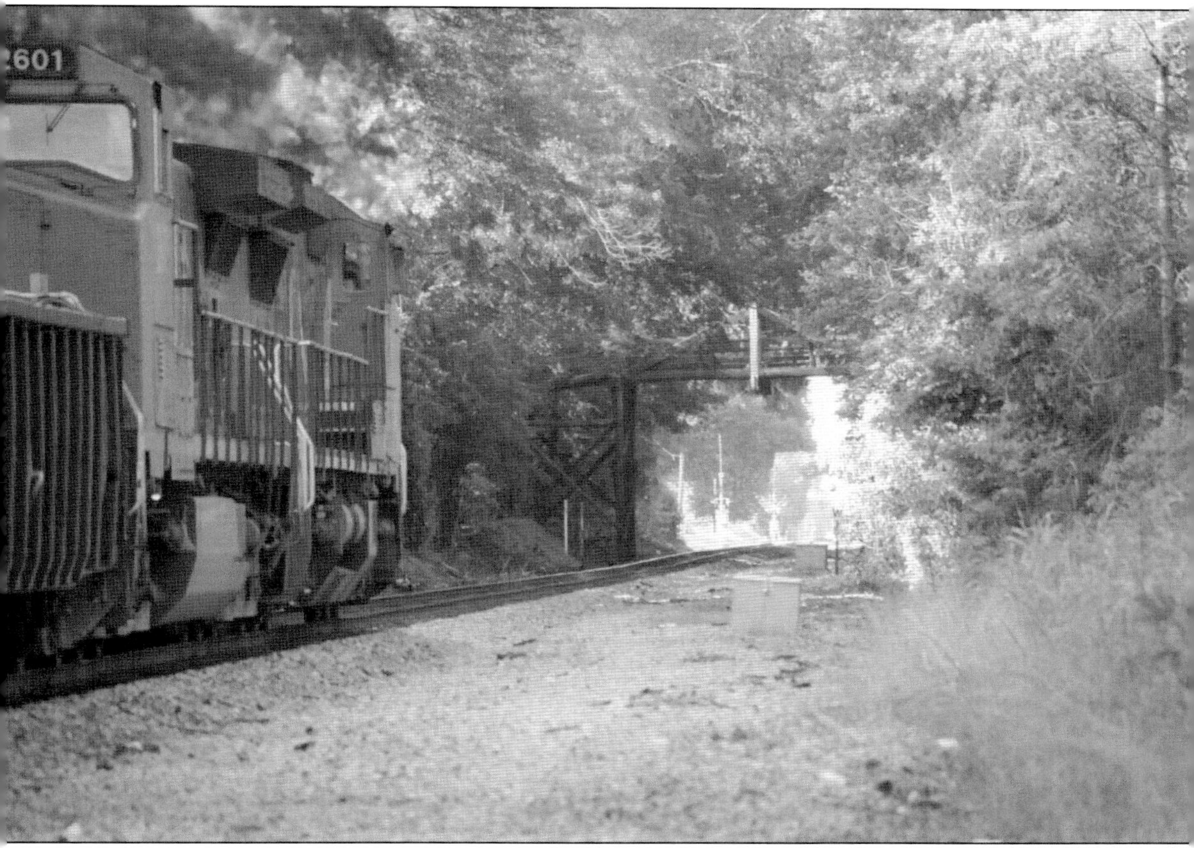

In 1903, the railroad was ordered to build a bridge over the tracks to connect the east and west sides of what is now Warren Avenue. Shown here is the overhead bridge, now closed, which gave drivers a thrill as they attempted to drive over it. Travelers never knew what was coming from the other side and would blow their horns as a warning in case someone was coming from the other direction. (Tammie Santos Brewer.)

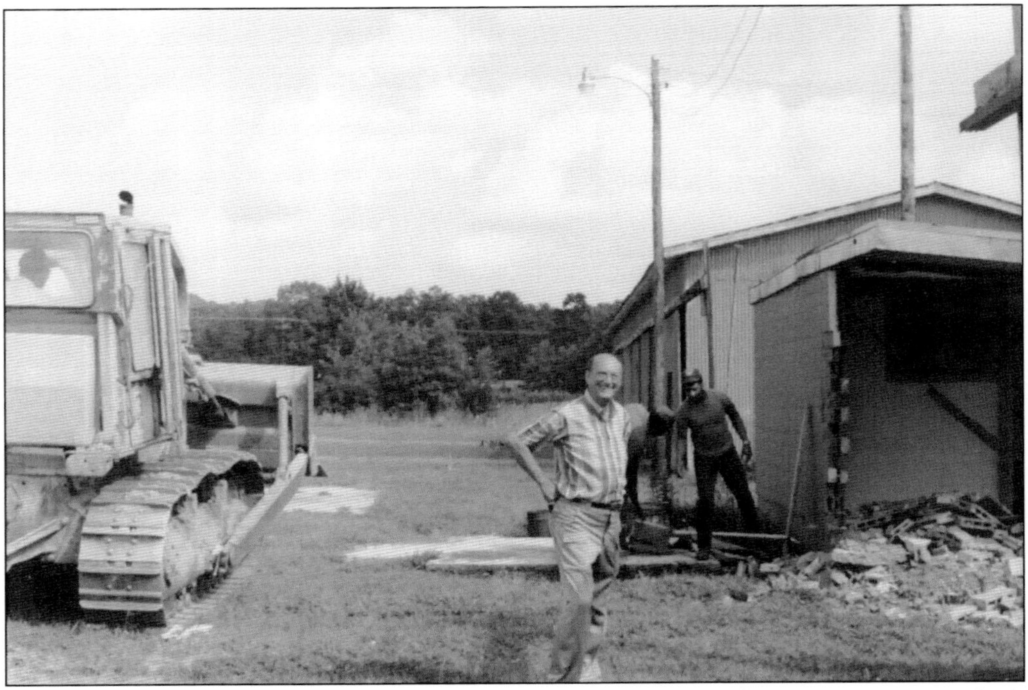

Dr. Jim Barnett was instrumental in modernizing Brookhaven-Lincoln County's airport, which is located on 146 acres off Old Highway 51. The land for the original airport was purchased from Mrs. Pink Mason in 1951 for $26,000. A terminal was built some years later and was torn down in 1986. A modern terminal was built in its place, with Barnett overseeing its construction. The airport began with a 3,000-foot grass runway. It now has a 5,000-foot asphalt runway. (Roberta Barnett.)

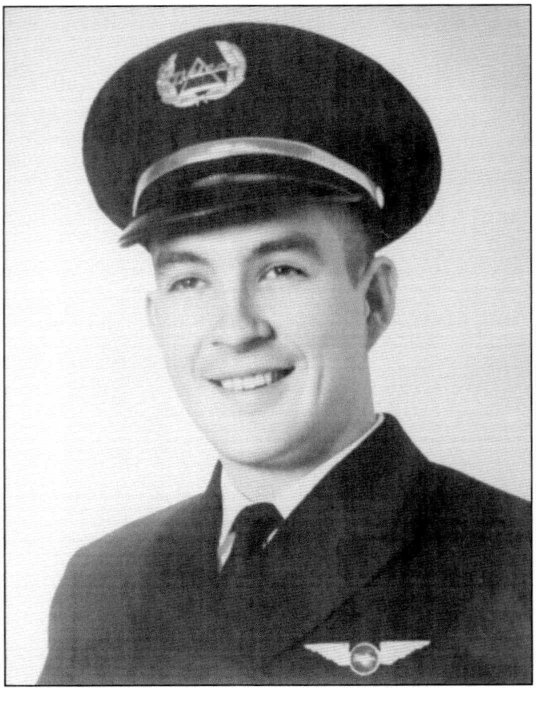

David Eugene Posey was born on November 25, 1941. While a freshman at Mississippi College, Clinton, he cut classes and the required chapel services to take flying lessons at the Jackson airport. With support from his parents, he purchased a small plane and opened the first flying service at Brookhaven. At that time, he was the youngest Cessna dealer. Later, he was hired by Delta Air Lines and, in 1967, lost his life in a training flight at Kenner, Louisiana. (Bettie Posey Bullard.)

Five

Focus on Education

Education was very important to most of the early Lincoln County settlers. From the very beginning, they taught children in their homes until they could arrange for a teacher to live in the community for a small salary and room and board. A classroom would contain as many as eight grades. Many lessons had to be memorized, and students would file to the front to recite.

As residents became more affluent, one-room, one-teacher schools were combined with schools nearby, later merging into larger schools.

Schools with creative names, such as Love, East's Mill (later Red Star, named for the red star on the Thomas East store), Grange Hall (later named Loyd Hall), finally consolidated with Red Star and became Loyd Star. In 1925, there was a move to further consolidate schools in the state. Loyd Star was chosen to combine Reed, Grafton Hall, Macedonia, Love, Beaver Creek, Mount Zion, Friendship, and Grange Hall.

It was not until 1936, however, that the remaining small schools were consolidated. West Lincoln was designated a high school and swallowed Pleasant Grove, R.E. Lee, Cross Road (Flea Hop), Byrd, Gum Grove, and Oak Grove. Previously, high school students had to go to Lucien or Independence in Franklin County, or Arlington or Fair Oak Springs in Lincoln County. The Works Progress Administration (WPA) enabled schools to build auditoriums and classrooms.

Higher education was always a priority for the founders of Brookhaven. Whitworth College, the nation's first college to offer degrees to women, opened its doors in Brookhaven in 1856, after the original structure, located in Washington, Mississippi, burned to the ground.

Currently, there is one county school district with four community K-12 schools, one municipal district, and several private and parochial schools and kindergartens. Brookhaven is also fortunate to be home to the Mississippi School of the Arts, located on the grounds of Whitworth College.

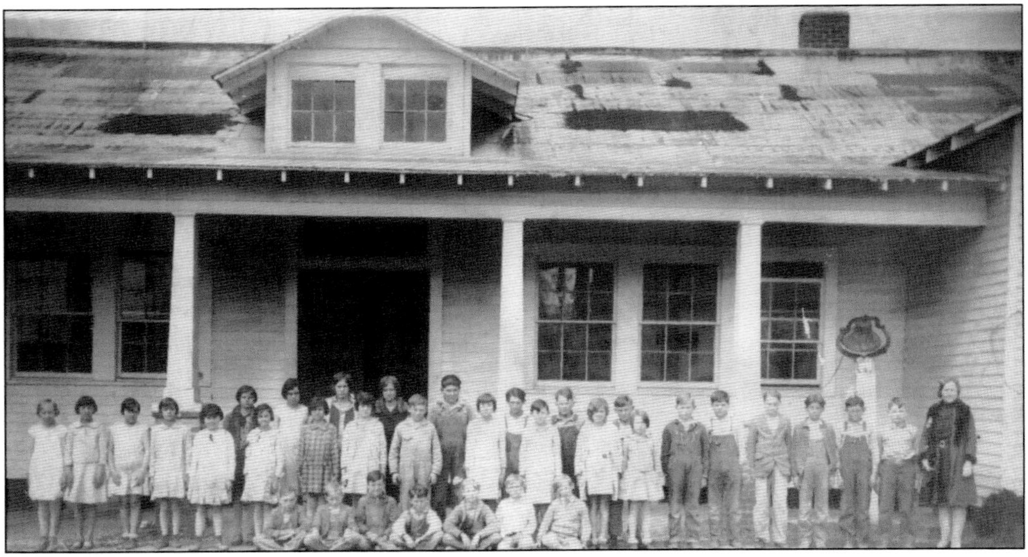

Auburn School was located in the southernmost part of Lincoln County. This is a class from the 1929 school year, when H.B. Roberts was the superintendent. Harold Porter is pictured fourth from the right. (Donald Porter.)

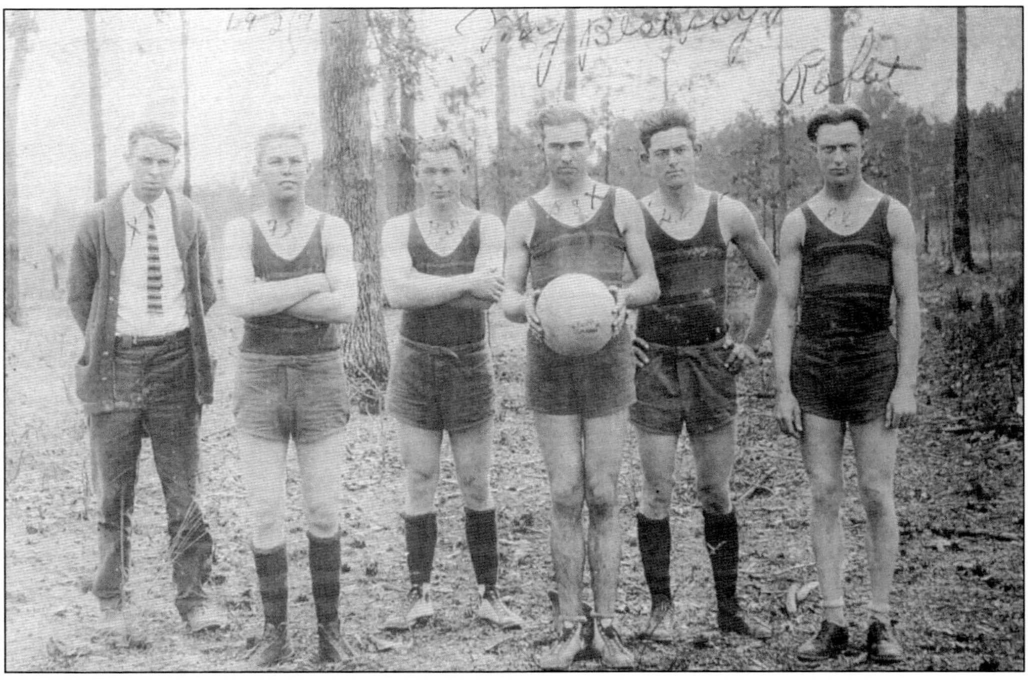

The Friendship basketball team is shown in 1927. Pictured are, from left to right, coach Pearlie Lofton, Fred Smith, H. Smith, Barney Smith, Leslie Vaughan, and Robert Vaughan. The team played on a dirt court near the church in the Vaughan community. (Elliott Smith.)

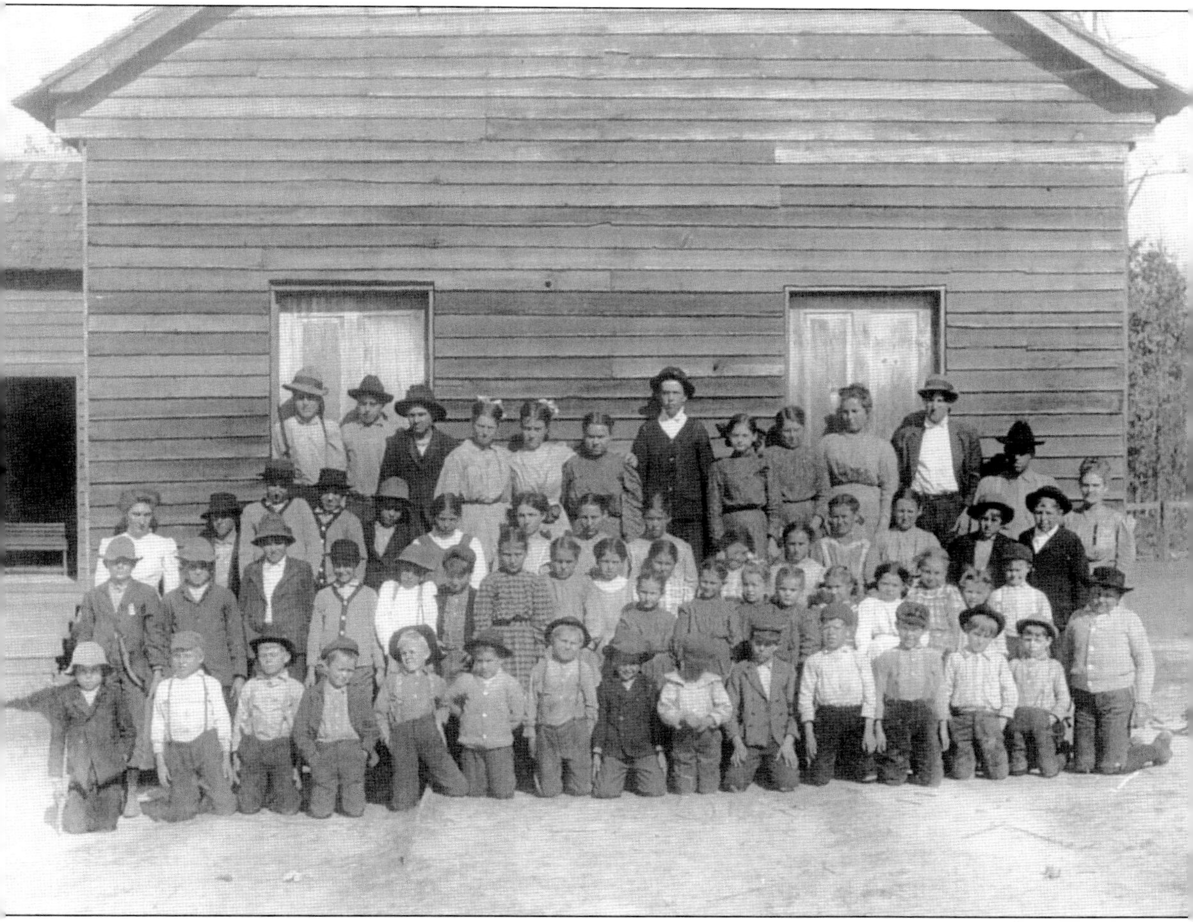

Macedonia School students pose in front of the school in 1906. It was located off Highway 550, between the highway and Red Star Road. Many of the children were from the Britt, Case, and Smith families. (Seth Allen.)

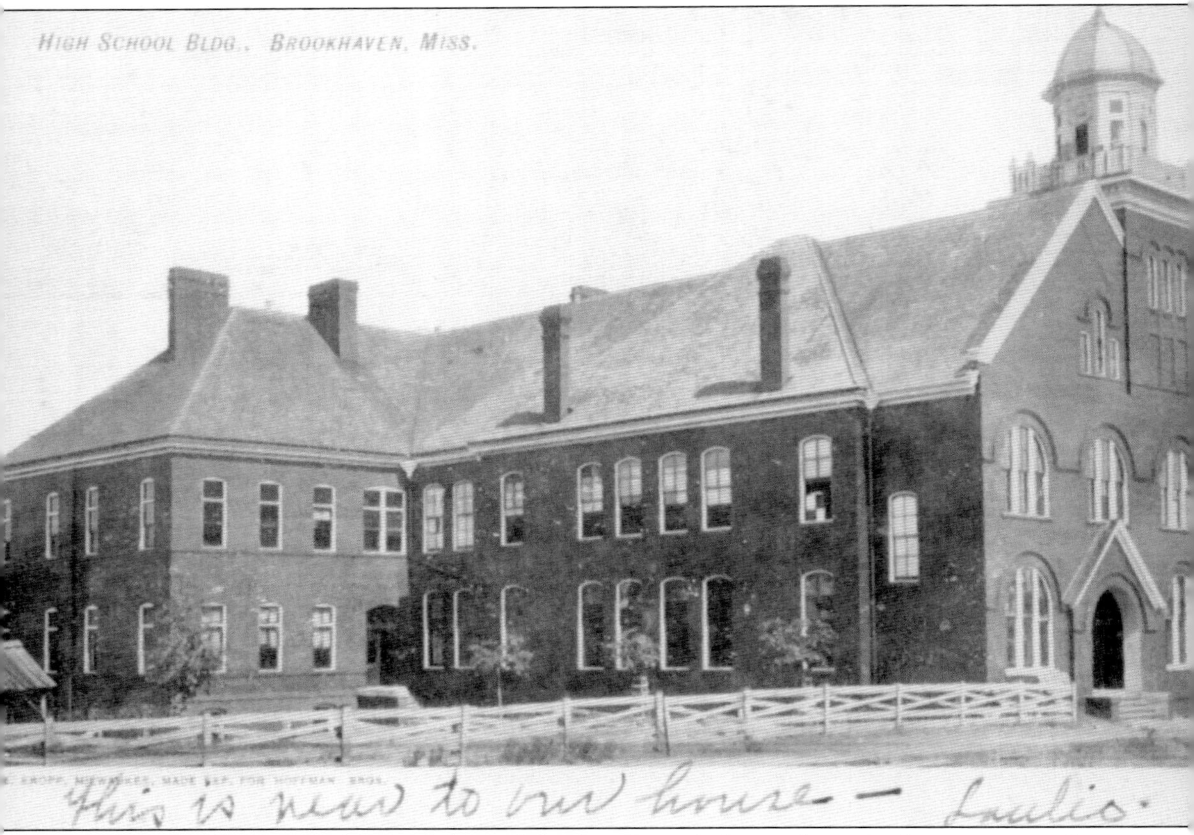

This building, erected in 1890, housed the first through the tenth grades for many years. It was known as the Little Red School. There were 110 students enrolled the first year. Until it was built, school was held in an old skating rink on Court Street. In 1923, a new building was erected for grades nine through twelve on East Monticello Street. This building remained the elementary school until 1940, when it became necessary for a new building to be erected. (LLF.)

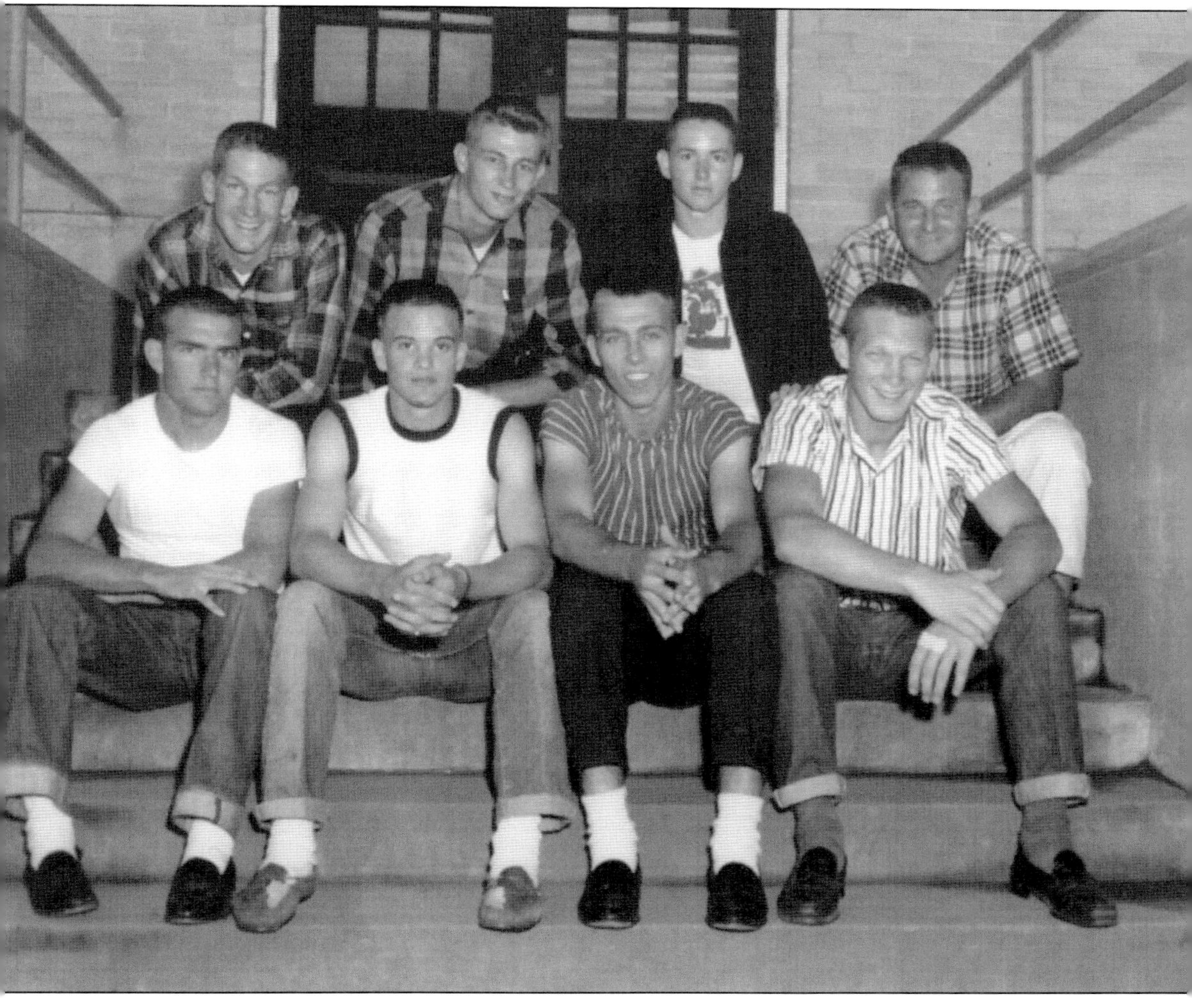

The Brookhaven High School 1957 track team poses for a photograph with the coach. Shown are, from left to right, (first row) Norman Minton, Lance Alworth, Ralph Smith, and Don Estes; (second row) Jerry Pevey, Henry Hoskins, Terry Jones, and coach Paul Moyer. All of these young men played multiple sports, and at least two lettered in four sports during the school year. Alworth went on to play for the University of Arkansas, the San Diego Chargers, and the Dallas Cowboys. Estes played for Louisiana State University, the San Diego Chargers, two Canadian-league teams, and the Houston Oilers. Minton played for Mississippi College and then coached its Choctaw team for many years. Smith played for the Philadelphia Eagles, the Cleveland Browns, and the Atlanta Falcons. (Shirley Estes.)

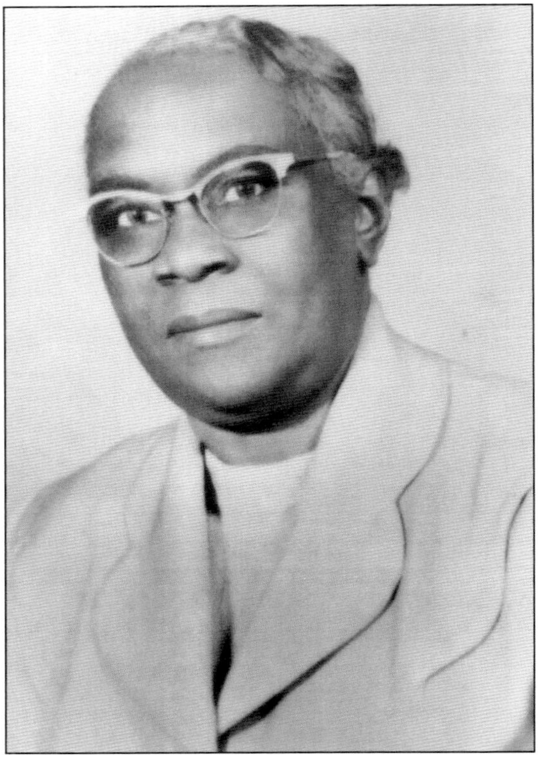

Eva Hall Harris was born at Union Church about 1902. She was the first black female from Mississippi to be awarded a scholarship for study toward a master's degree at Northwestern University and has the distinction of being the first black female to have a high school named after her. Later, she was awarded the honorary degree of doctor of humanities at Prentiss Institute, where she served as trustee. She was the Lincoln County Jeanes agent (liaison between blacks and whites) and organizer of the county Head Start Program. She founded two Federated Clubs: the Bethume Literary and Arts Club, and the Bertha L. Johnson Literary and Garden Club. She was married to Rev. V.H. Harris. (Maxine Allen.)

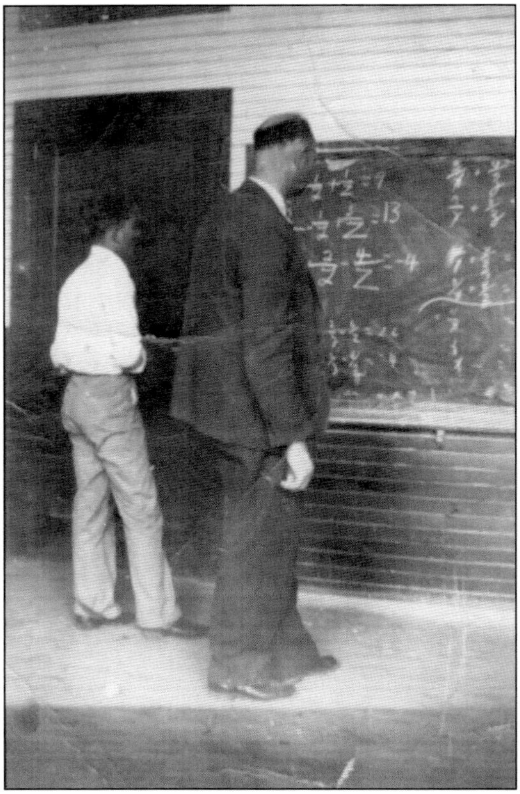

Shown at the blackboard is William "Willie" Henry Calcote, first superintendent of West Lincoln, which was consolidated in 1937 from Pleasant Grove, Cross Road, Byrd, Gum Grove, Oak Grove, and possibly others. Calcote formerly taught at Lucien and was later a state representative. (Kay Calcote.)

Mary Beacham stands with a few of her students at Bailey Branch School, which was located in the East Lincoln community in the early 1900s. (Anita Nettles.)

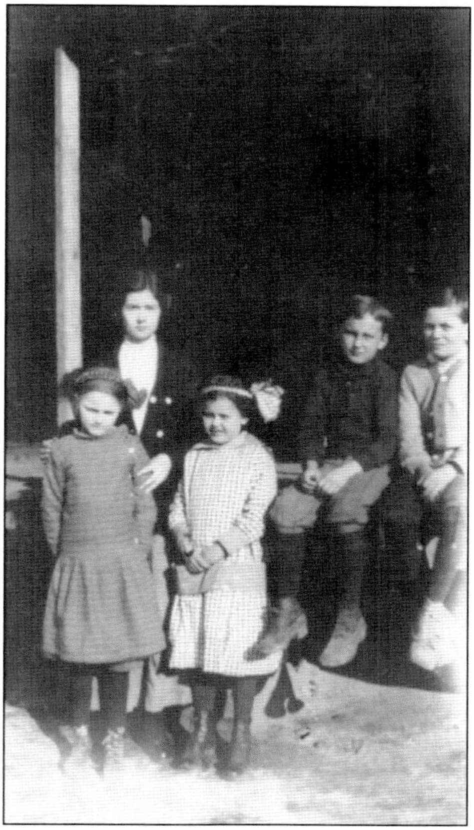

Grange Hall School students pose for a photograph in front of the school in the early 1900s. The school was located in the northwestern part of Lincoln County, near the Caseyville community. (Anita Nettles.)

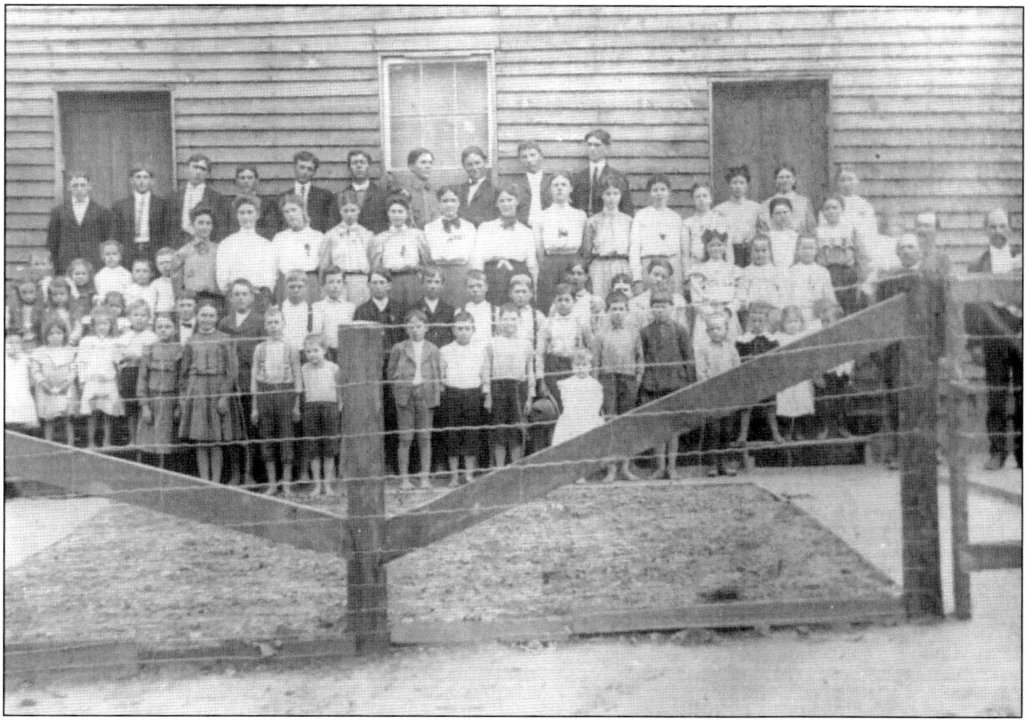

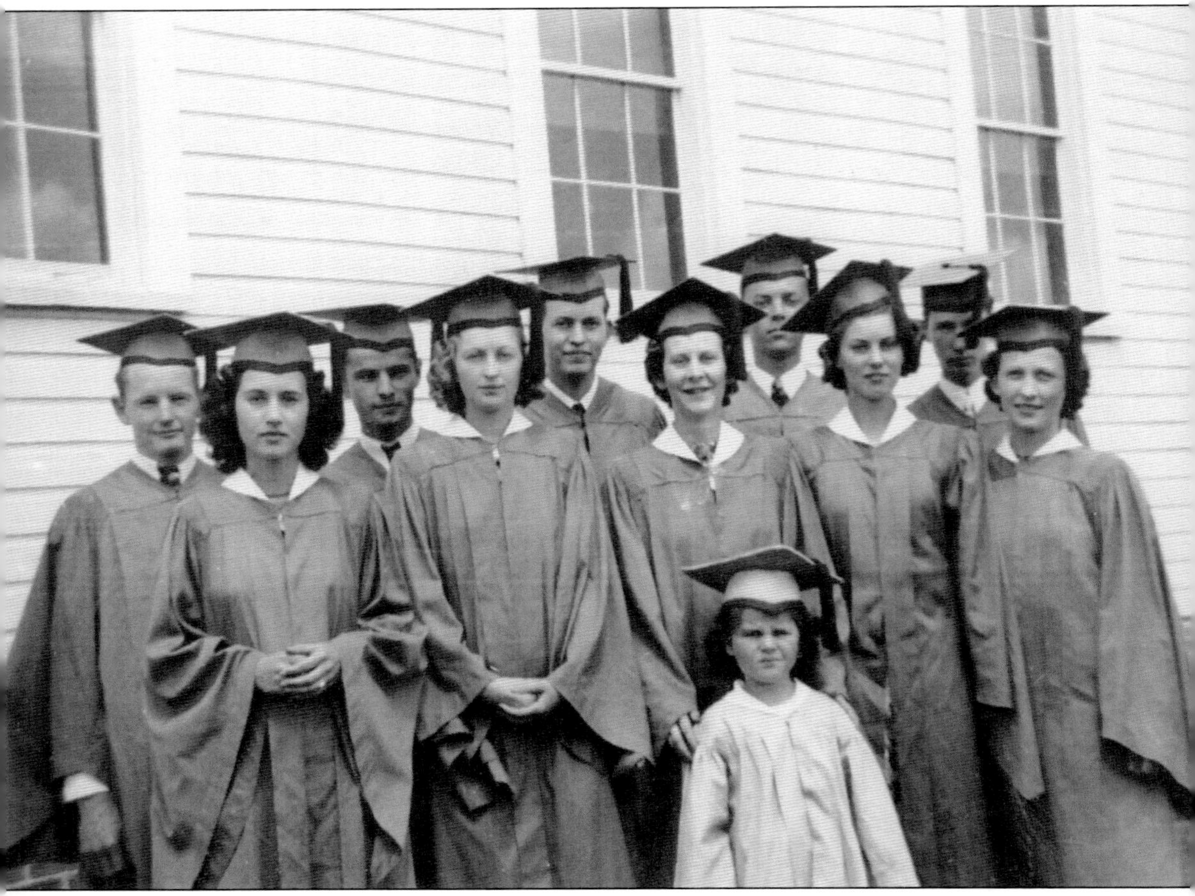

Dot Clark (child in white), daughter of Floyd L. Clark, is shown with unidentified members of the 1940 graduating class of Ruth High School. (Martha Sinclair.)

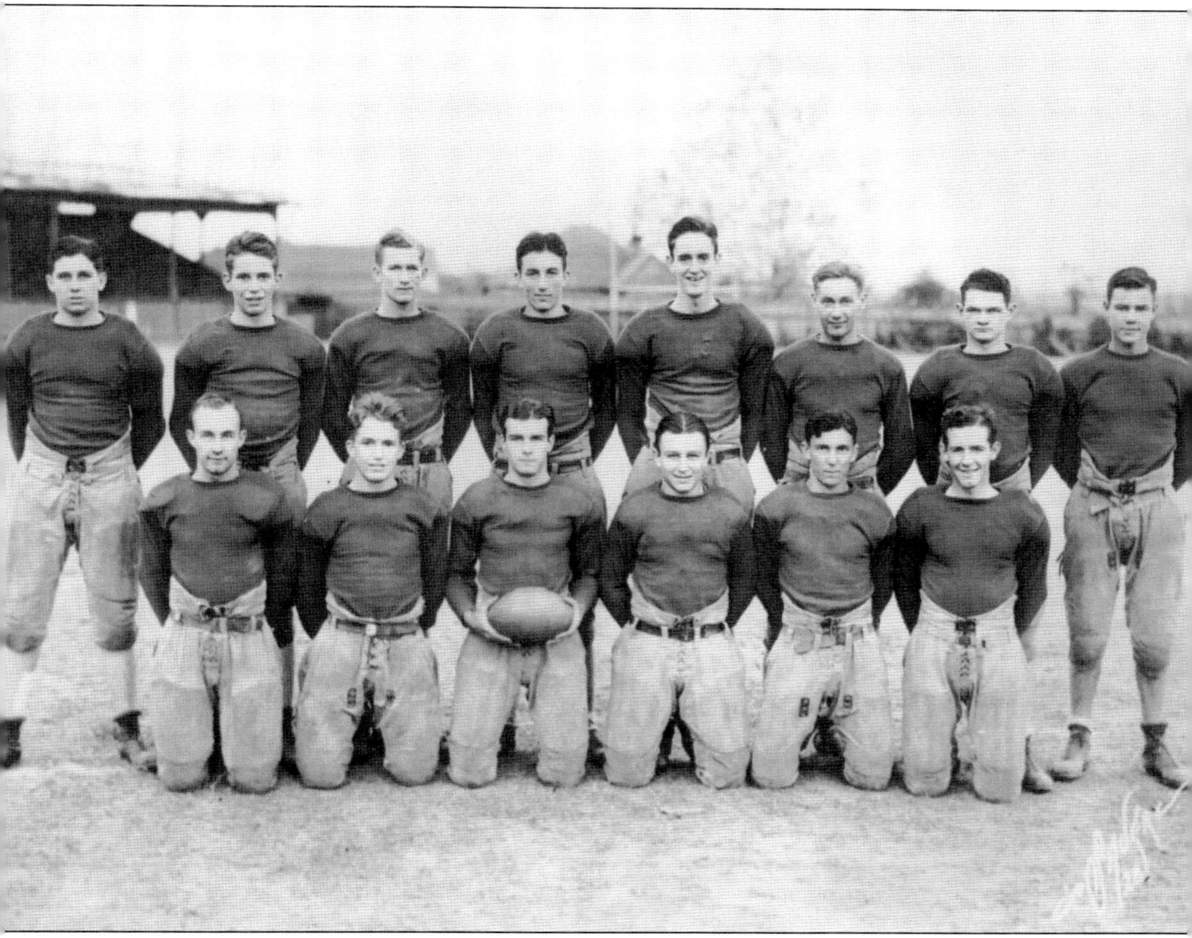

Members of the 1928 Brookhaven High School football team are, from left to right, (first row) Donald Coke, Jack Bowen, Meredith Wood, Bill Day, Alden Evans, and Cleul Scovill; (second row) R. Davis, Kent Bowen, Harold Hollis, James Evan, Bud Taylor, Buchman Stamps, Homer Kees, and Harvey Wood. The photograph was taken and signed by Albert Sauer. (Carroll Montgomery.)

Founded in 1858 as a four-year women's college, Whitworth College was incorporated in 1860 in fulfillment of the dream of the Reverend M.J. Whitworth. The first building was constructed under the guidance of young architect A.E. Moreton, and the first graduate was Mollie Noble. The Civil War interrupted the dream, and the college was closed—first in 1861, and again in 1862, when the facilities were converted into a hospital for troops. The college is now the home of the Mississippi School of the Arts. (Phyllis Spearman.)

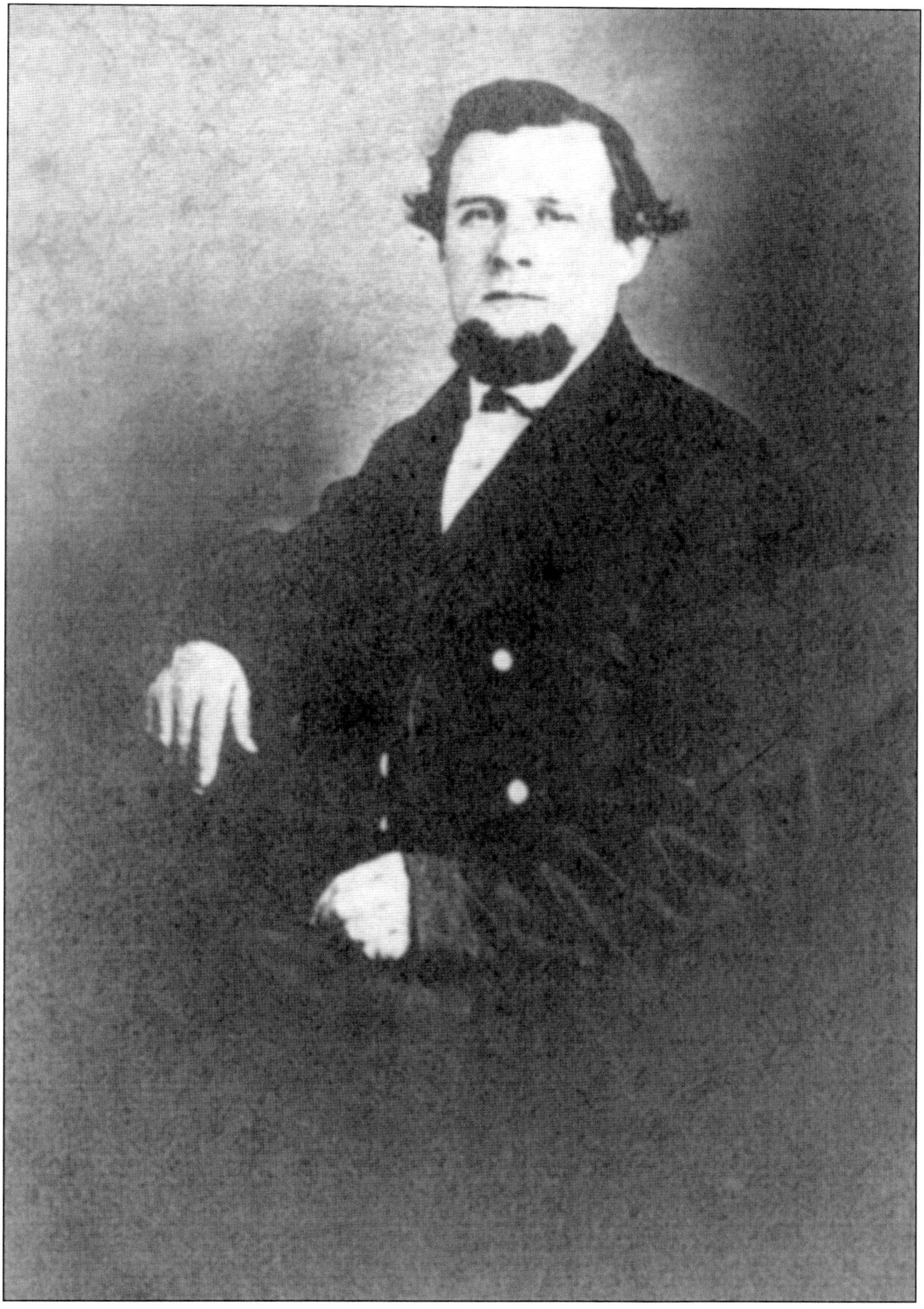

Harvey Fletcher Johnson was an attorney, legislator, Methodist minister, and longtime president of Whitworth College. He was married to Margaret Bates. Johnson was the great-grandfather of Phyllis Spearman. (Phyllis Spearman.)

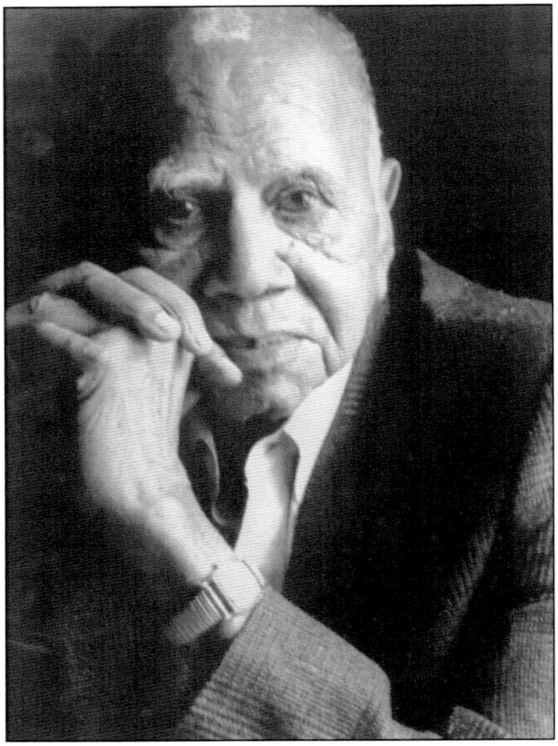

Archie Alphonso Alexander was born about 16 miles southeast of Brookhaven. He attended Hughey School, a "one-teacher" rural school, from the first through eighth grades. He was accepted to Jackson State University and received a bachelor of arts degree in science and economics in 1928. Alexander went on to receive a master of arts degree in school administration from Northwestern University and did postgraduate work at Atlanta, Cornell, and Rutgers Universities. In the 1932–1933 school year, Alexander was appointed to serve as principal in the Brookhaven Public School System. In later years, Alexander High School would be named for him. He also served as supervisor of education, Mississippi State Department of Education, and special consultant for Title IV (desegregation of schools) at Mississippi State University. (Maxine Allen.)

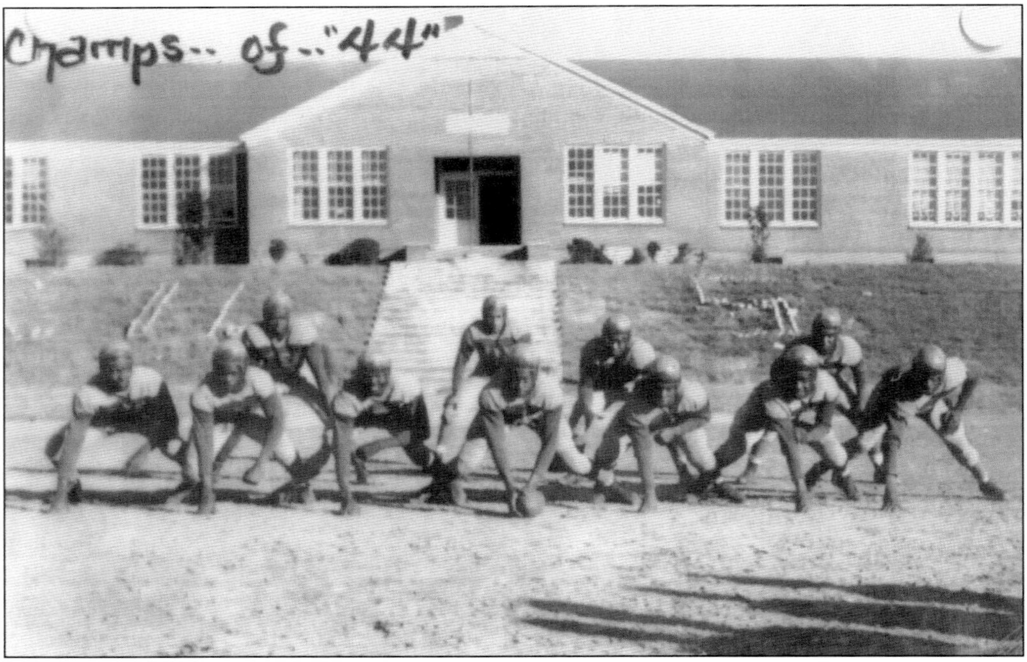

The Alexander High School football team of 1944 was declared the "champs." Behind the players is the old school, which was destroyed by fire in 1952. It would take several years for a new campus to be completed, and it was opened to students in 1956. (LLF.)

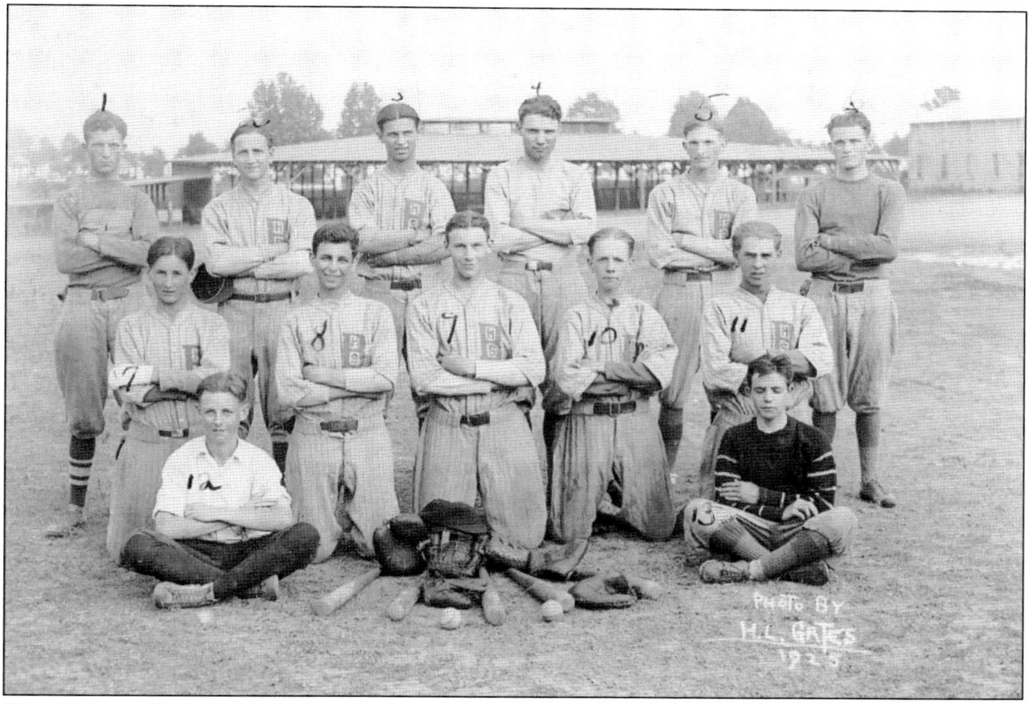

Brookhaven High School's baseball team was the 1925 Southwest Champion. Names of the players are listed on this photograph taken by H.L. Gates. The surnames include Alford, Decell, Smith, Nevins, Tibbs, Cheairs, Brueck, Lewinthal, Middleton, Massengill, Herring, and Johnson. (LLF.)

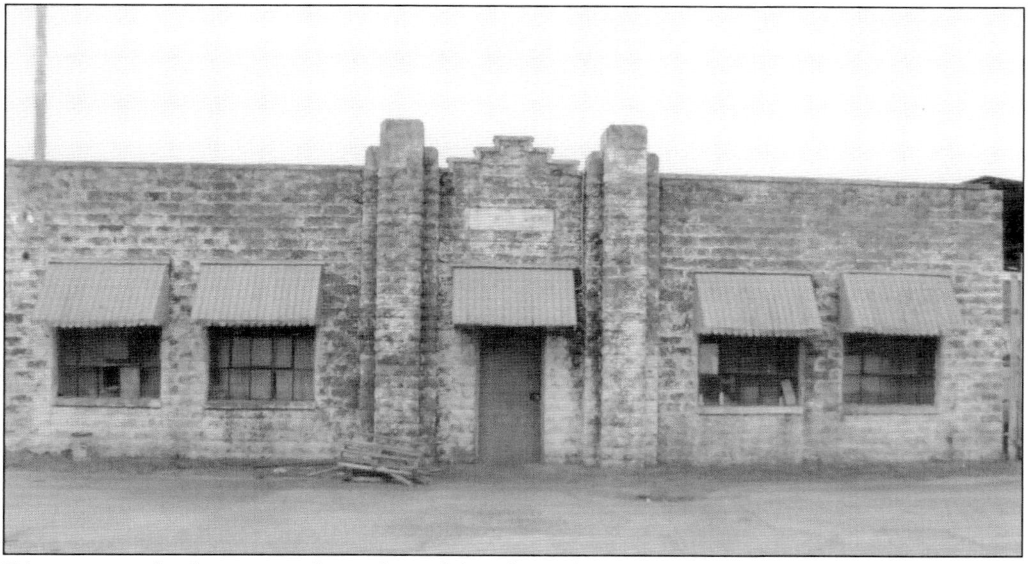

Education and job training for male and female students, ages 16 to 25, from "relief" families was the goal of the National Youth Administration. Shop skills for boys, a sewing room for girls, and a handicraft room for both were offered in the Brookhaven facility. This program was originally part of the 1935 Works Progress Administration. The program was transferred to the Federal Security Agency in 1942 and closed in 1943 as a part of the War Manpower Commission. (Marti Parker.)

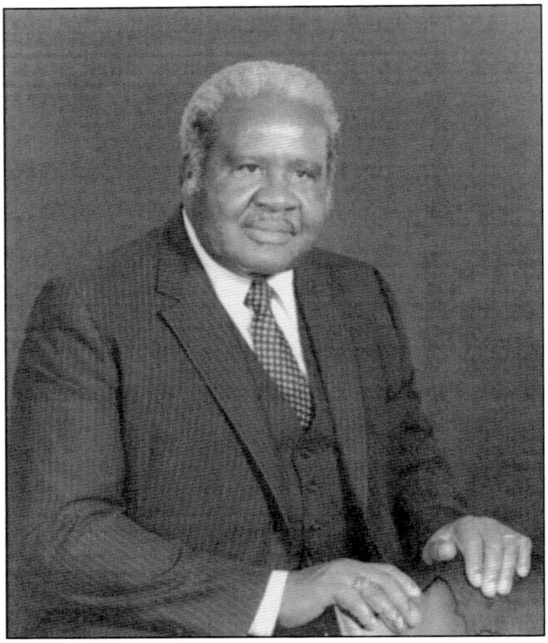

John Dow Sr. began his professional career at Alexander High School in Brookhaven in 1950 with multiple positions, including assistant coach. In two years, he was promoted to head football coach. Through the years, he served as principal at Mullins Elementary and Alexander Junior High. Later, Dow was assistant superintendent in Lincoln County and the first black appointee to the Copiah-Lincoln Community College District Board of Trustees. (Maxine Allen.)

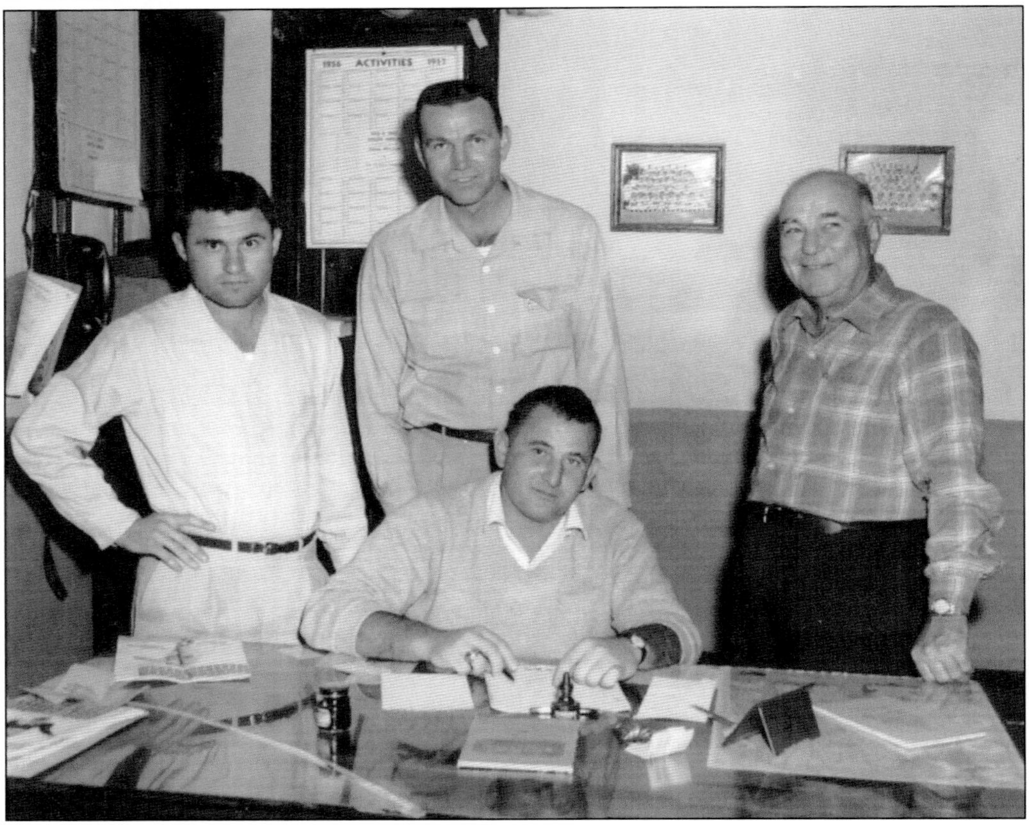

The Brookhaven High School coaches in 1956 pose for a photograph. They are, from left to right, Eddie Langford (football), James Sinclair (basketball), Paul Moyer (head football coach), and Robert L. Therrell (girls' basketball and track). (Miriam Moyer.)

Six

Worship as a Priority

Beginning in 1540, Hernando de Soto led a band of Spaniards across the wild, uncharted New World. With him were Catholic priests intent on Christianizing the "heathen" Indians. Mississippi's population was concentrated at Natchez, with an influx of people mainly from the river. Spain and Catholicism failed to have a lasting influence. Near Natchez, in 1791, Rev. Richard Curtis had organized Salem, the first Baptist church, even though public services were forbidden. Then, two years later, the Spanish government ordered Curtis to stop preaching or leave the colony.

Moving southward from Virginia and the Carolinas were subsistence farmers, very different from the rivermen, plantation owners, merchants, trappers, and Indians of the western part of the territory. Spiritual needs of these colonizers were met by preaching services only once a month, with a circuit rider traveling from one congregation to another; or by camp meetings lasting up to two weeks under tents or roofs supported by wooden beams, lighted by kerosene lamps.

Revival flamed when Methodists Lerner Blackman and C.T.N. Barnes persuaded the fiery Lorenzo Dow, who had been preaching to the Presbyterians in Kentucky, to join them. Churches of several denominations evolved, meeting first in homes and later building small structures for worship. Blacks were members of established churches until the Civil War, when they began to form their own churches.

As the population grew, residents sought organization and ways to have a minister nearby at times of weddings, illnesses, and deaths. Methodists were the first to organize as a formal ecclesiastical body for mission to settlers in the piney woods, in November 1813. The formation of the Presbytery of Mississippi was three years later, followed by the Episcopal Diocese of Mississippi and the State Baptist Convention. Formal organization of the Lutheran Synod of Mississippi was 42 years in the future, and it was not until 1844 that the Disciples of Christ created a state association.

The life of the community revolved around the church, establishing the moral, cultural, and spiritual character of Lincoln County.

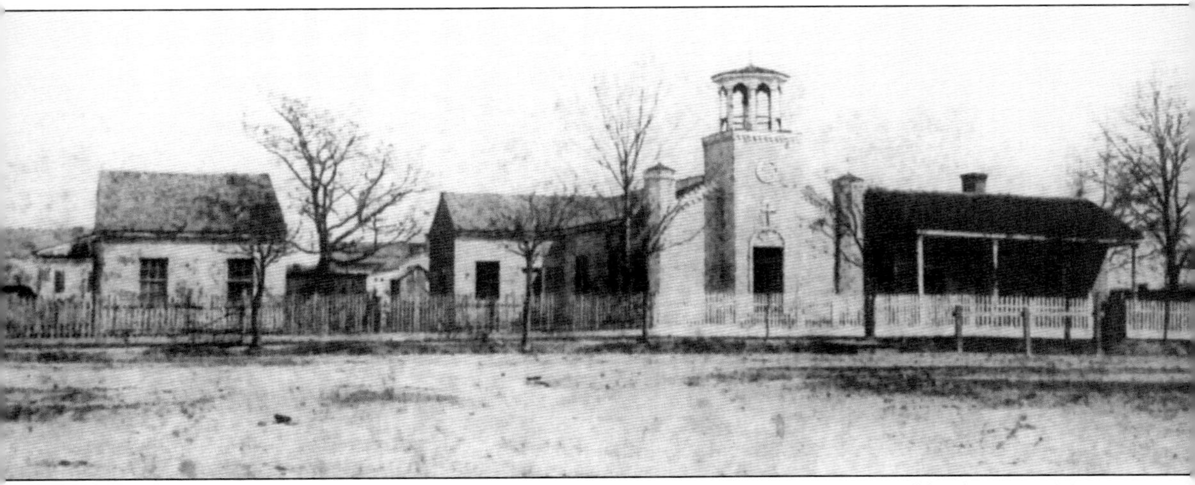

The original St. Francis of Assisi Catholic Church (pictured) was destroyed by fire in 1873. It is reported that the first masses were celebrated in the homes of Pierre Becker and the Stafflers in 1858. Land for the school, church, rectory, and cemetery was procured in 1860, and Father Henry Picherit was the priest as St. Francis was established as a mission station. The priest shown standing in the gateway is Father Strake, who succeeded Father Picherit in 1869. Rosa Grant, daughter of Patrick and Mary Welch Grant, was the first child baptized into the church. In 1866, St. Francis was changed from mission to parish status. (Bettie Hatcher Cox.)

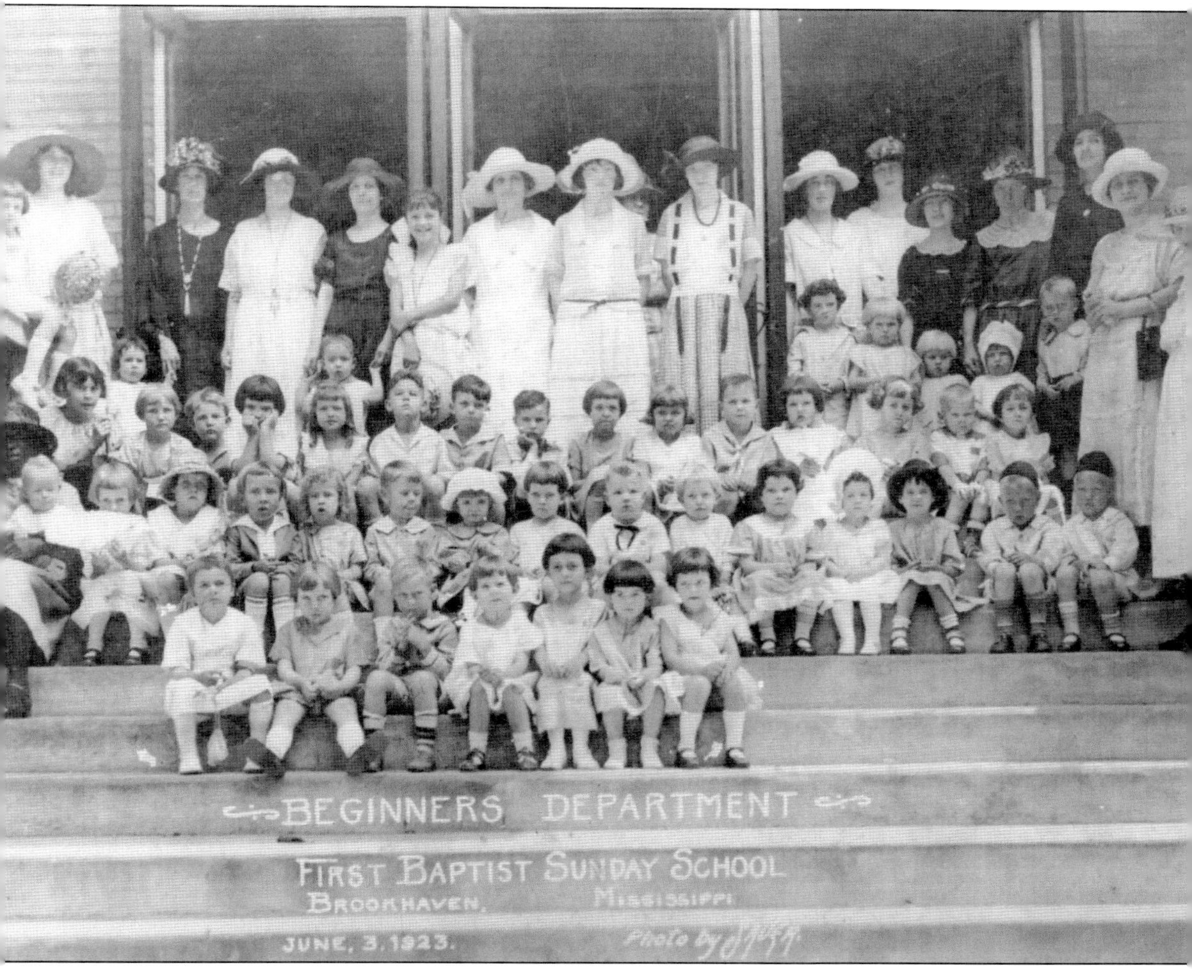

The original First Baptist Church in Brookhaven was established during or after the Civil War, but it was dissolved a few years later "rather than permit names of members upon the roll who brought reproach upon the cause by their recreant lives and conduct." The present church was organized in 1872 by the efforts of Rev. J.R. Farish, who became the first pastor. In this photograph taken on June 3, 1923, members and teachers of the Beginner Sunday School pose on the steps of the second sanctuary, completed in 1914. (Carroll Montgomery.)

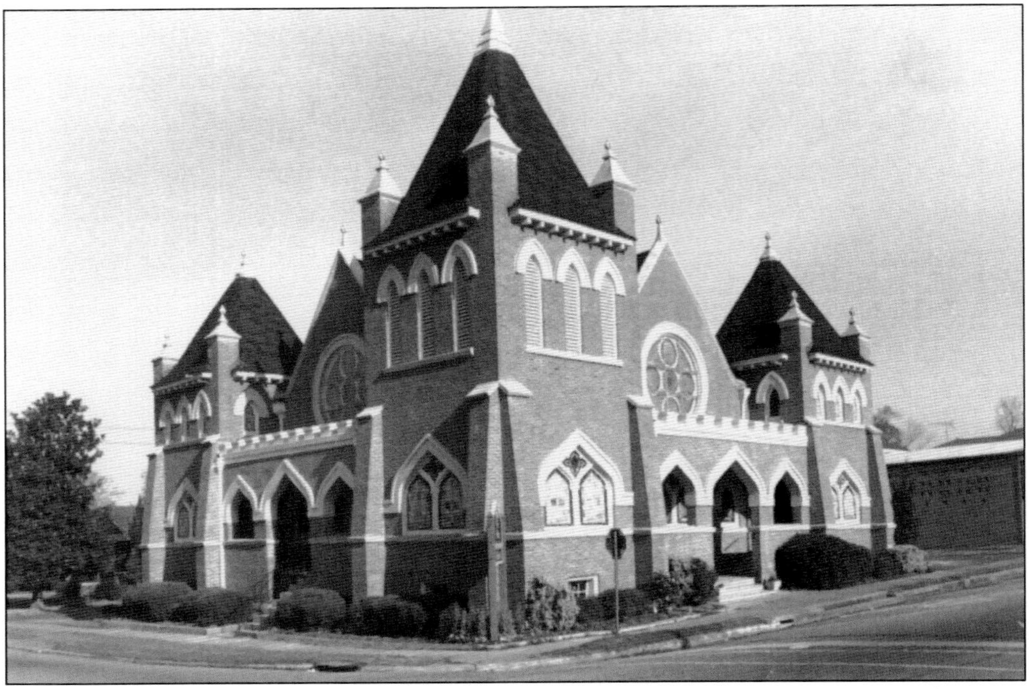

One of the most beautiful examples of architecture in Brookhaven is the First Presbyterian Church. The congregation was formed in August 1857, and Milton Whitworth donated land for the first church to be established. It was later torn down, and a new building was constructed at the corner of South Jackson and West Chickasaw Streets. The present building was constructed in 1906, and its first service was held on February 17, 1907. Later years would see the congregation dissolved and the building used as an events center. (LLF.)

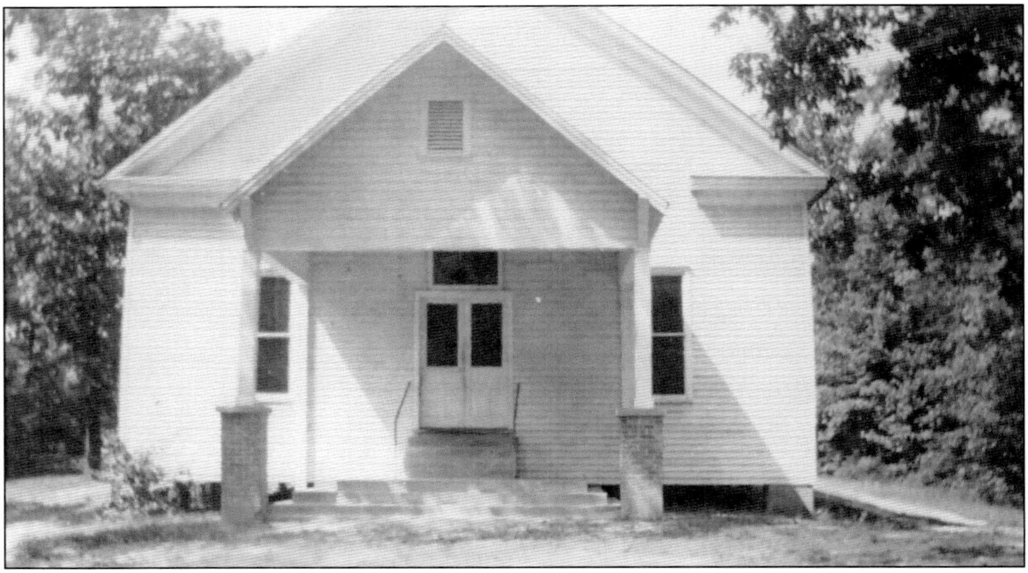

Friendship Baptist Church was established in 1809. Founded by Stephen Smith, the church was not constituted, however, until 1818. By that time, sawmills were planing logs cut from pine forests along Old St. Stephens Road (now Zetus Road), opening up a land route for settlers and traders from the St. Stephens post on the Tombigbee River in Alabama to Natchez. (Laverne Smith.)

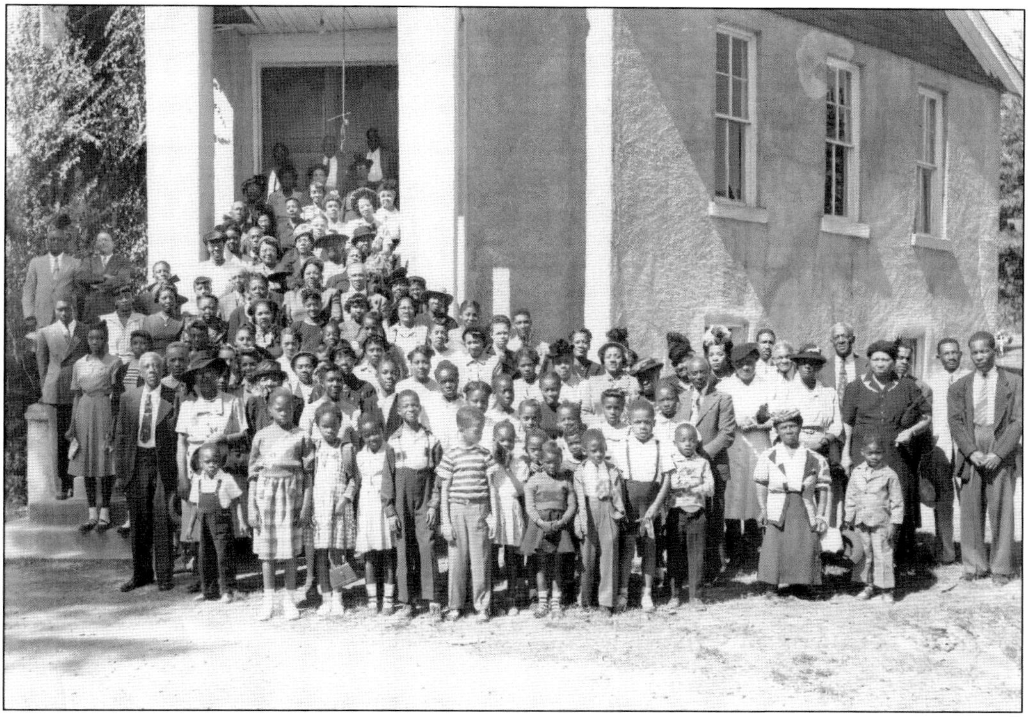

Members of St. James Missionary Baptist Church were photographed at the old church, located on the corner of Minnesota and Second Streets. The original church was established in 1866 on South First Street by the Reverend George Black. The congregation eventually moved to a new building on East Monticello Street. (LLF.)

The First Baptist Church in Brookhaven was disbanded, and the second First Baptist Church was organized in 1872, two years after Lincoln County was formed. In 1873, the first building was erected on what is now the front campus of Whitworth College. Rev. J.R. Farish was the first pastor; Mayor W.P. Baggett and K.R. Webb were the first deacons chosen from a membership of only 13. Within 10 years, growth necessitated a new building. Constructed on the block where the present church stands, the new edifice was completed in 1885 on a lot purchased for $400. Its domed structure was, and remains, very unusual in Baptist architecture. A large tapestry, created by Chinese artisans, hangs in the baptistery. (LLF.)

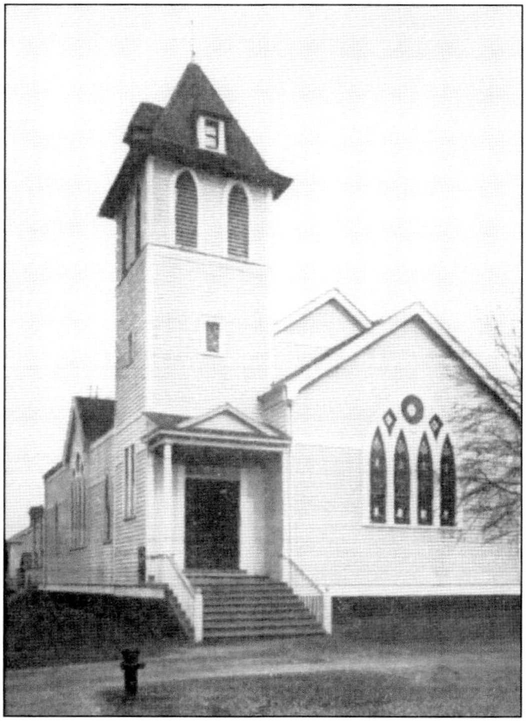

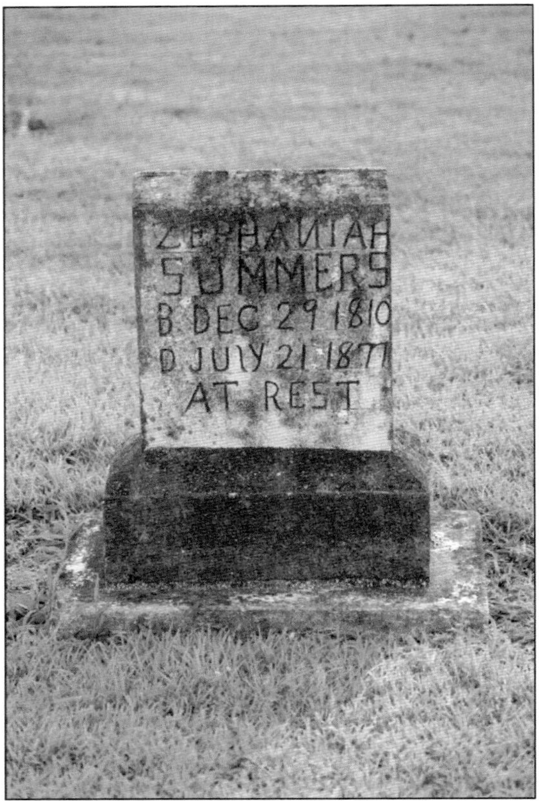

The tombstone of Zephaniah Summers (1810–1877) marks one of the oldest graves at Union Baptist Church, organized on June 15, 1869, in what was then Lawrence County. Organizing members' surnames included Boyte, Chandler, Coon, Cummings, Albritton, Martin, McGuffee, Stewart, and Summers. The first pastor was the Reverend J.L. Chandler. (Tammie Santos Brewer.)

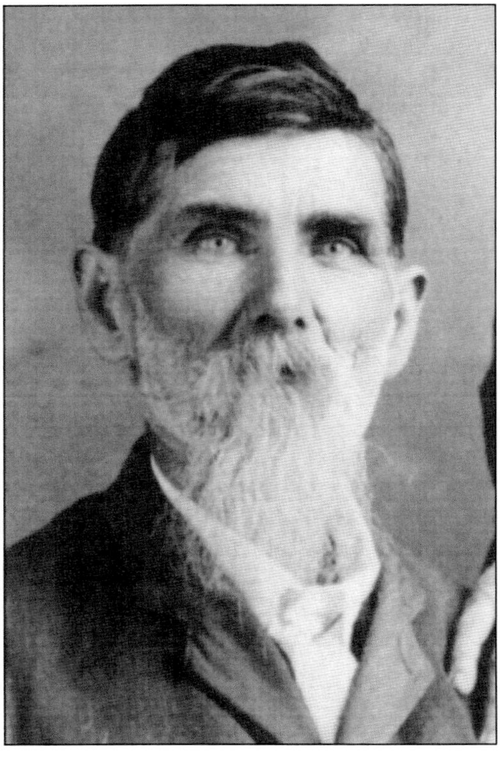

It was the year 1896, in late afternoon, when two young men, missionaries for the Church of Jesus Christ of Latter-day Saints, better known as the Mormons, approached the Mayberry Britt home. Britt (pictured) allowed them to spend the night. The following day, a cottage meeting was held. Britt and his wife, Arabella, along with Joseph B. Reed, a neighbor who had joined the church the year before, formed the foundation of the Mormon Church in Lincoln County. The first chapel was built on property of Mayberry Britt in the Red Star community in 1909. It was destroyed by fire two years later. The new building of 1913 was destroyed six years later, also by fire; in 1928, the third was established, which endured until 1960. (Ralph Calcote.)

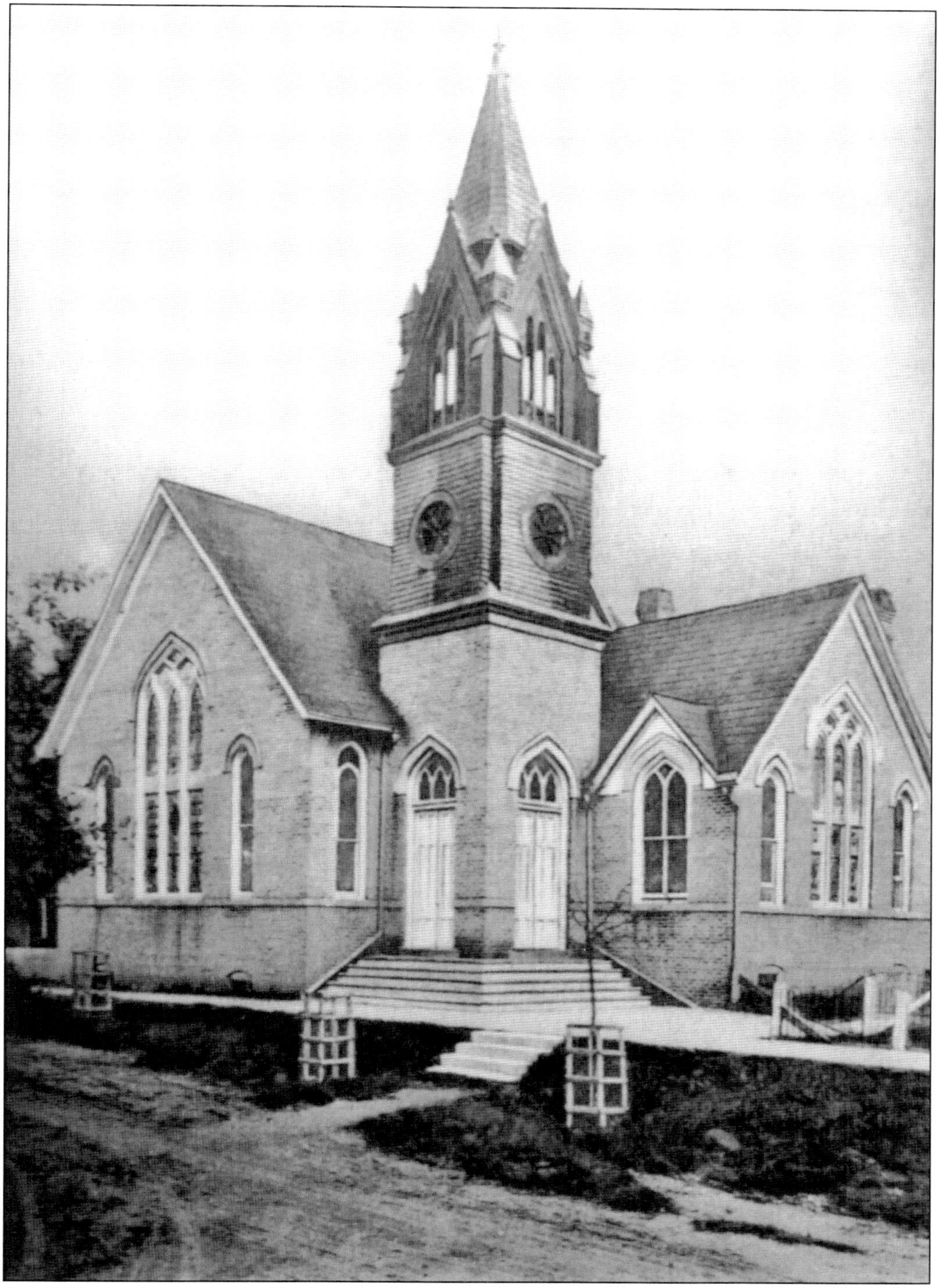

In 1858, Brookhaven was still a forest with wild deer running through the area when construction of the First Methodist Church was in progress. Milton J. Whitworth donated most of the funds for the building. The original plot was on what was part of the Methodist-owned Whitworth College campus. The current structure was completed in 1917 to accommodate the tremendous growth in the early 1900s. Rev. Archibald B. Nicholson was the first pastor. (Raymond Roberts.)

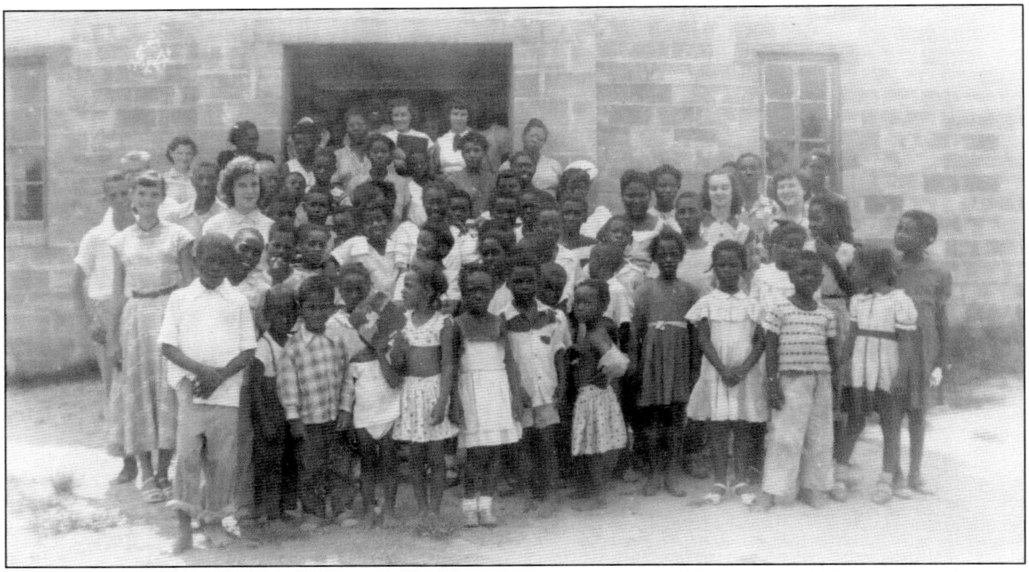

This photograph was taken at Mount Olive Missionary Baptist Church in 1953. It highlights the cooperation and goodwill between blacks and whites that existed in Lincoln County, contrary to what many people believe. The youth at Vacation Bible School include children from the church and Pleasant Grove Baptist Church. Those who have been identified are, in no particular order, Fred Herring Jr., Ann Herring Rushing, Laurie Fauver Goetz, Johnnie Smith Jackson, Patricia Watts Case, Bettie Posey Bullard, and Shirley Byrd Nations. (Bettie Posey Bullard.)

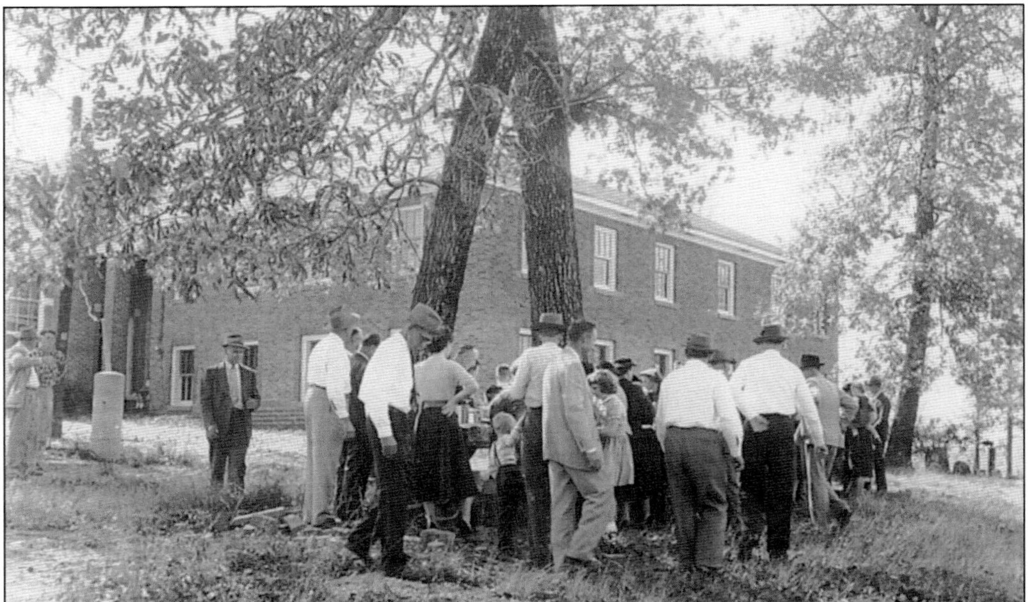

Homecoming, such as this one at Macedonia Baptist Church in 1956, was always a special time in Southern rural churches. Families came home from jobs in nearby cities and even other states to attend church and eat on the church grounds with friends and relatives who were part of their lives from childhood. They saw new babies, young married couples, and the tombstones of those who had passed on during the previous year. Many descendants of the original members of the early Britt, Case, East, and Smith families still attend church at Macedonia. (Seth Allen.)

Seven

Downtown in Brookhaven

Downtown Brookhaven, now built around the New Orleans, Jackson & Great Northern Railroad, was first located about a mile and a half south of the present site, on land purchased by Samuel Jayne in 1833. Jayne established a community he named after his hometown, Brookhaven, Long Island, New York, and operated a gristmill, a small store, and the post office.

There is evidence in court records in Monticello that Jayne expected the railroad to come through his property and that the railroad company would purchase the land needed from him, but Milton J. Whitworth, who owned property just west of Jayne's, offered to donate land for the right-of-way and for the location of a depot.

When the railroad was built, the town moved, taking the name with it. The old location became known as Old Brook, and for years, it was a favorite swimming and picnic place.

Enterprising men started businesses, such as general merchandise stores, hardware stores, livery stables, and even a jewelry store. The Bowen House and the Commercial Hotel were two of several lodging places located close to the railroad.

The town continued to grow and was incorporated in 1873. Then, in 1879, when funds were available, it was possible to build the first of four courthouses. Land was purchased from Mrs. F.A. Brooks, and the contract was given to Capt. Alfred E. Moreton, who built the two-story brick structure.

Also located in the downtown area was Whitworth College for Females, organized shortly before the Civil War by the Reverend Henry J. Harris and Milton J. Whitworth. Whitworth College was once called the "Arts Center of the South" and is today the location of the Mississippi School of the Arts.

This chapter includes images of the streets and stores and other buildings along the major streets of Brookhaven, the county seat of Lincoln County.

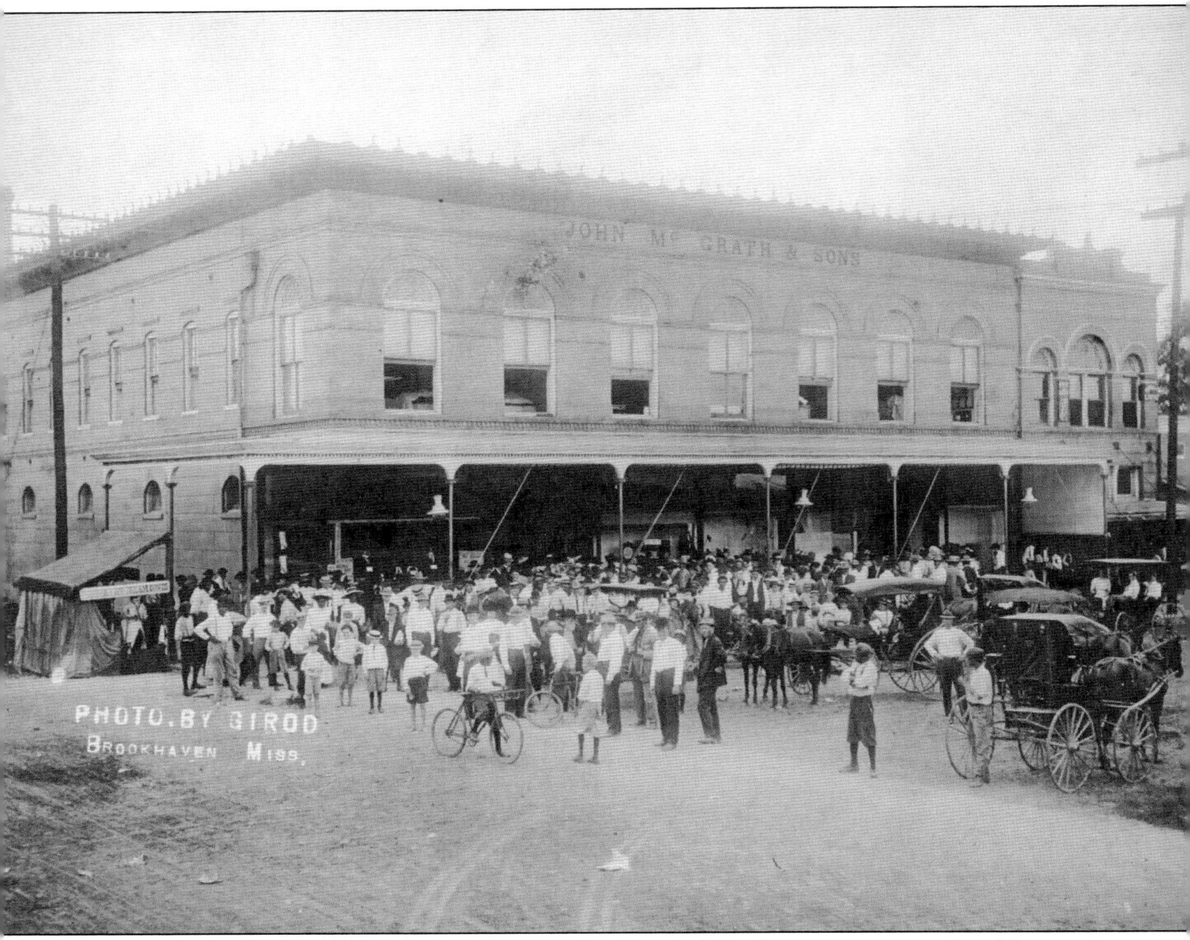

In February 1878, John W. McGrath opened a dry-goods and grocery store in Brookhaven that proved to be a very successful business. He advertised that he had no overhead, because he employed his sons as clerks. McGrath managed the store until his death in 1902, when his son John Jr. took over. He was in charge until his death in 1922. It was told that John Jr.'s last words were "Good-bye, Brookhaven friends." (LLF.)

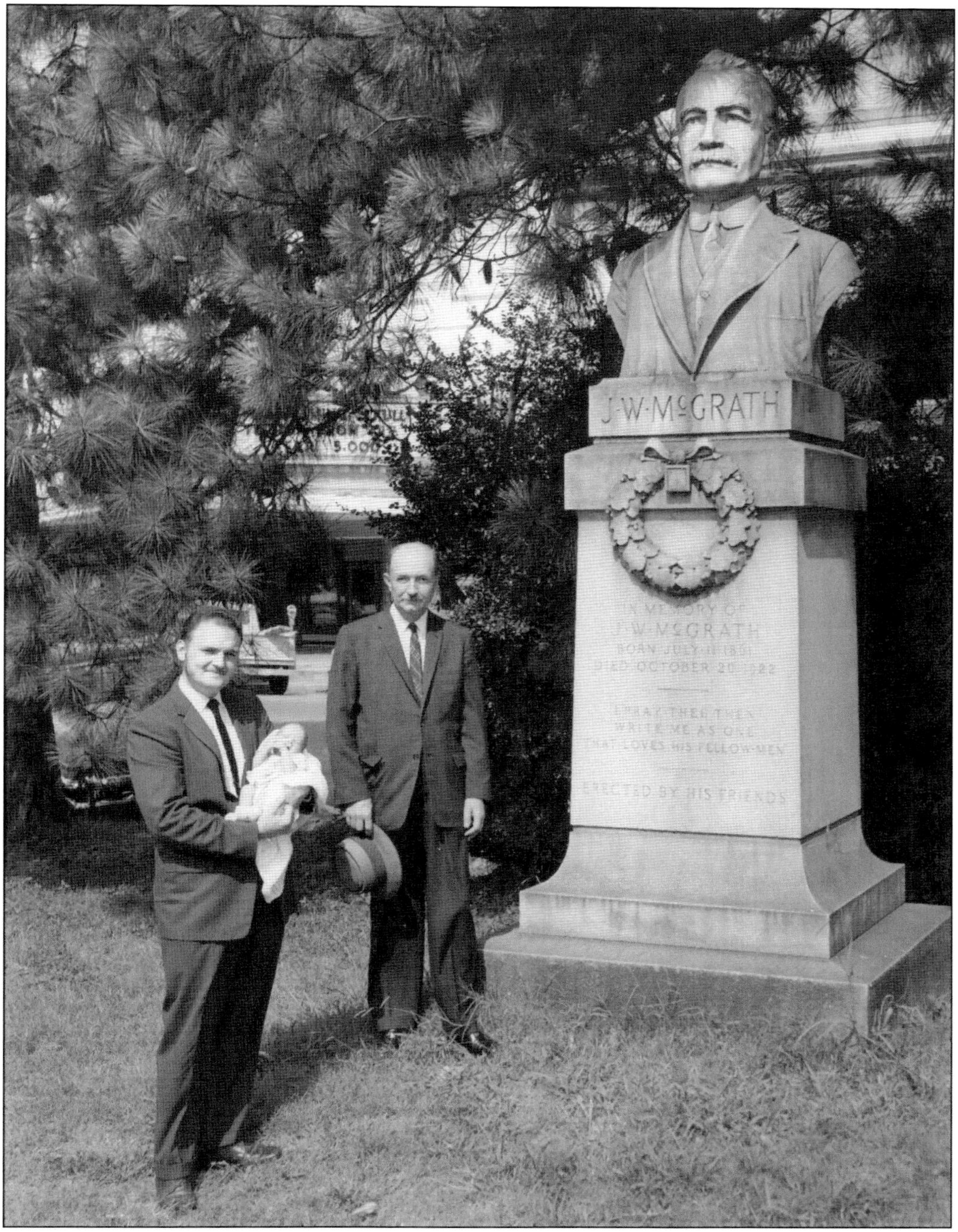

After the death of John W. McGrath Jr. in 1922, a drive was started to erect a memorial to him. Donations came from as far away as Texas and Illinois. McGrath was admired by all who knew him. He supported anything he thought was good for Brookhaven and was always willing to lend a helping hand to those in need. He was known for his infectious smile and loyalty to his friends. Albert Weidlen of New Orleans was commissioned to do the monument, and an unveiling ceremony was held on December 23, 1923, in Railroad Park just across the tracks from McGrath's Department Store. Pictured here are four generations of the family (including the bust), all named John W. McGrath. (LLF.)

FALL STYLE PAGEANT

—OF—

JOHN McGRATH & SONS

THURSDAY, SEPTEMBER 18, 1930

High School Auditorium

8:15 P. M.

I've Got My Eyes on You.........................Ellen Johnson and Dancing Chorus

Modeling of Coats

Autumn Leaves—Interpretive Dance....................................Patricia Vance

Modeling of Sport Frocks
Men's Sport Togs

With My Guitar and You......................................Roger Noble and Orchestra

If I Had a Talking Picture of You..
.... Mary Clare and Lewis Decell assisted by Juvenile Chorus

Modeling of Street Dresses
Men's Business Suits

Military Tap Dance (Uncle Sam Gets Reminiscent)..................Elsie Moodie

Swinging in the Hammock..................Miss Alpha Williams, Homer Powers

Modeling of Afternoon Dresses
Men's Street Suits

Come a Little Closer (Solo Dance) ....Miss Irma Brent

It Must be an Old Spanish Custom .... Peggy Grafton, Ellen Johnson

Modeling of Dinner Dresses

Selection ....Orchestra

You Darlin'.............................Homer Powers, Elsie Moodie, Dancing Chorus

Modeling of Evening Gowns
Men's Semi-Dress Suits

Finale ....Ensemble

—CAST—

Dancing Chorus—
Aline Brister
Anita Cox
Eloise Guess
Regina Morton
Seymour Phillips
Lucille Schwem

Juvenile Chorus—
Betsy Bee
Betty Bowlus
Katherine Hardy
Cecilia Moore
Phyllis Johnson
Henry Ware Hobbs

—MODELS—

Mesdames—
James Alford
Bessie Blake
Leon Oberschmidt

Misses—
Mary Sue Burnham
Louise Craven
Eva Myrtle Henry
Roxie Moodie
Nannie Smith
Cleo Warren
Ruth Winfield

Messrs.—
Kent Bowen
Raymond Cohen
Lewis Decell
Sam Jones

Musical Director..........................Mrs. J. H. Johnson
Accompanist...........................Miss Dorothy Middleton
Stage Artist..Mr. John Gryder
Music ....Merrymakers

One of McGrath's seasonal promotions was to hold a style show with local entertainers, as illustrated in this program from 1930. John McGrath & Sons was in business for 85 years, closing its doors on February 1, 1963. (Phyllis Spearman.)

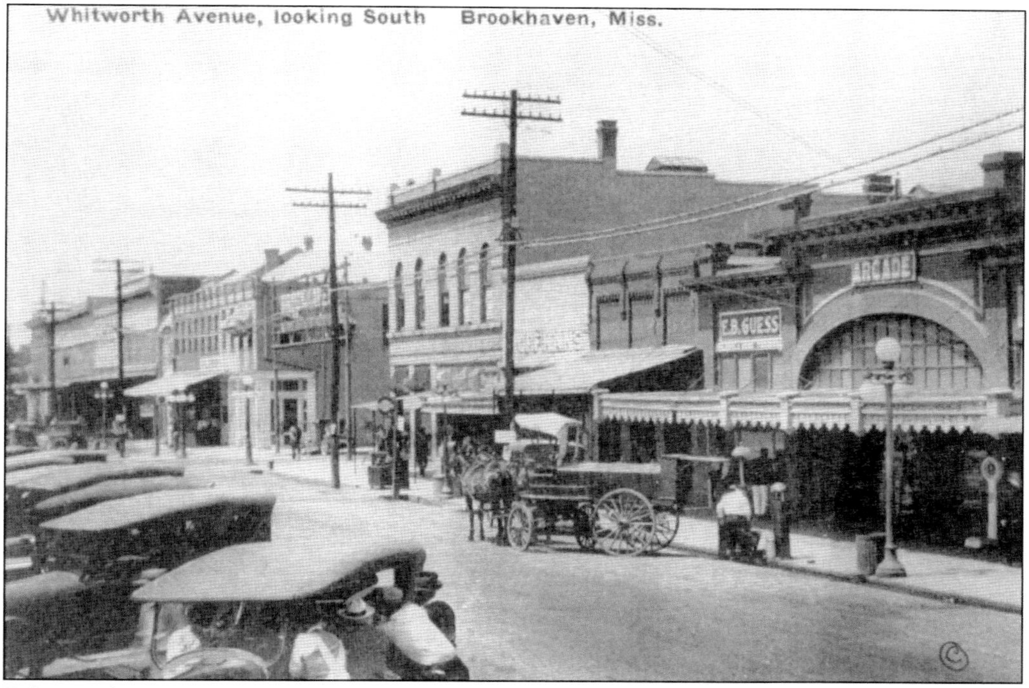

Whitworth Avenue, one of the main business streets in town, runs on the west side of the railroad tracks. The Arcade Theater was one of the early moving-picture shows in town and was the first to show talkies, in 1929. It was also the first theater in Brookhaven to feature movies just for children on Saturday mornings, in 1925. E.B. Guess Tailoring Company, Hoffman Drug Store, and Brookhaven Bank & Trust Company are other businesses pictured here. The Arcade moved from this location to Monticello Street in 1935. (LLF.)

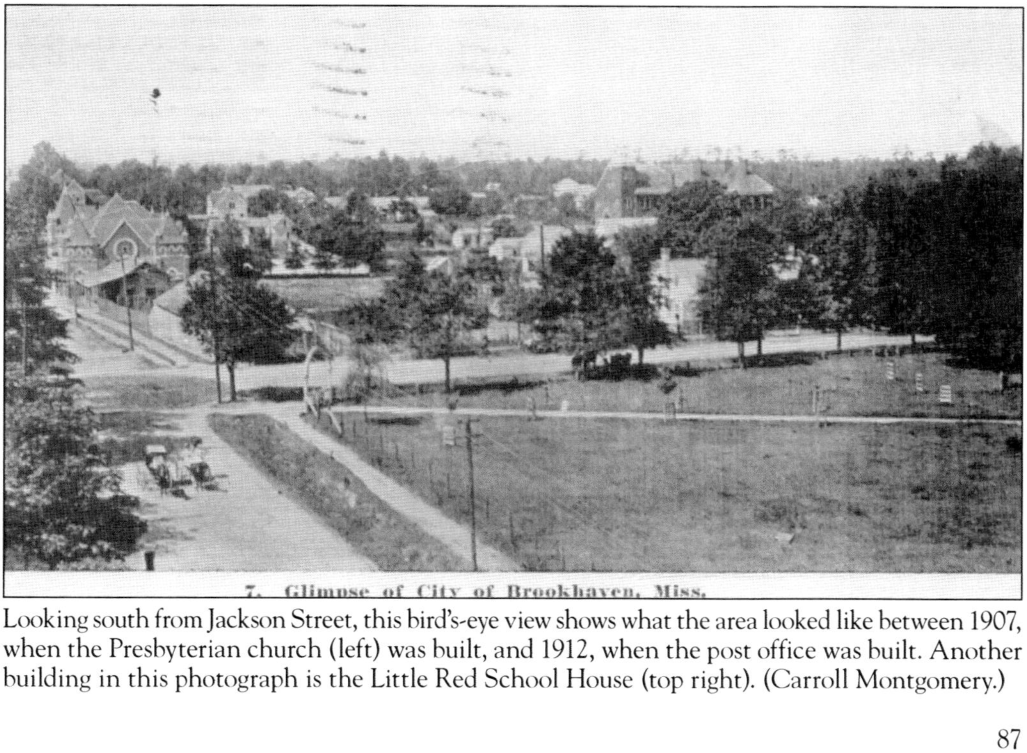

Looking south from Jackson Street, this bird's-eye view shows what the area looked like between 1907, when the Presbyterian church (left) was built, and 1912, when the post office was built. Another building in this photograph is the Little Red School House (top right). (Carroll Montgomery.)

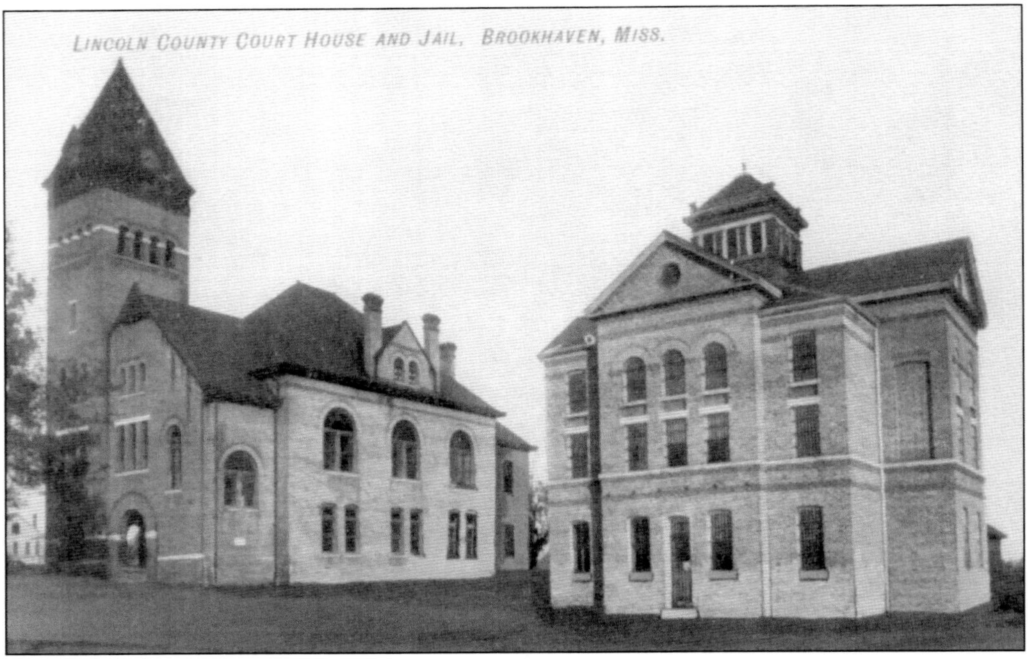

Capt. Alfred E. Moreton constructed the third building that served as a courthouse for Lincoln County (left) in 1894. Architect Andrew J. Bryan commented that Moreton was doing an excellent job and had done more than his duty by making the walls thicker than had been specified. In 1979, after serving the county for 84 years, the courthouse "came down with reluctance," as described by the *Daily Leader*. The building on the right served as the county jail. (Terry Pappas.)

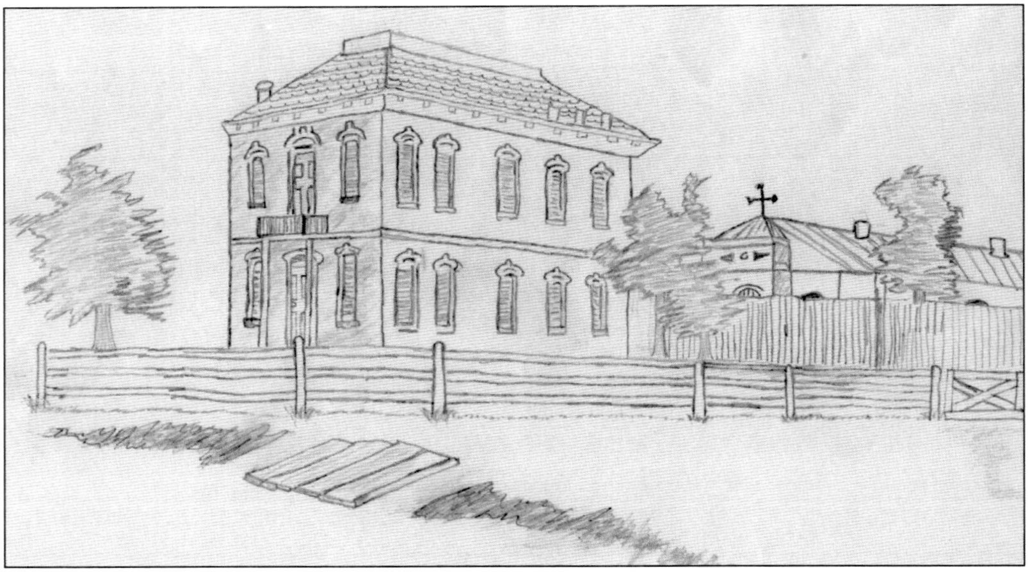

This drawing is believed to depict the second courthouse serving Lincoln County. The first one, built by Capt. Alfred E. Moreton in 1879, burned down in December 1884. A fire was discovered in the second courthouse about 2:30 on the morning of November 6, 1893, and an alarm was sounded. All efforts to save the building and its contents failed. Captain Moreton was again awarded the contract for a new courthouse, which was completed in 1894 at a cost of $15,000. (Ben Hartzog.)

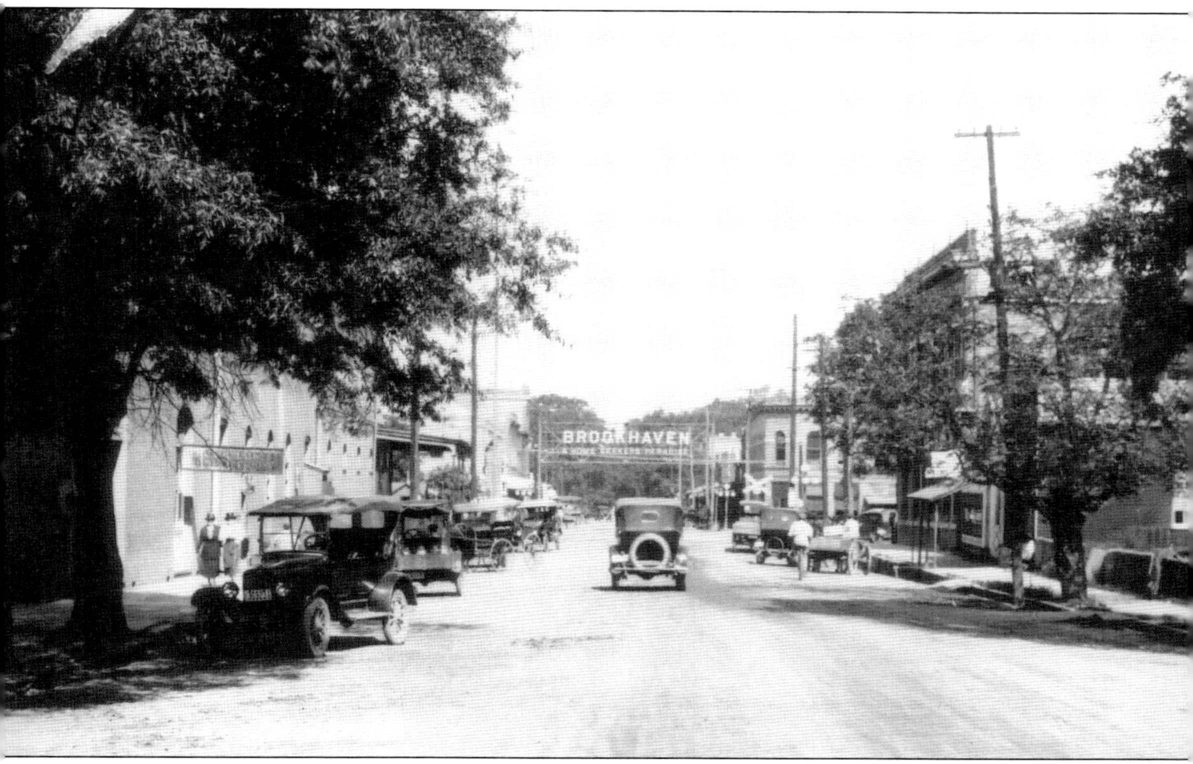

Cherokee Street and Brookhaven's A Home Seekers Paradise sign are shown in the early 20th century. Milton Cohen won $5 for the winning slogan, A Home Seekers Paradise, during a contest by the Brookhaven Board of Trade (later the chamber of commerce). The light for the original sign was first turned on in November 1915 when the Liberty Bell was brought through Brookhaven. The sign was taken down during World War II to aid with the war effort at the suggestion of students from Brookhaven High School. A replica of the sign was erected on November 16, 1996. (Terry Pappas.)

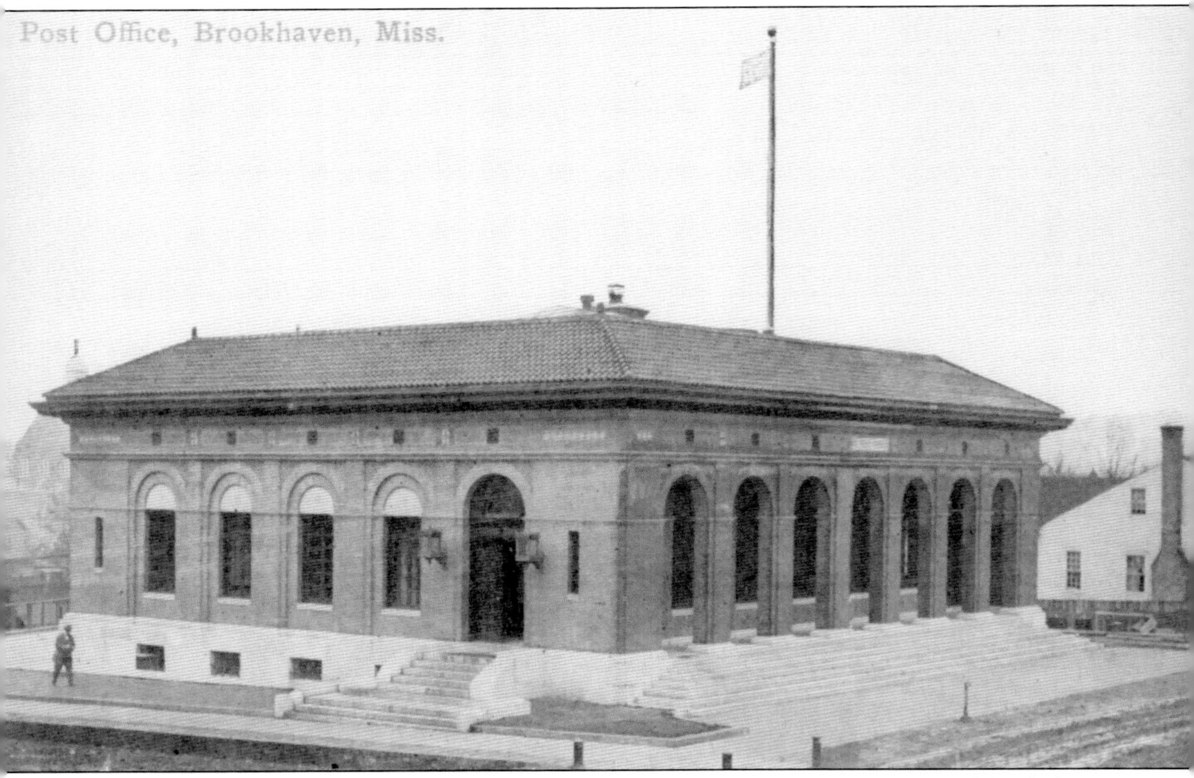

Finished in 1912, Brookhaven's post office, built with bricks made at the local brick factory, cost $70,000. It was erected by Stuart and Randall of Oklahoma. The lot was purchased from Capt. A.E. Moreton for $8,000. The site was chosen because of its location one block from the railroad. (LLF.)

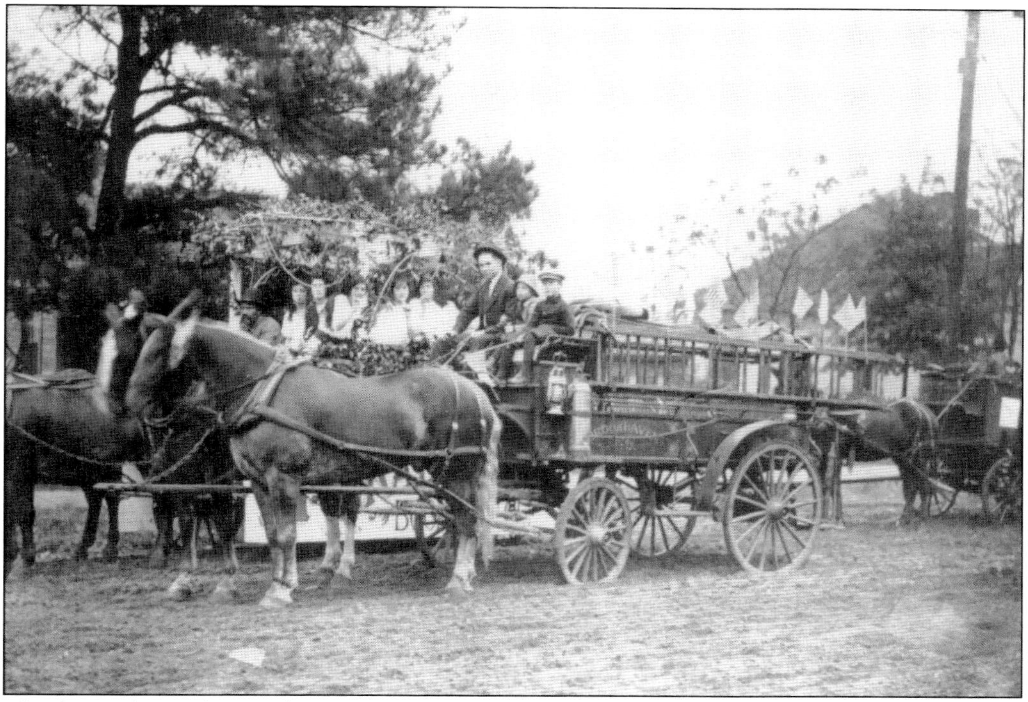

This horse-drawn fire truck waits for the parade to start on an unknown occasion. The driver is Shelby Cowart, and his two companions are Clay Abrams (center) and Stanley Guess (right). The horses were trained by Dan McCarthy for use by the fire department. (Carroll Montgomery.)

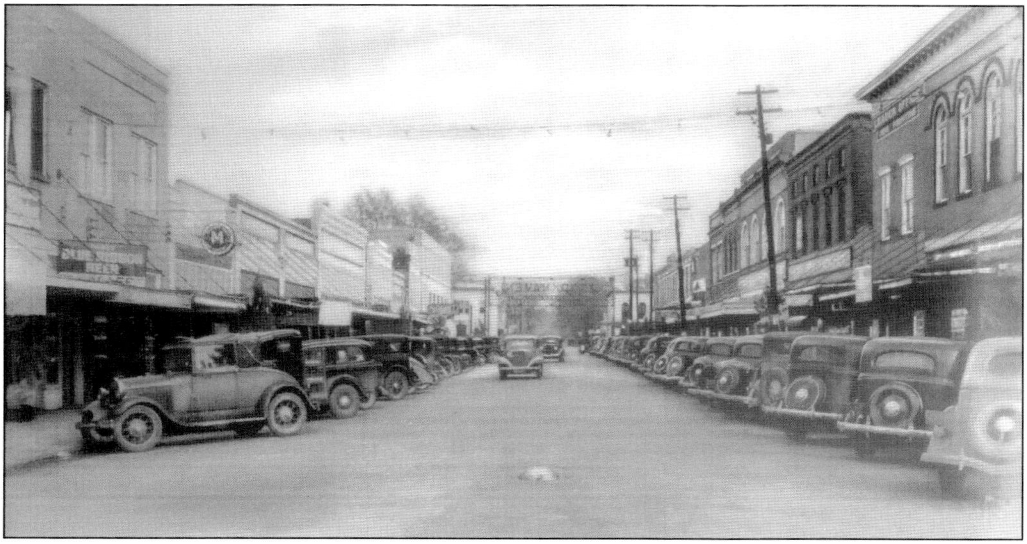

Vehicles line Cherokee Street in this undated photograph. Note the many businesses on each side of the street, including the Leader Office, a job printer and newspaper. (Terry Pappas.)

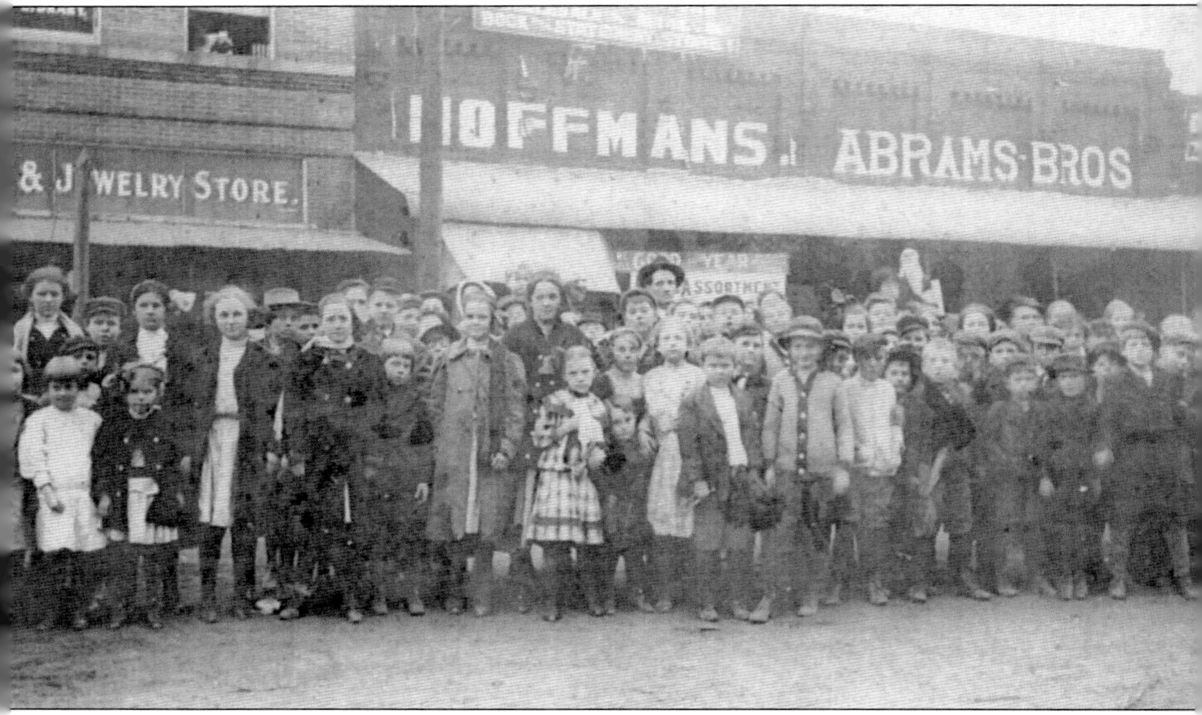

Behind the many people lining the street, on the left side of the photograph, is Price Drug & Jewelry Store. Next to it is Hoffmans, and at right is Abrams Brothers. Both Price and Hoffmans were taken in by the bank and are now part of the Trustmark Building. Abrams Brothers carried hardware and basic farm supplies, such as saddles, bridles, and other livestock equipment, until it closed. (LCHGS.)

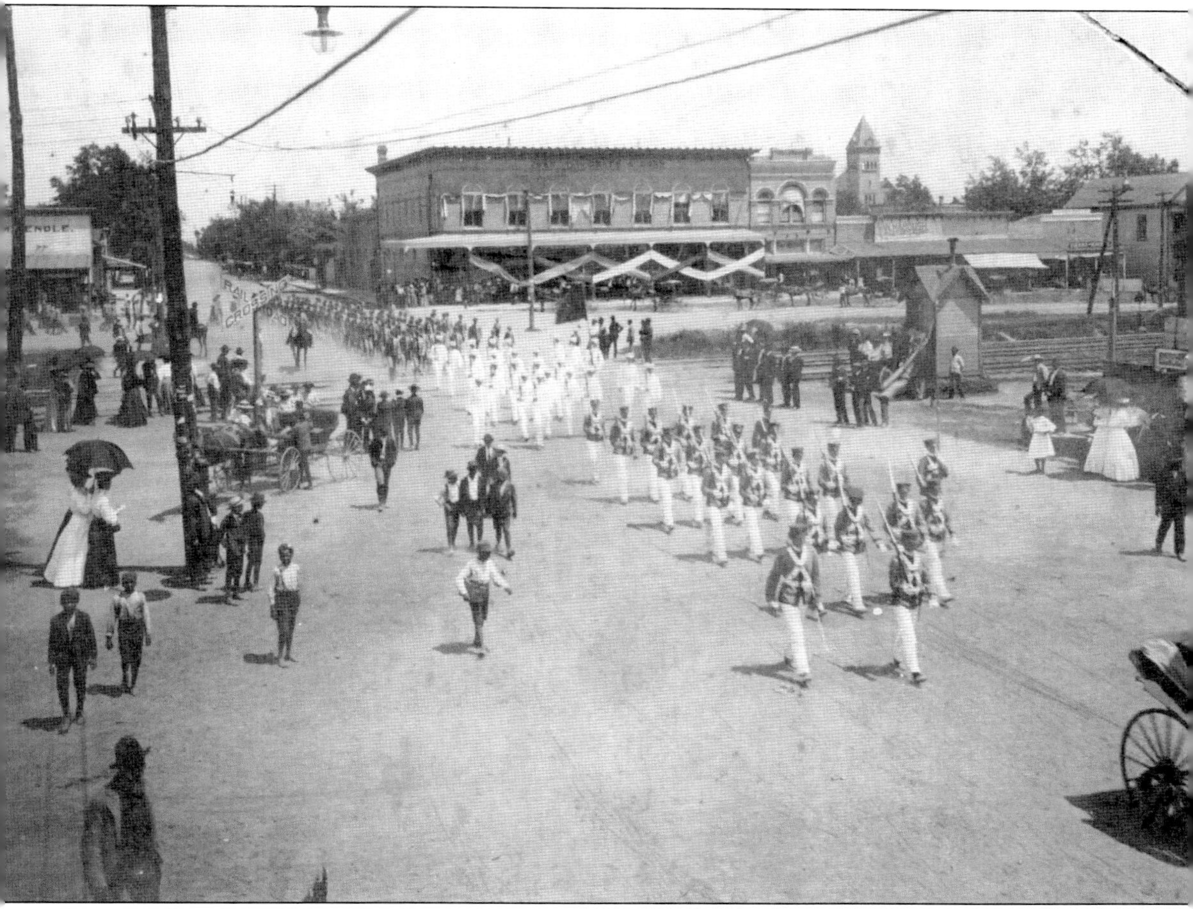

Everyone loves a parade. This photograph is believed to depict a parade on Cherokee Street honoring veterans at a Confederate soldiers reunion around 1909 or 1910. In the background is McGrath's big store. (LLF.)

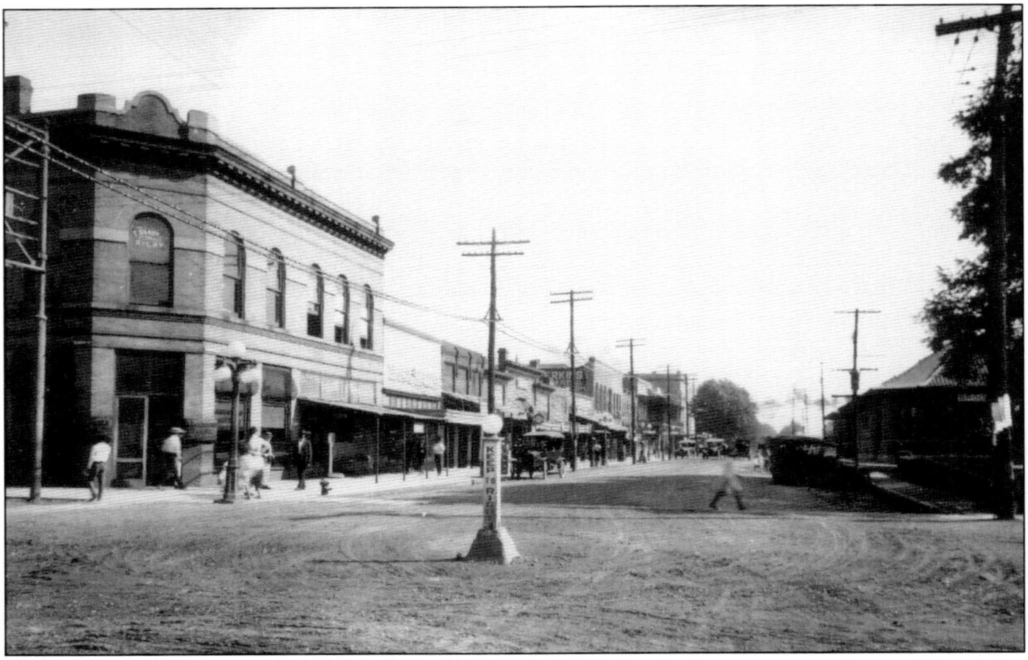

Whitworth Avenue is shown here about 1919. The Keep to the Right sign in the middle of the street was placed in an effort to control traffic. (LLF.)

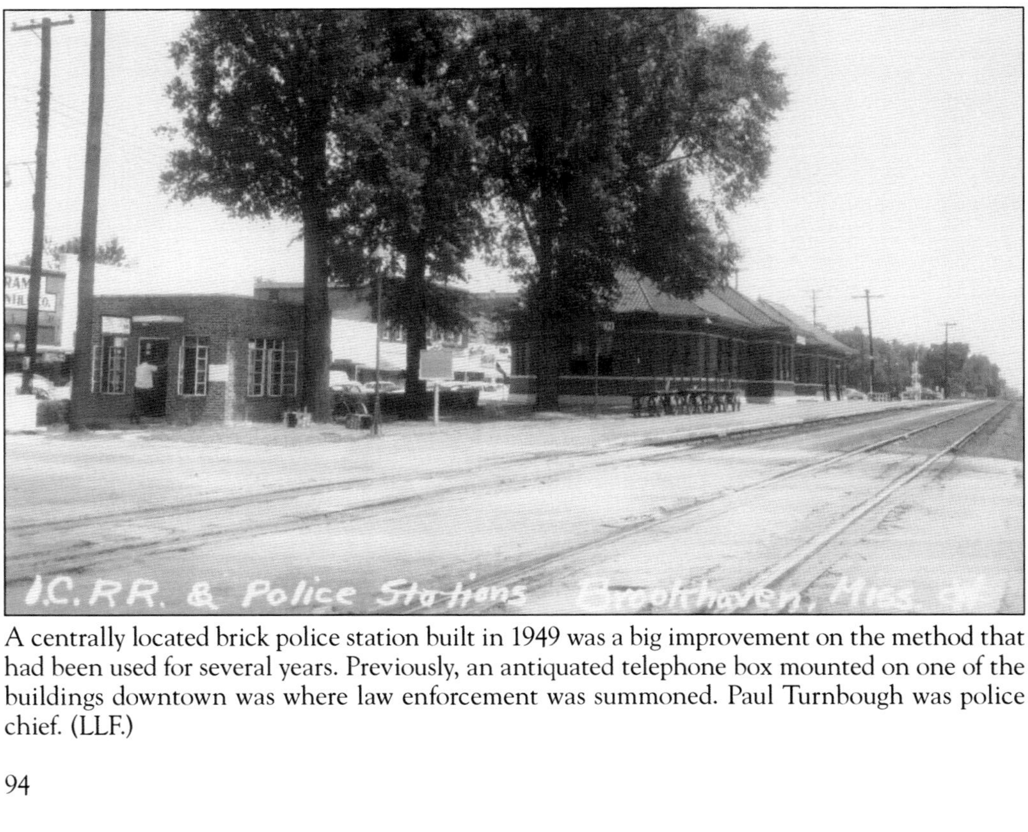

A centrally located brick police station built in 1949 was a big improvement on the method that had been used for several years. Previously, an antiquated telephone box mounted on one of the buildings downtown was where law enforcement was summoned. Paul Turnbough was police chief. (LLF.)

Eight

Time for Entertainment and Leisure

Many early families moving to unsettled areas that later became Lincoln County were deeply religious. Traveling ministers would hold campground meetings, sometimes lasting as long as two weeks. Families camped out and socialized between the services.

In between these meetings, families held barn raisings, hog-killings, and quilting bees to help each other. When the work was over, they gathered to share stories, sing, or play musical instruments.

Men and boys enjoyed attending livestock auctions, horse shows, and competitions. By the early 1900s, fishing, football, baseball, basketball, and swimming were popular pastimes. Women enjoyed teas for various occasions and showers for young couples marrying or expecting a child. Clothing magazines and favorite recipes were treasured and shared with friends.

Often, traveling acting companies were booked for a few nights in town to perform at Heuck's Opera House. Van Cliburn, the famous concert pianist, performed a benefit concert at the high school when he was only 12 years old.

With the arrival of the railroad, entertainers came to perform at Whitworth College and Heuck's Opera House, which was located across from the college. Whitworth students and the students of various music and oratory instructors held musical programs or recitals, dramatic plays, and oral interpretations. Local residents were always eager to show their talent by performing before an audience to raise money for their church, club, or Rosehill, the city cemetery.

About 1900, social clubs—including Cadmus, Climbers, and Peripatetics—were formed. The Masons, Shriners, Elks, and Woodmen of the World (now WoodmenLife) also provided recreation.

Local businesses sponsored summer baseball teams. The stores in town would close early so that everyone could go to the game. In the 1920s, a semipro baseball team formed, playing in the Cotton States League. City and county schools had their own basketball and track teams. Brookhaven had a football team.

Soon after the development of moving pictures, movie theaters were built. The first theaters located here were the Picto and the Lomo. Later, the Arcade, Haven, Rex, and Dixie were constructed. The Haven is now home to Brookhaven Little Theatre.

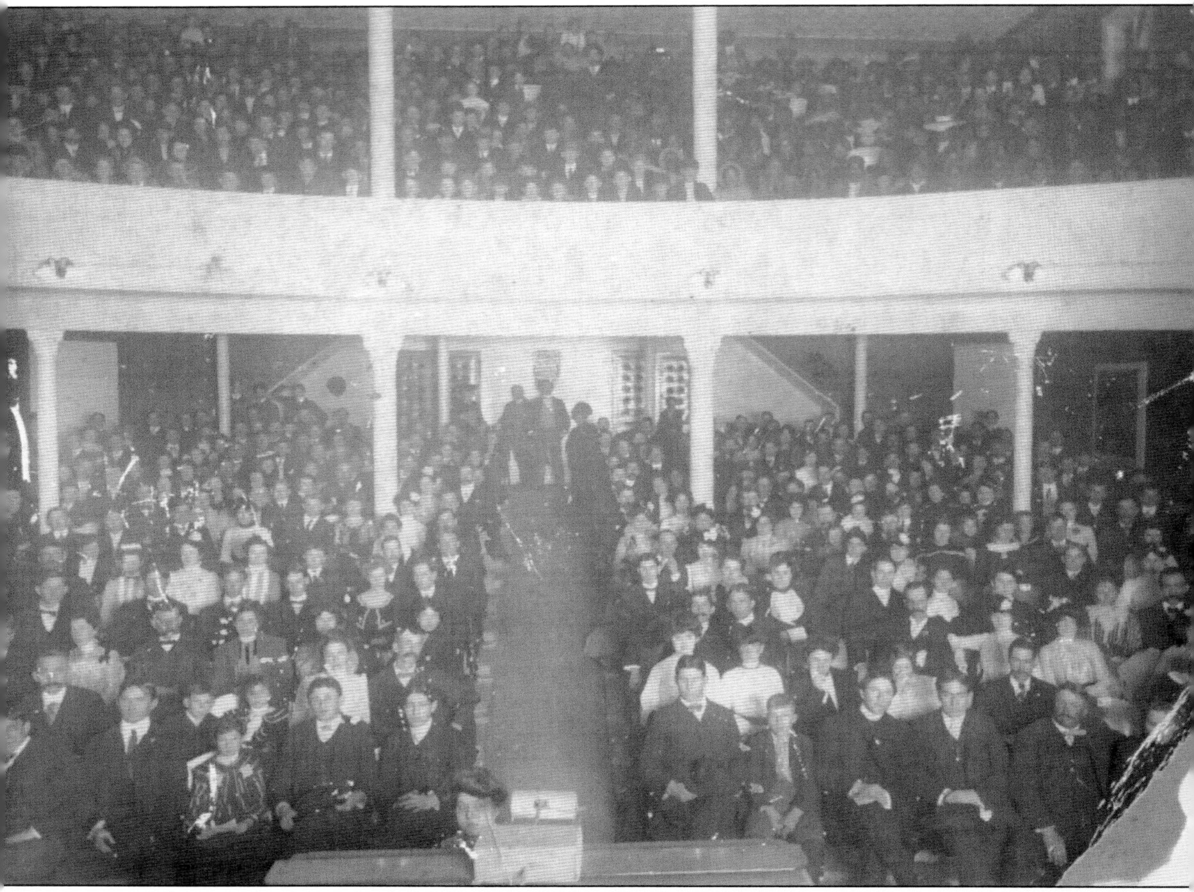

Heuck's Opera House, built in 1902, at a cost of $8,500, was the place to go see the most popular traveling groups of the day. It was built by Chris Larsen and decorated by John Grant. The two-story structure was heated by 12 radiators, lighted by 200 electric burners, and had a seating capacity of 650. Weddings and intercollegiate oratorical contests were held there also. Owned and operated by Charles Heuck, the opera house was located at the corner of South Jackson and West Monticello Streets. (Carroll Montgomery.)

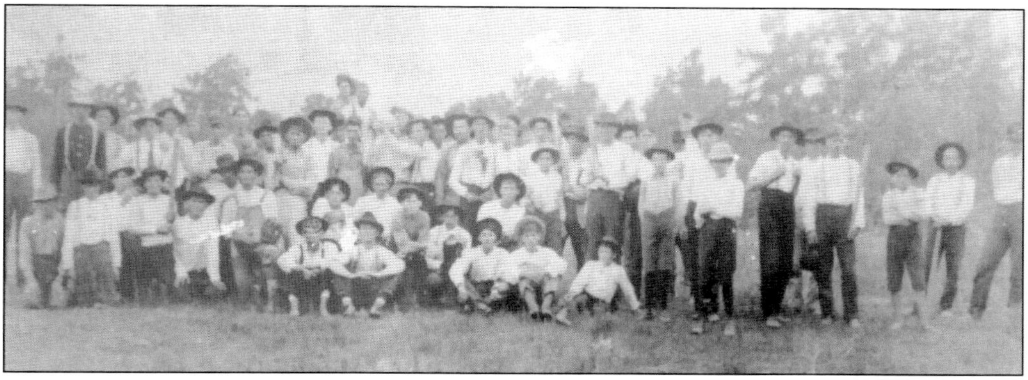

The Roberts family and their cousins, the Terrell family, were farmers who grew cotton and corn. When the men had free time, a game of baseball was just the thing to do to pass an afternoon. The families are shown here around 1900 in the West Lincoln community. (Seth Allen.)

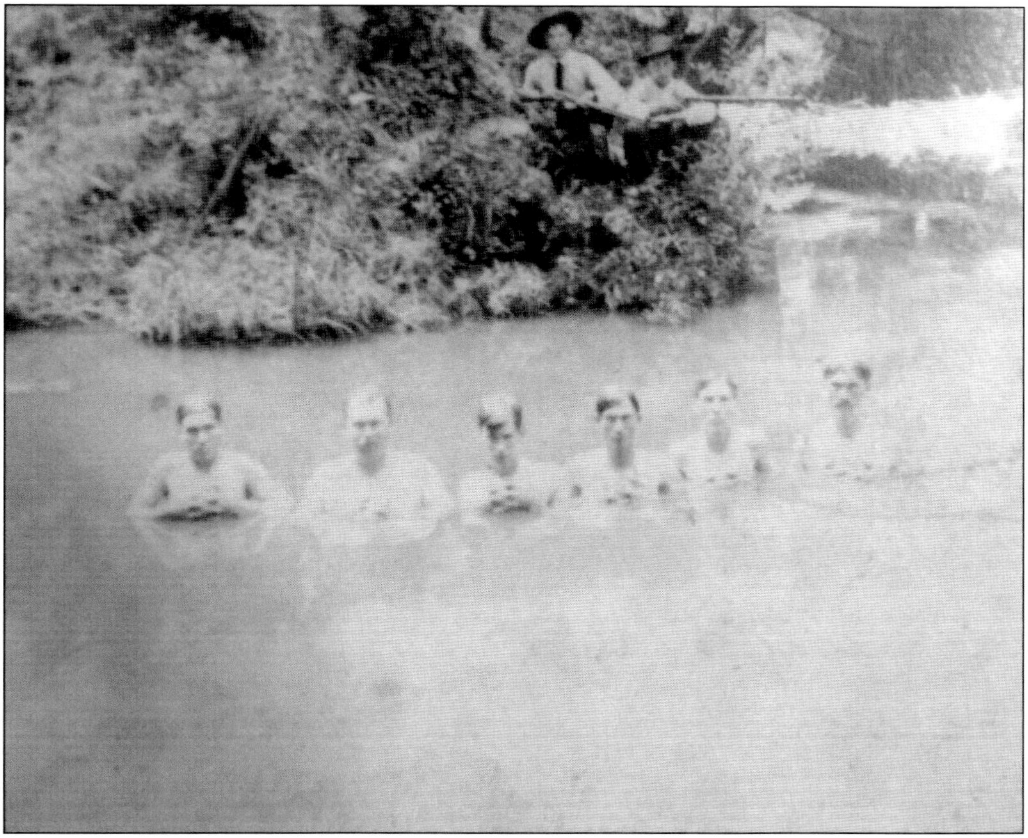

Cooling off in the Roberts' swimming hole on a hot summer day around 1900 in the West Lincoln community are, from left to right, William Thomas Roberts Sr., J.S. Terrell Sr., unidentified, Jim Morgan, unidentified, and Johnny Morgan. On the bank holding rifles are Jim Roberts (left) and Jack Roberts. This photograph represents a favorite summer pastime of Lincoln County youth. (Seth Allen.)

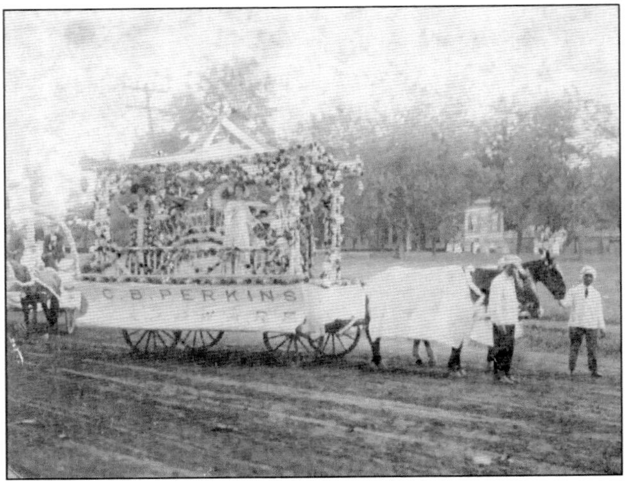

Among the earliest leaders in business and civic life, members of the Perkins family were very active in the community and great supporters of First Methodist Church. John Randolph Perkins established Perkins Hardware Store, one of the earlier businesses in Brookhaven. Perkins Furniture Store was founded by Thomas Hoyte Perkins Sr. in 1865. John R. Perkins (August 1, 1823–March 25, 1895) was the first Perkins male to settle in Lincoln County. He is buried at Rosehill Cemetery. (Betty Ann Perkins.)

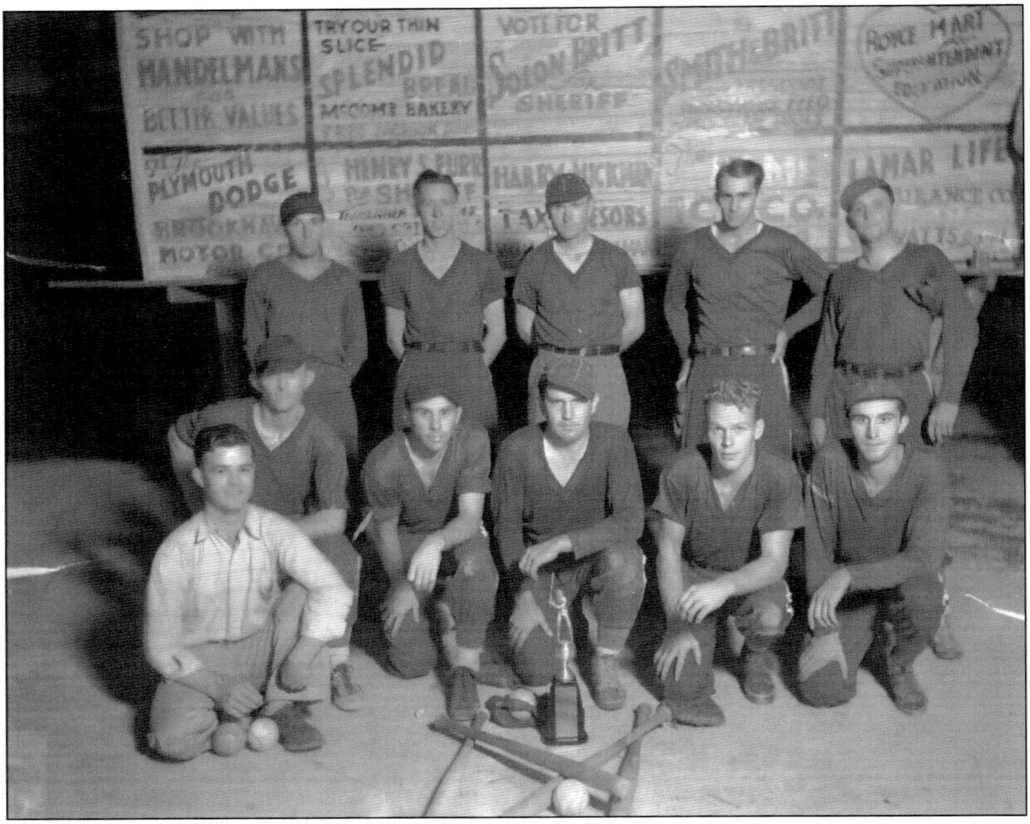

The Chicago World's Fair brought softball into the spotlight in 1933. Teams and leagues began popping up around the nation, such as the Suds Softball team sponsored by Brookhaven Steam Laundry. The team is shown here in 1939. The bat boy, George Herring, is seated at left. The others are, from left to right, (first row) Clyde Allgood, coach Otho Cross, J.P. Reeves, J.C. Reeves, and L.P Ward; (second row) J.E. Brister, Roy Adams, Ralph Blades, Fetch Ward, and Lee Martin. The Suds won the city championship and went to the state finals in Jackson, where they lost to Mississippi Power & Light. Cross was also Brookhaven's football coach. (LLF.)

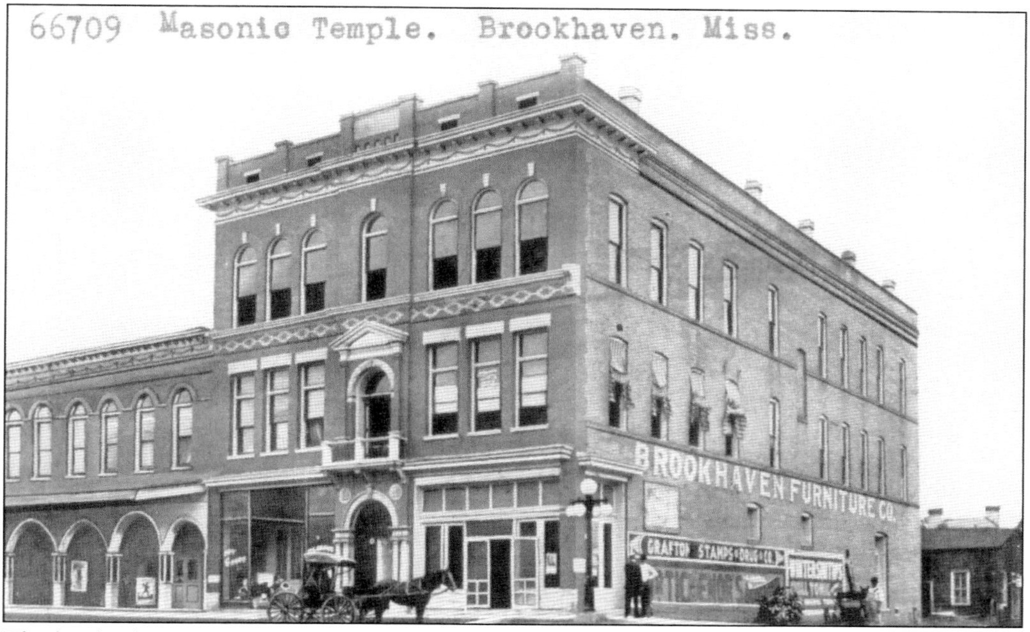

The brick, three-story Masonic Temple was built by Chris Larsen and finished in January 1900 at a cost of $17,500. The first floor was used by two local businesses, the second for club rooms, and the third for local lodges. On March 27, 1951, a fire that had been intentionally set by a 14-year-old boy totally destroyed the building and damaged the one next to it, causing $300,000 in losses. (Both, LLF.)

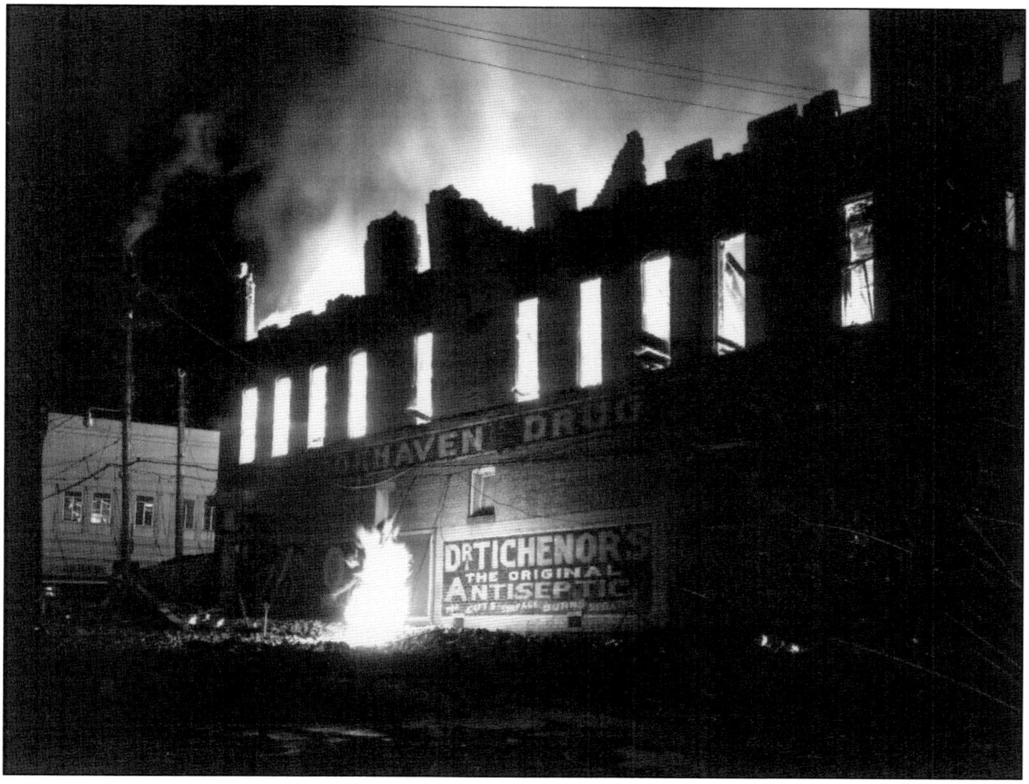

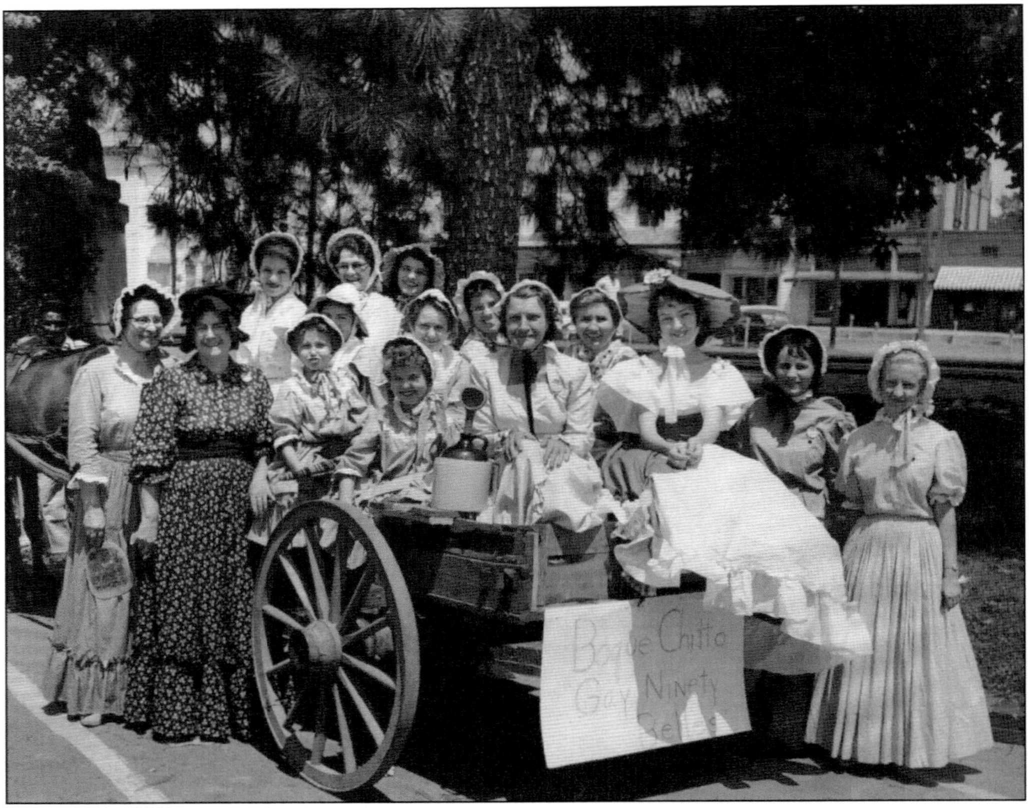

Brookhaven celebrated its 100th birthday in August 1959 with street dances, a beard-growing contest, a beard-shaving contest, and a big parade. People from every community in Lincoln County joined in the fun. (Both, LLF.)

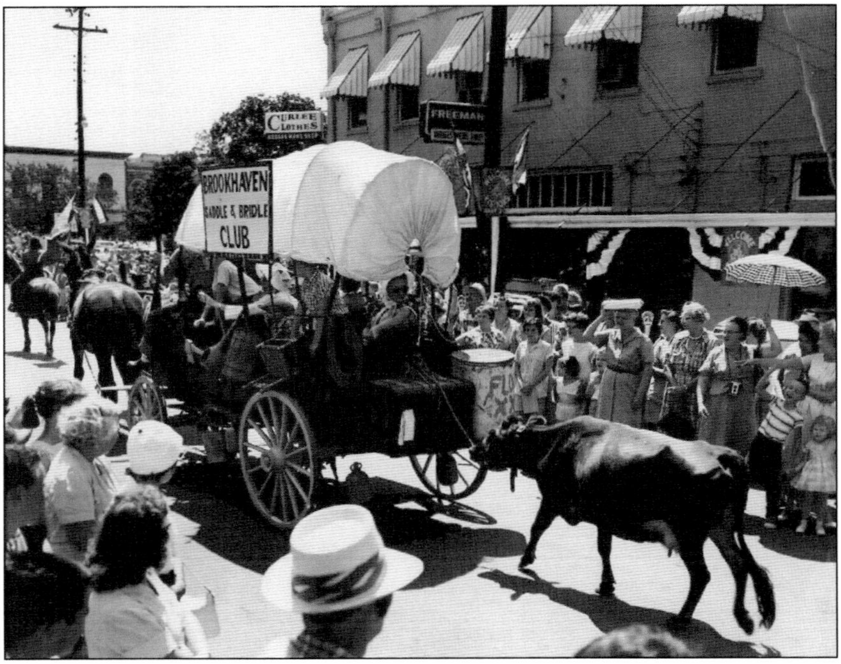

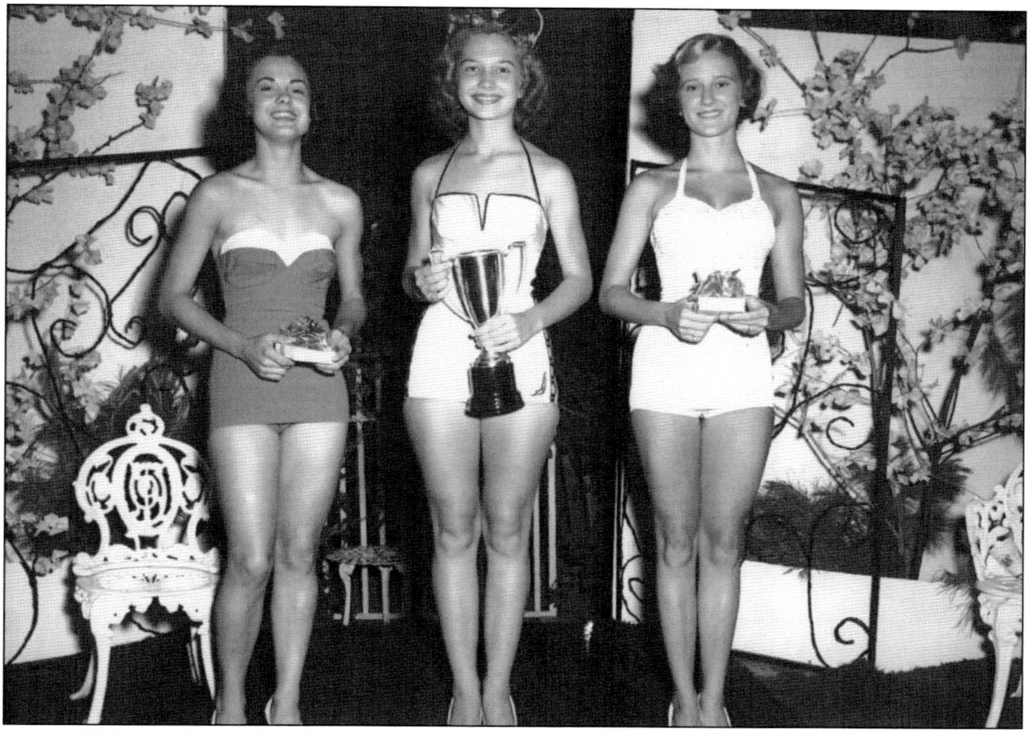

Lions Club Water Carnival contestants in 1953 are, from left to right, Ann Alworth, Mary Sue Covington, and Judy Entrican. The Lions Club held the carnival at the pool located on the Brookhaven High School campus. The annual contest is still held today as the Lions Club Beauty Pageant. (LLF.)

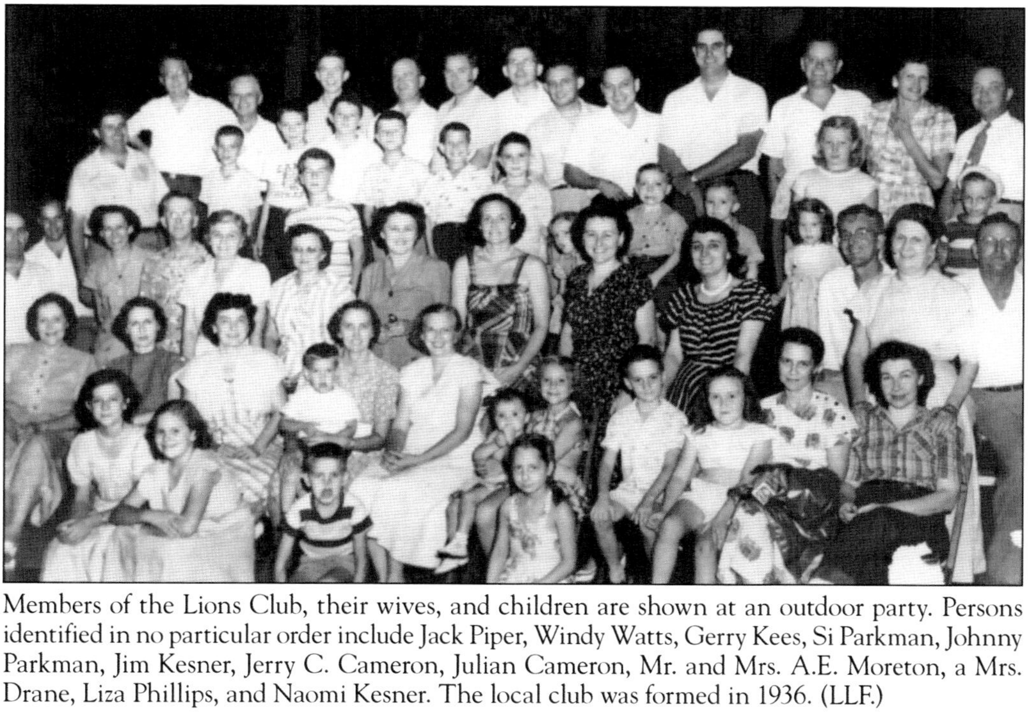

Members of the Lions Club, their wives, and children are shown at an outdoor party. Persons identified in no particular order include Jack Piper, Windy Watts, Gerry Kees, Si Parkman, Johnny Parkman, Jim Kesner, Jerry C. Cameron, Julian Cameron, Mr. and Mrs. A.E. Moreton, a Mrs. Drane, Liza Phillips, and Naomi Kesner. The local club was formed in 1936. (LLF.)

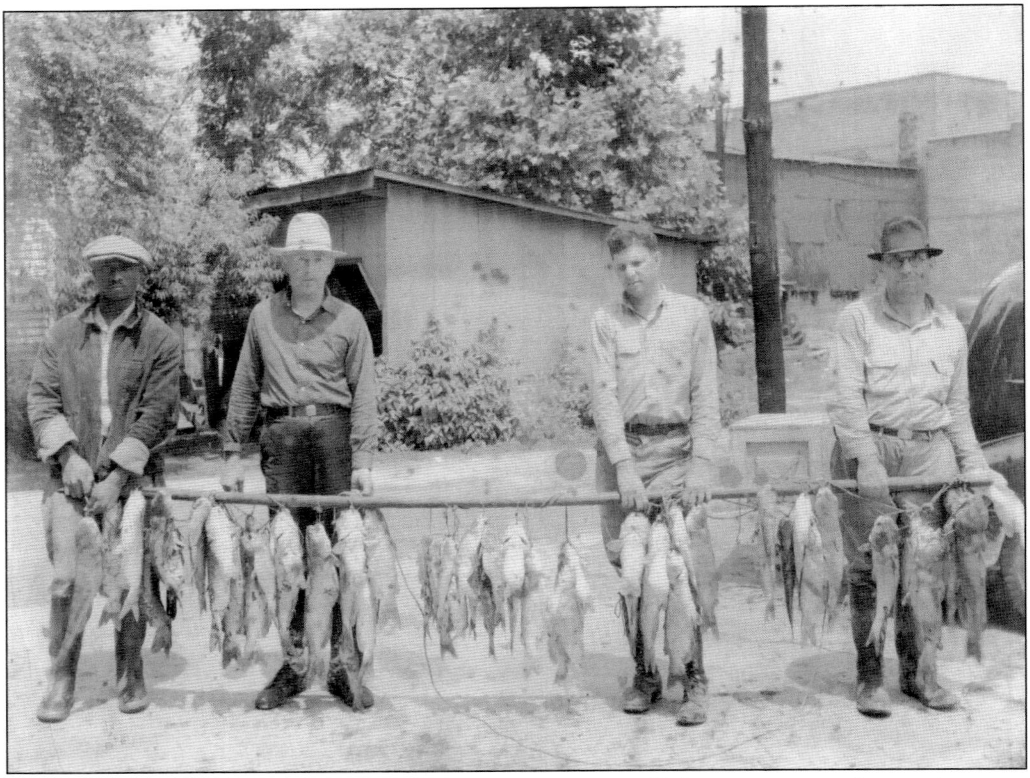

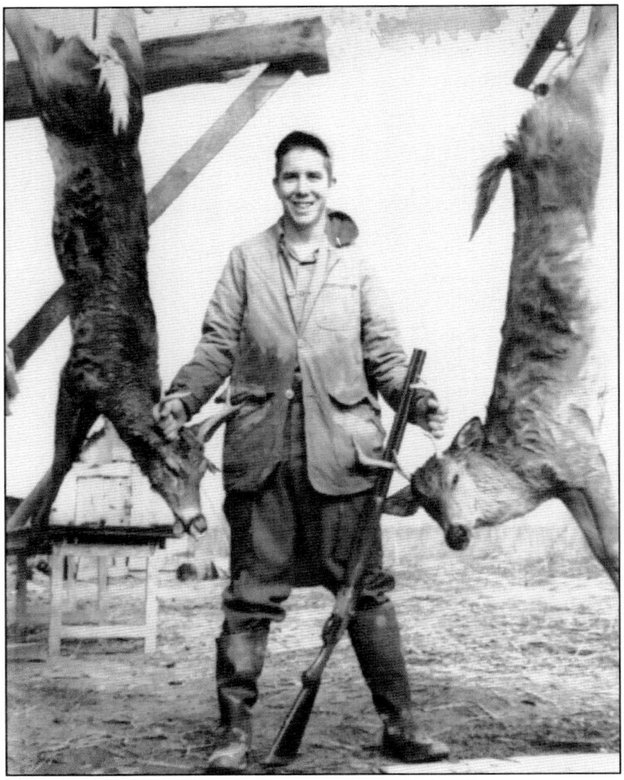

Fishing was a popular pastime in 1937, as evidenced by the number of fish caught by these men. They are, from left to right, unidentified, Luther M. Smith, Lee Martin, and a Mr. Berryhill. The photograph was taken behind the downtown fire station, which was located behind city hall. (Mary Jane Russell.)

Hunting, specifically deer hunting, was a popular pastime in Lincoln County. Many families relied on the meat to supplement their meals. (LLF.)

Cyrus Martin Shipp, original owner of Shipp's Florist, is pictured with his daughter Ruth Hanna (rear, left) and her daughters Allison Hanna (lower left) and Kathleen Hanna. At the time, Shipp was visiting San Francisco. Shipp's Florist opened in June 1950. (LLF.)

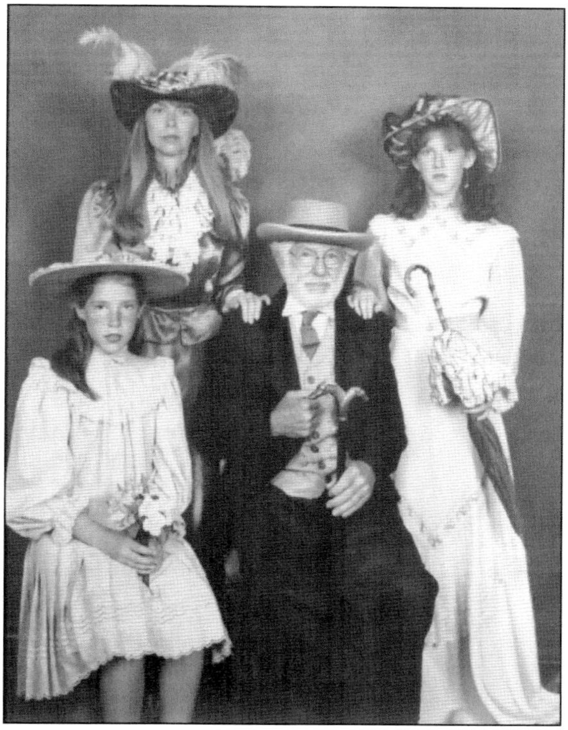

The Babe Ruth League was formed in 1951 to give boys between the ages of 13 and 15 a chance to continue playing ball during the summer. They could also enter tournaments and perhaps play in a World Series. Here, the Boling Motors team poses in 1954. Pictured are, from left to right, (first row) Tim Byrnes, Pat Reed, two unidentified players, Gene Spence, Glen Fallin, and O.C. Freeman; (second row) coach Loyd Edge, Roffie Burt, Richard Evans, Roland Byrd, Edwin Wallace, Paul Dennis Smith, Jerry Case, unidentified, and coach Willie L. Fallin. (Roffie Burt.)

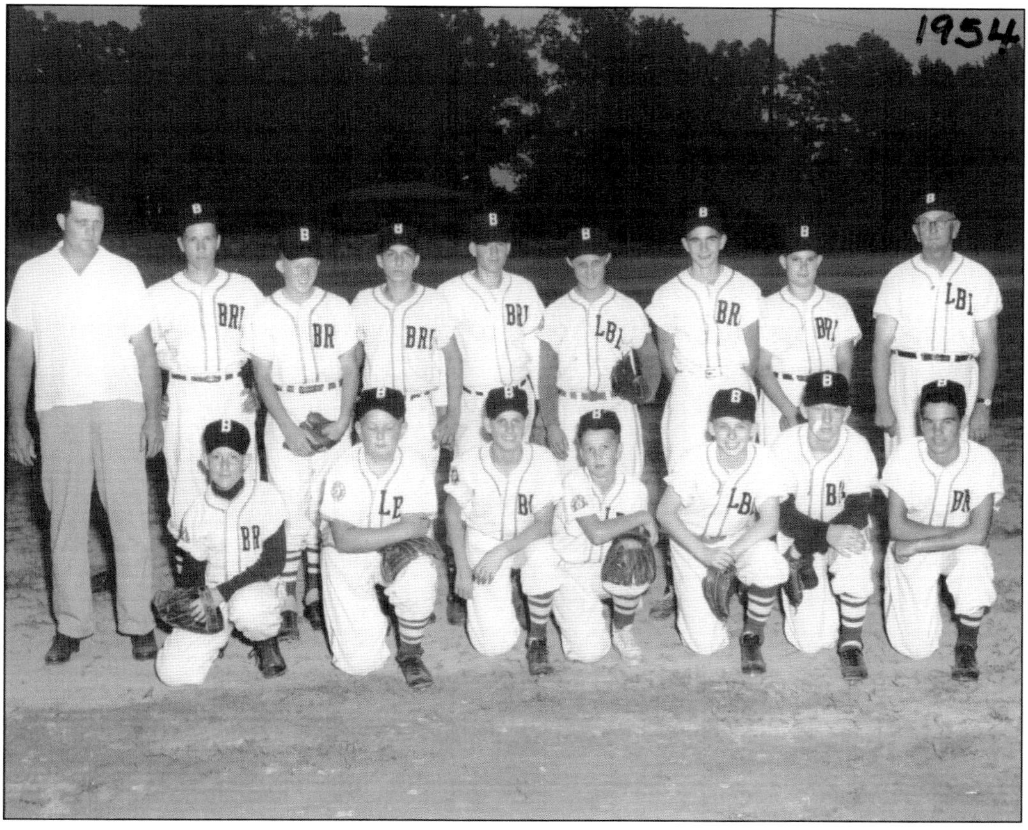

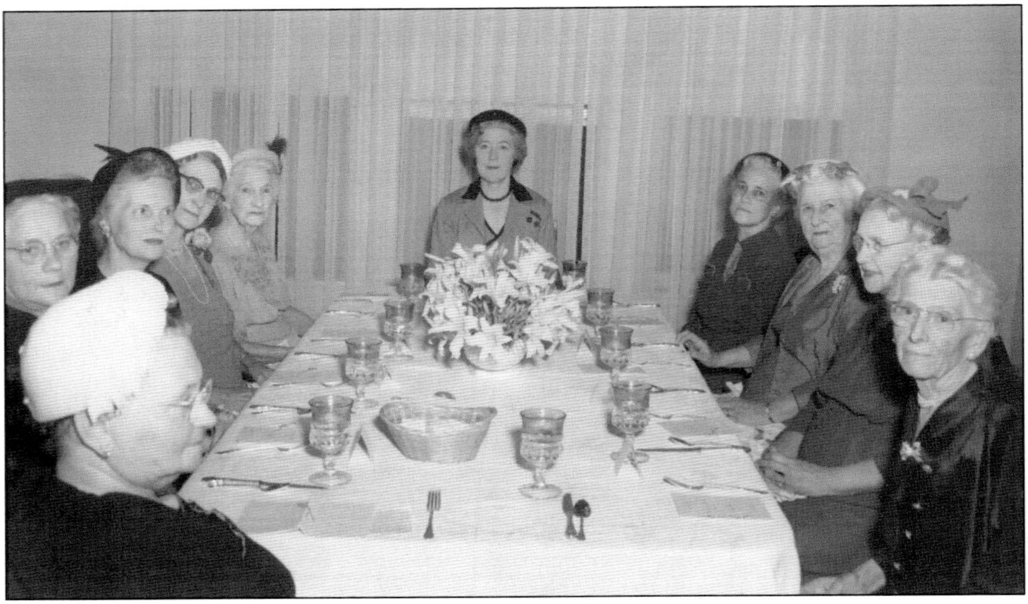

The Climbers Club began as a social club for women in the early part of the 1900s and continues today in Lincoln County. Seen here in the 1940s or 1950s are, clockwise from lower left, Mrs. Kees, Mrs. Sam Walker, Onita Nutt, Mrs. Flowers, Mrs. J.H. "Katie" Johnson, Mrs. Evelyn Oswalt, Mrs. Robert Eitel Smith, Maggie Moody, Mrs. C.B. Johnson, and an unidentified woman. (LLF.)

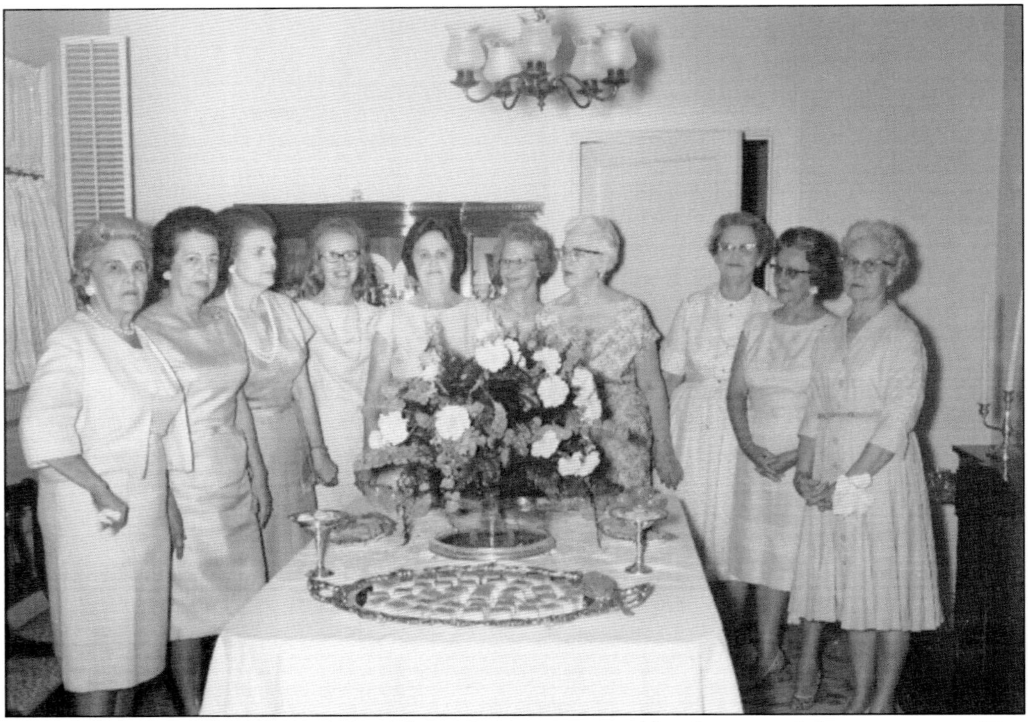

Many affluent ladies in the middle of the 20th century joined local society clubs as a pastime. The Climbers, Peripatetics, and Matinee Musicale were just a few that could be found in Brookhaven. These ladies are, from left to right, Lutie Powers, Marguerite Beel, Donna Lovell, unidentified, Clara Perkins, Willie King, Boopa Poole, Theresia Abshagen, and two unidentified. (LLF.)

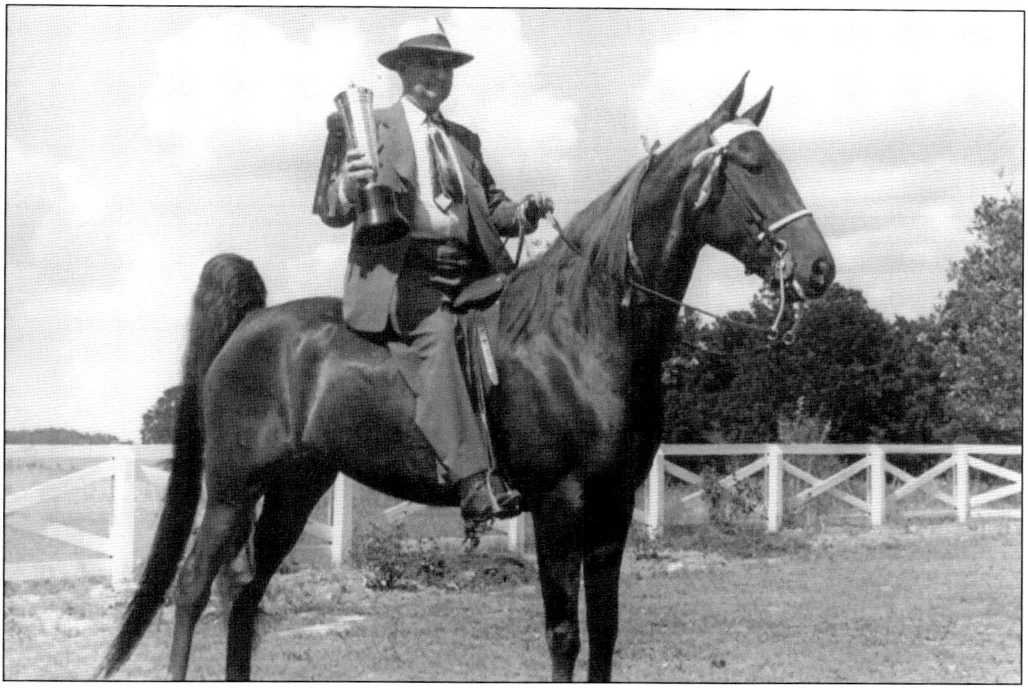

Stewart Day is shown astride a beautiful Tennessee walking horse. In the 1940s and 1950s, horse shows were frequently held on the south end of Brookhaven, on the property once belonging to Samuel Jayne and near the site of his original trading post. (LLF.)

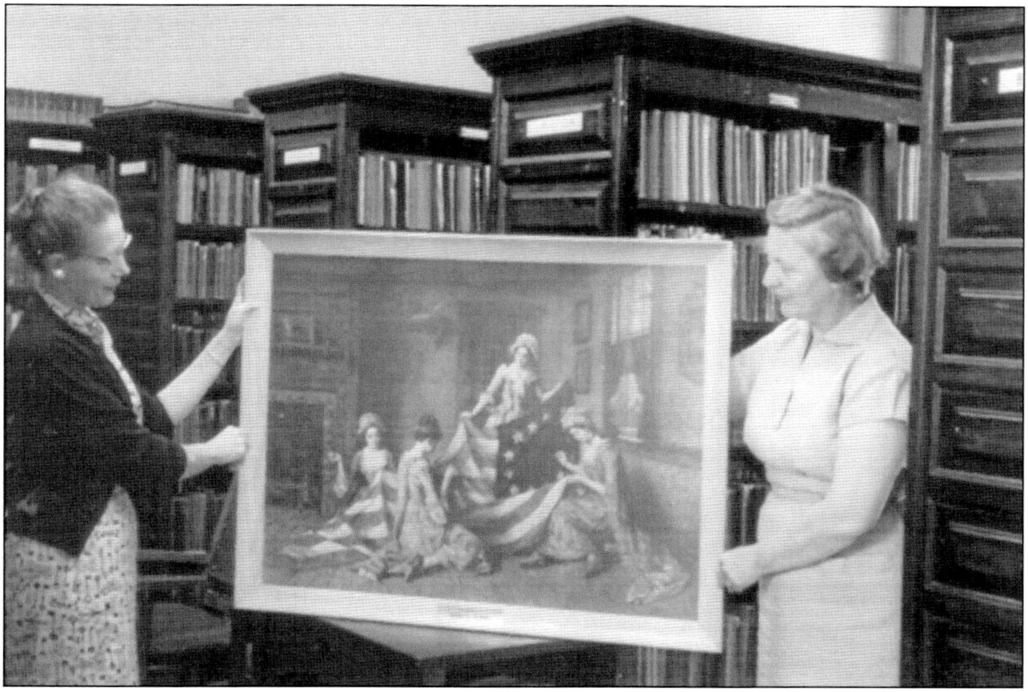

Iola Magee (left), director of the city library, and Pauline Vaughn, the driver of the bookmobile, hold a picture donated to the library by the Woodman of the World in the old library located in back of city hall. (LLF.)

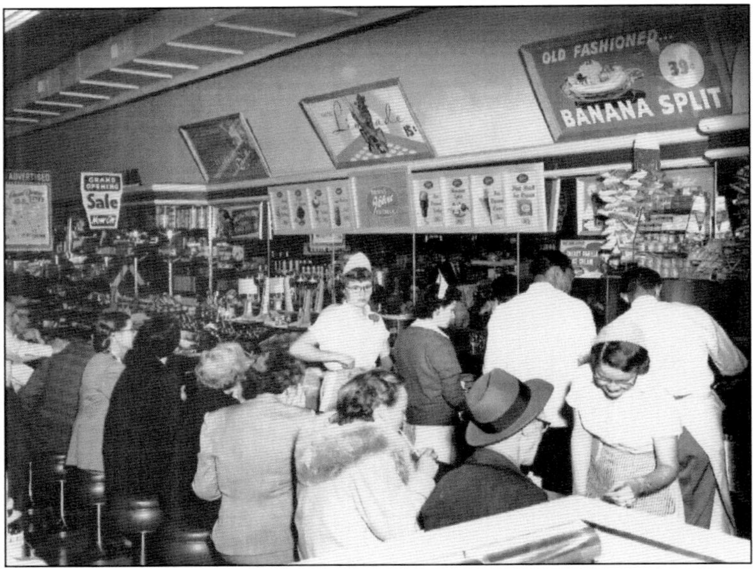

Clinton Bane opened his pharmacy on Whitworth Avenue, between the corner of Cherokee Street and Lofton's Department Store, in the 1950s. The most exciting part for young people was the soda fountain in the back. Here, many customers enjoyed a light lunch. After school, the store was crowded with teenagers purchasing French fries and Coca-Colas. (LLF.)

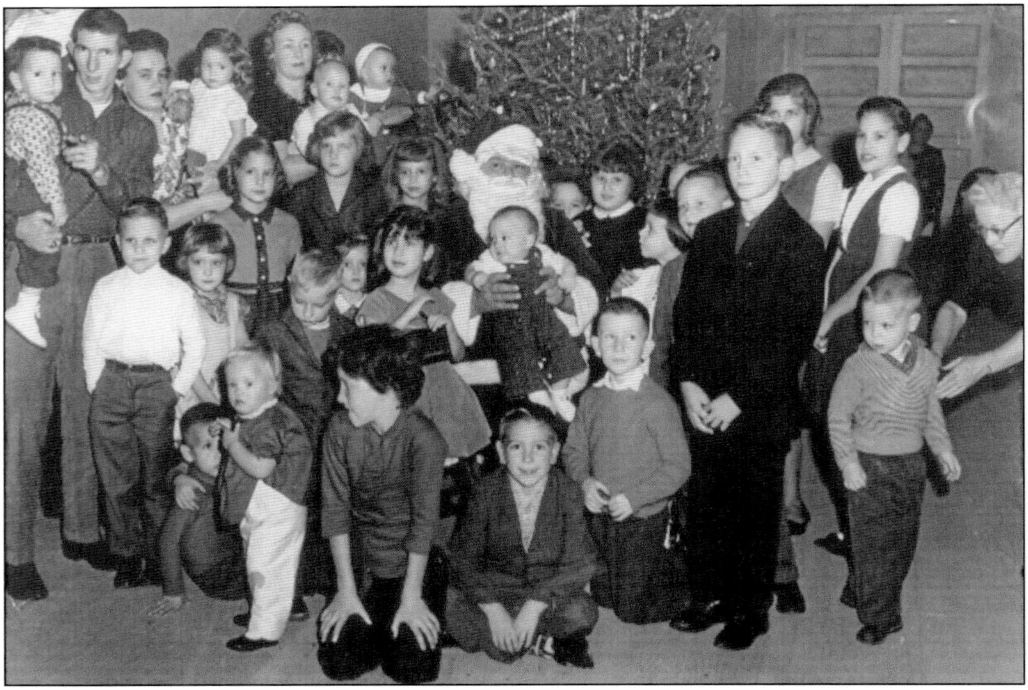

For men only, Woodmen of the World (WOW) was organized in Lincoln County by H.F. Sumrall on September 20, 1892. Designated Camp No. 9, it provided insurance and social activities. Later, the Woodmen Circle was formed for women. Freddie Nations (by Santa next to tree and partially obscured), Ginger Leggett (third from right), and Gene Leggett (second from right) are identified in this photograph, taken during a WOW Christmas party. (WoodmenLife Collection.)

Nine

The Way They Lived

To look at photographs of Brookhaven, one would think every Lincoln County family lived in a beautiful Greek Revival or Victorian home. Although the community has many of these beautiful homes, most of the earliest setters lived more modestly.

For most, a one-room log cabin built with a steep roof was the quickest way to obtain shelter, due to the availability of raw materials and the speed of construction. Adding a second cabin that shared a roof into the dogtrot house could expand these cabins, forming a wide hall between the two structures. Many adapted the Creole cottage of the French setters of the 1600s by adding a wide center hall between two wide rooms.

Around 1830, the "I" house, a little more formal and larger, with two stories (only one room deep), began to appear. It gave access to the second floor via stairs outside the structure. Larger families and more-affluent citizens frequently built "planter's cottages." Built in towns instead of in agricultural settings, these small, one- or one-and-a-half-story houses had a center hall and were usually either one or two rooms deep. Wealthier builders added a gallery or porch for family members to relax in the evenings and on Sundays.

After 1850, construction began on larger homes throughout the county. These homes, built in the Federal, Greek Revival, Italianate, and Victorian styles, are still loved and maintained for their architectural beauty.

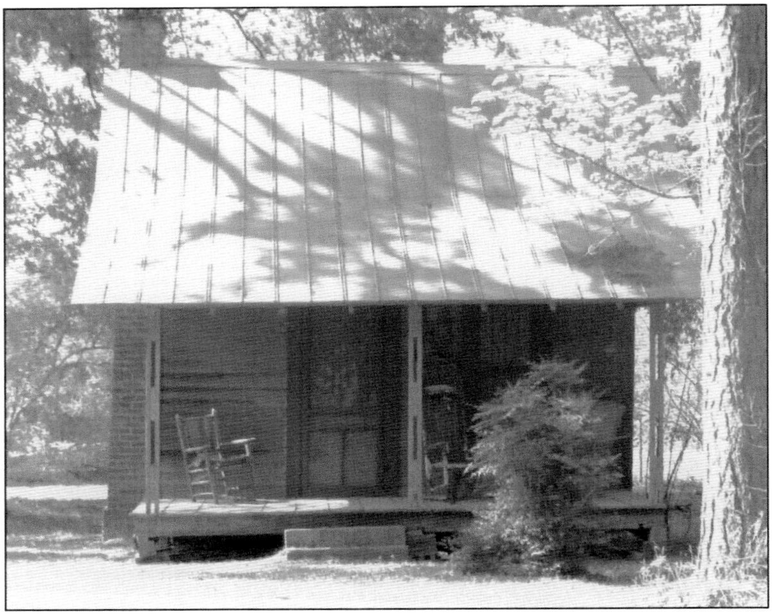

This small cottage stands lovingly restored in Lincoln County. At one time, homes of this style, with the high-rise roof, were common throughout the area. Usually, a ladder was attached to the wall inside to allow children to sleep in the loft. Most family life took place in the large main room. Cooking was done both outside and in the fireplace. (Marti Parker.)

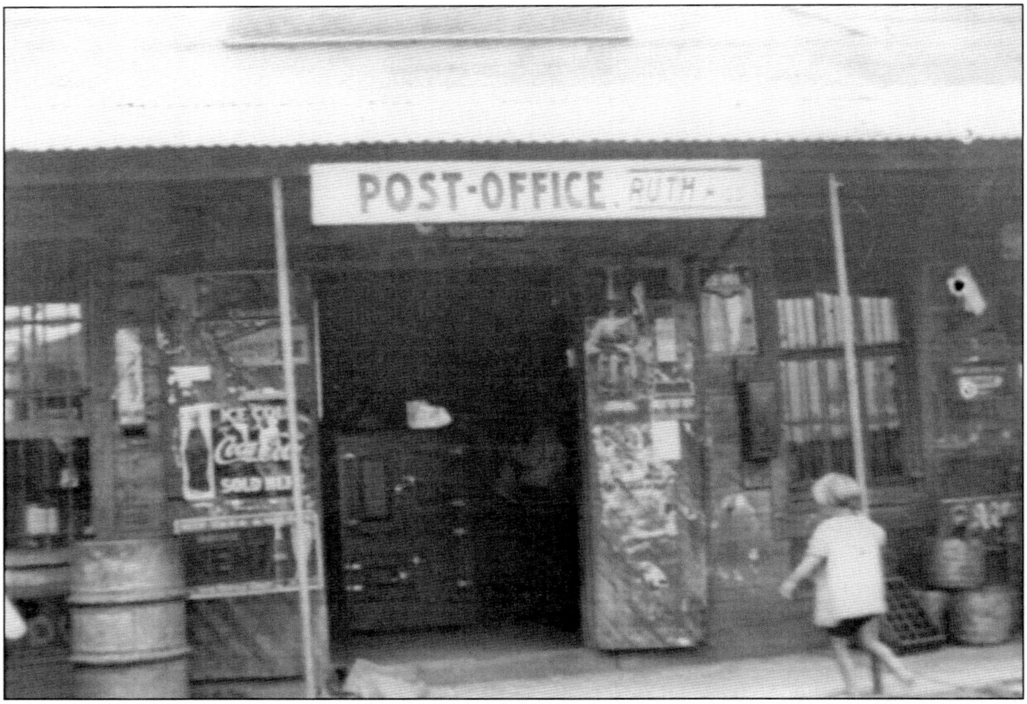

The Ruth store, like many community stores, often had a counter set aside for mail delivery. This store was built by Floyd Lafayette Clark at what is now the crossroads of Highway 583 and Ruth Drive. Dorothy Clark, age three, is seen running into the store. In the 1930s, at the age of 20, Clark, who succeeded her father in business, built a new, larger store across the road. (Martha Sinclair.)

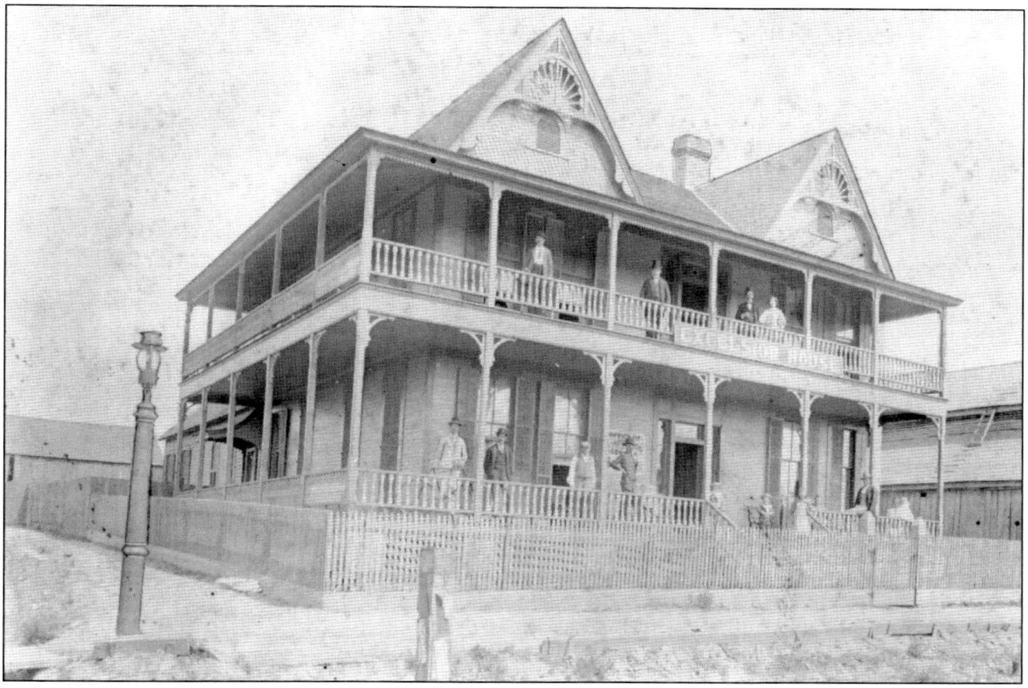

Mrs. Z.Z. Turnbough was the owner of this boardinghouse in downtown Brookhaven, located conveniently near the railroad station. In 1899, a fire was discovered in the building. Although the volunteer fire department responded quickly, there was a delay in getting full water pressure. But the firefighters did a magnificent job in saving the lower portion of the house and the neighboring buildings. The fire originated from a lamp that was left burning. (LLF.)

Built in 1895 by Chris Larsen for Richard T. Scherck, this beautiful home is located on South Railroad Avenue. In 1906, planning to move to New Orleans, Scherck sold it to Judge Pleasant Z. Jones and his wife, Maggie. This was the last house built in Brookhaven by Larsen. It remained in the Jones family until recent years. (LLF.)

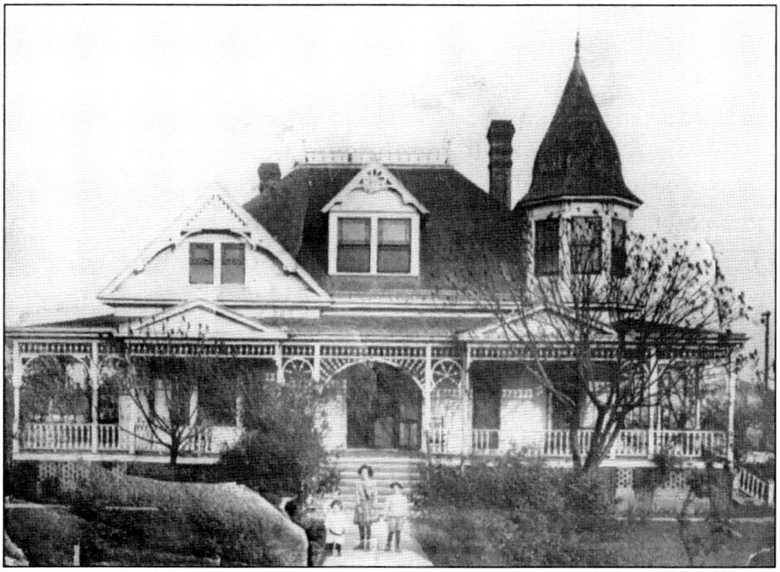

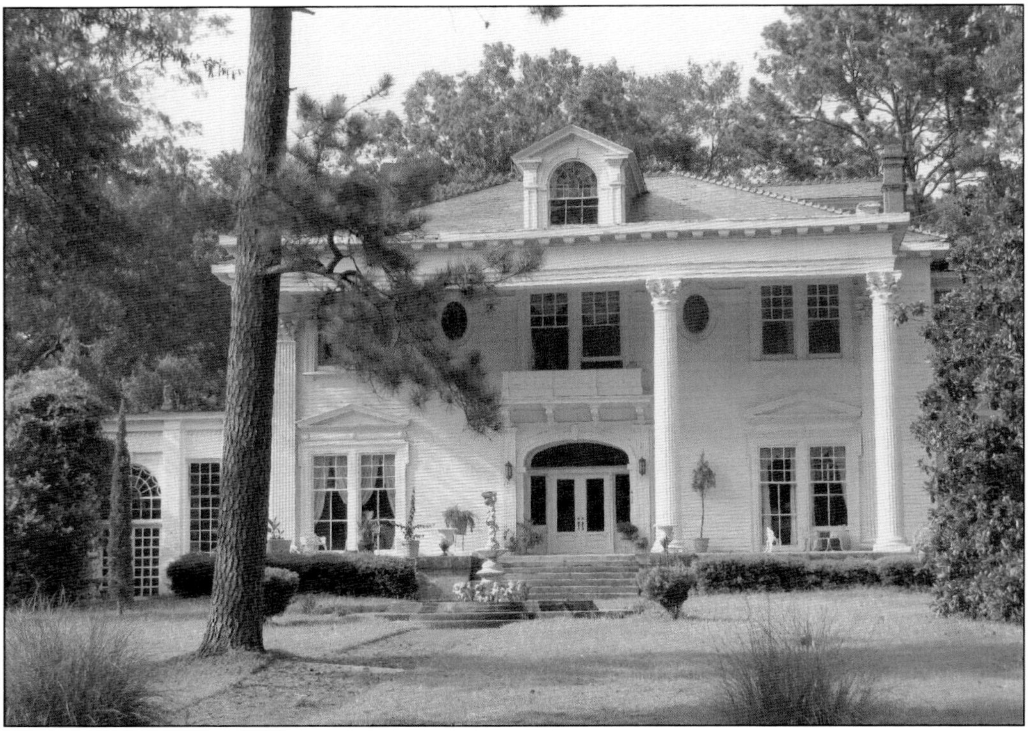

Charles Spencer Butterfield (1864–1935) built the Greek Revival home Edgewood for his second wife, Vivienne Emma Horn Butterfield (1877–1968), around 1910 at a cost of $75,000. Butterfield's first wife, May Lavina Millsaps Butterfield (1870–1903), died. His father, John S. Butterfield, along with partner Fred W. Norwood, established sawmills in Lincoln County and the town of Norfield, which was named for the men. Charles served as president of the company in later years. After the lumber business was sold, he continued with other business adventures, including Bank of Brookhaven, later Brookhaven Bank & Trust Company. As Charles neared his 60th birthday, he sold his mansion on Storm Avenue for $14,000, in addition to all of his business holdings. He and Vivienne moved to Florida, where they both died and are buried. (Marti Parker.)

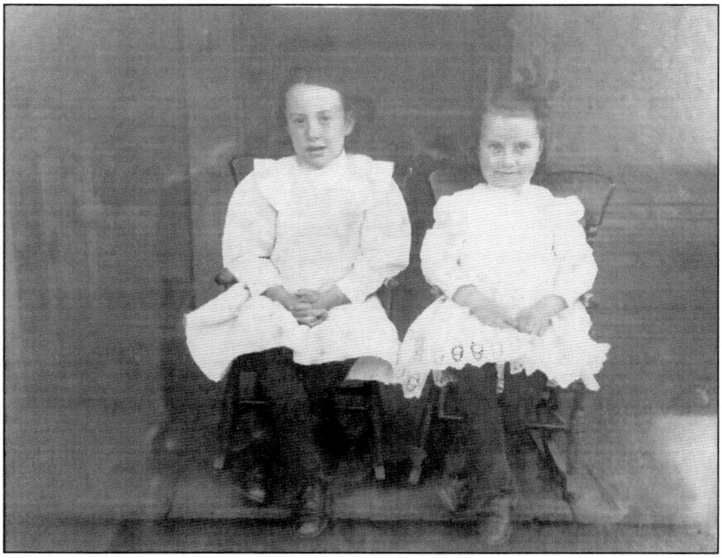

Una Tanner (left) and Myrtle Tanner sit on the porch of their Lincoln County family home around 1910. Porch photographs were very common in the early 1900s. (Mary Ann Smith.)

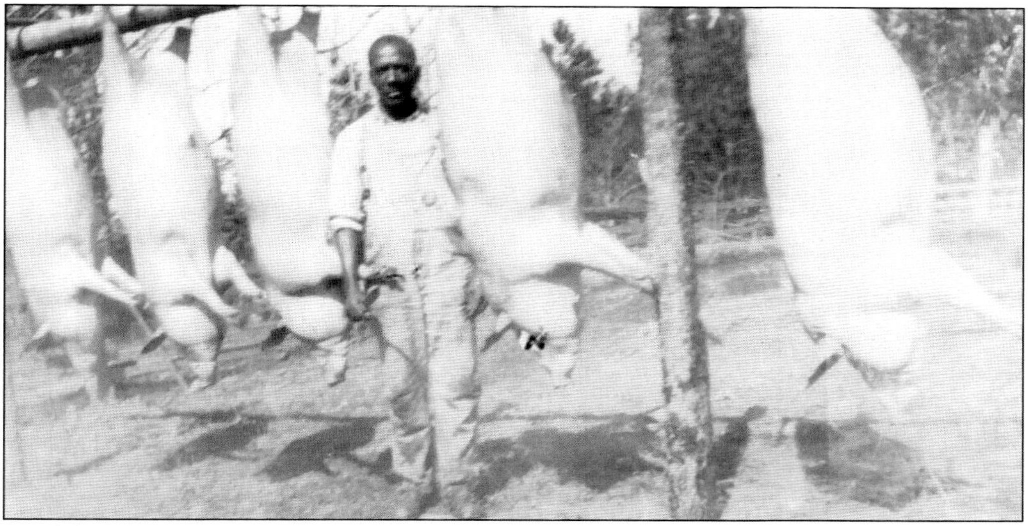

Hog killing was a way of life for county farmers in the 1930s. Here, ? Smith poses with several hogs that were being butchered on "hog day." Typically, tenant farmers and hog owners would gather on a cool winter day and slaughter many hogs at once. (Anita Nettles.)

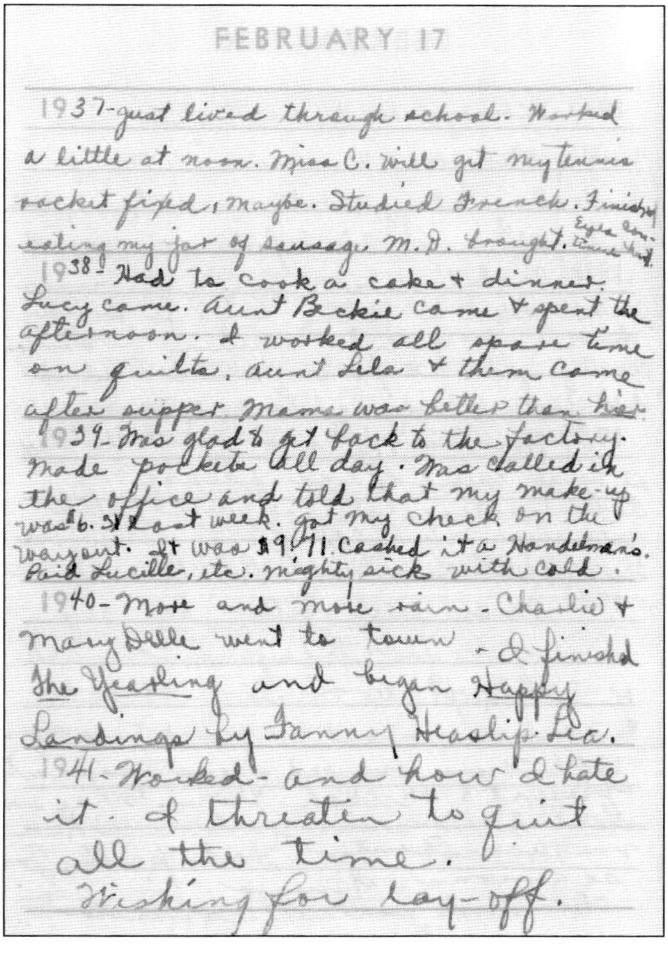

FEBRUARY 17

1937-just lived through school. Worked a little at noon. Miss C. will get my tennis racket fixed, maybe. Studied French. Finished eating my jar of sausage M. D. brought. [illegible]

1938- Had to cook a cake & dinner. Lucy came. Aunt Beckie came & spent the afternoon. I worked all spare time on quilts. Aunt Lela & them came after supper. Mama was better than [illegible]

1939- Was glad to get back to the factory. Made pockets all day. Was called in the office and told that my make-up was 6.[illegible] last week. got my check on the way out. It was $9.71. Cashed it a Handelman's. Paid Lucille, etc. mighty sick with cold.

1940- More and more rain. Charlie & Mary Belle went to town. I finished The Yearling and began Happy Landings by Fanny Heaslip Lea.

1941- Worked- and how I hate it. I threaten to quit all the time. Wishing for lay-off.

Journal entries from 1937 to 1941 are recorded in this diary. It was common in that era for young women to write down their thoughts. This young woman writes about school, work, cooking, and reading. (Bettie Posey Bullard.)

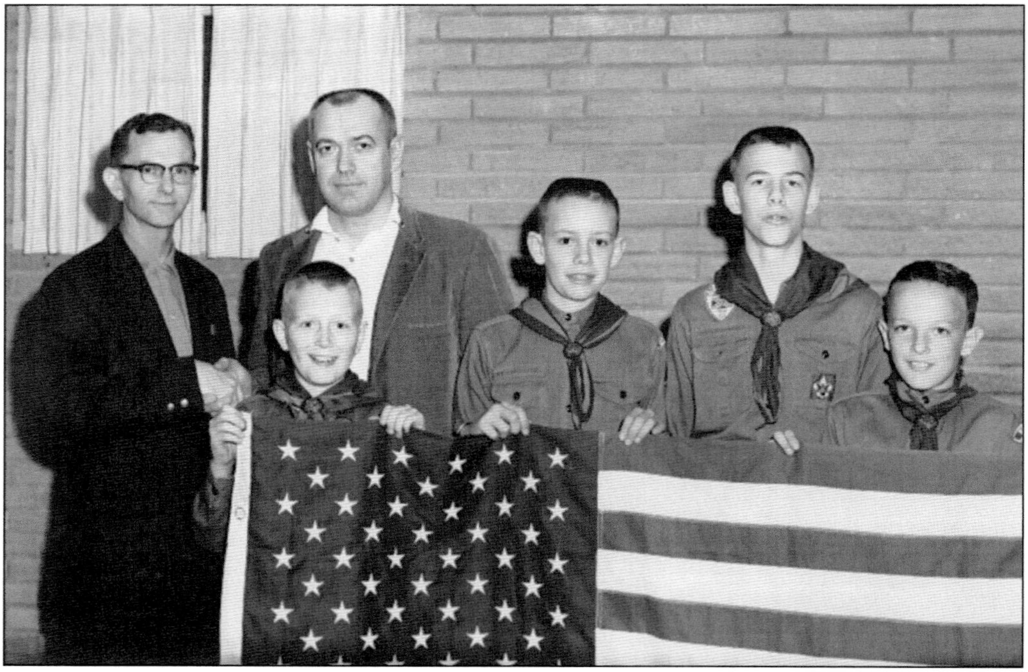

Boy Scouts and Girl Scouts were popular activities for Lincoln County youngsters. Here, Elmer McInnis (left) is shown with a few local Boy Scouts, including his son Elmer Jr. (fourth from left). (WoodmenLife Collection.)

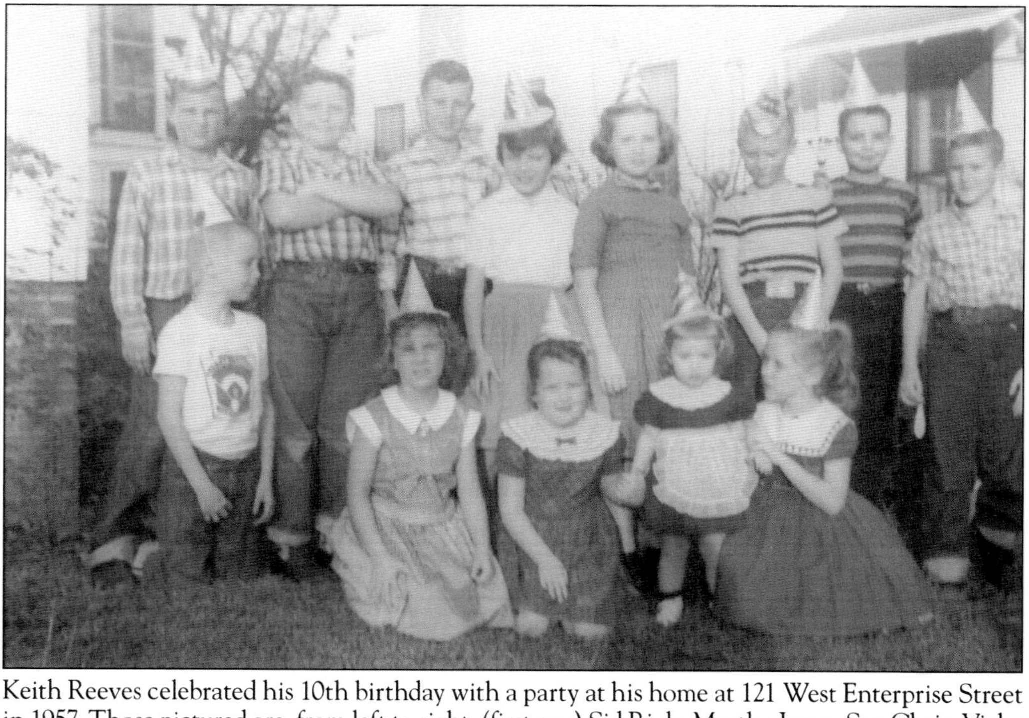

Keith Reeves celebrated his 10th birthday with a party at his home at 121 West Enterprise Street in 1957. Those pictured are, from left to right, (first row) Sid Rials, Martha Jones, Sue Chris, Vicky Nunnery, and Sue Beeson; (second row) Kenneth Bowman, Buren Lynn Jones, Barney Ray McEwen, Montiel Beeson, Iris Laird, Reeves, Winston George, and Bill Weaver. (Keith Reeves.)

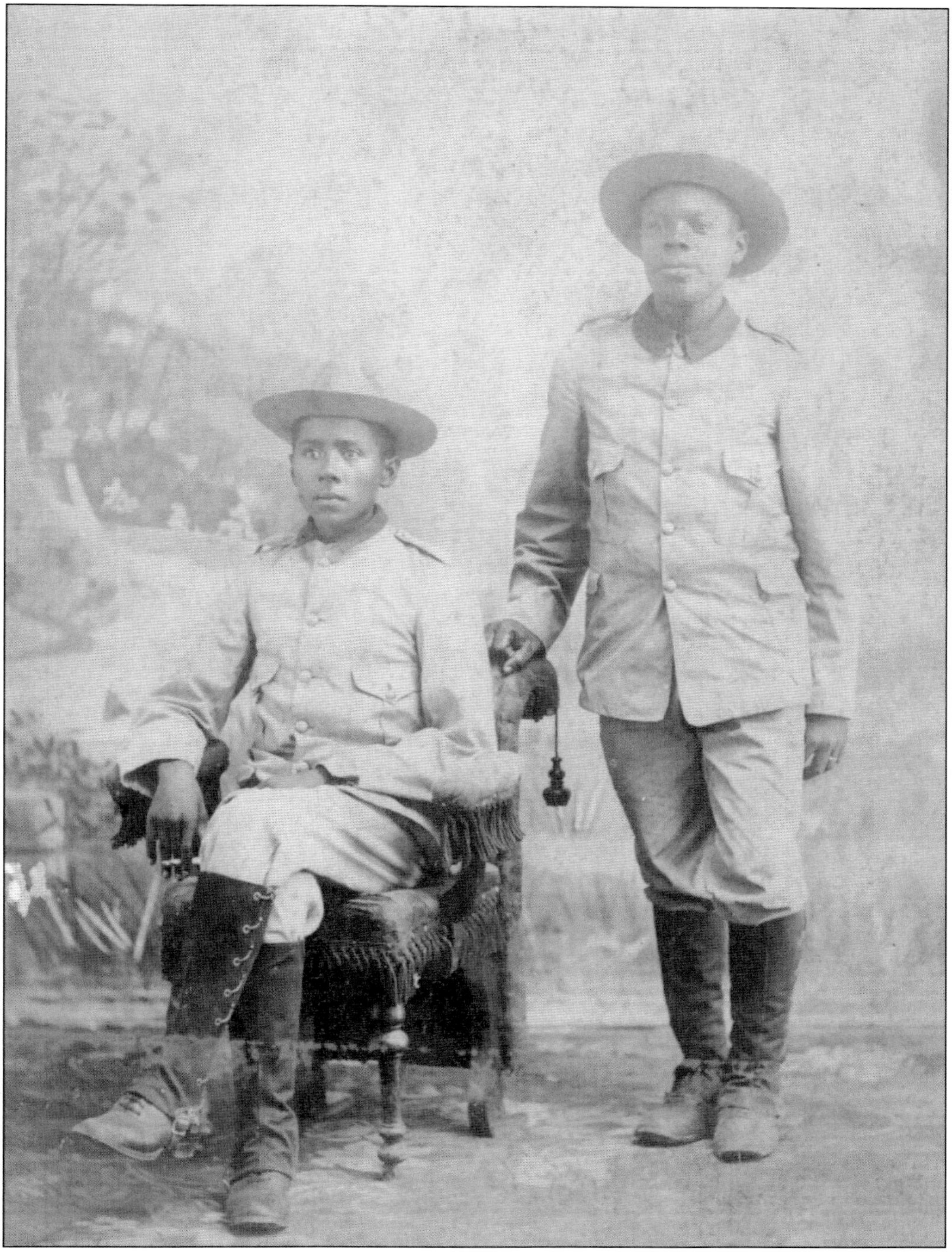

Edward D. Manson (right), born on August 1, 1877, and this unidentified soldier served in the Spanish-American War. The war with Spain began in April 1898, when Maj. Gen. William Shafter, a former commander of the 24th Infantry, led an expeditionary force of over 17,000 men, including nearly 3,000 black regulars, into Cuba. Manson was a corporal in Company C. After the war, he returned to the States, married, and later became minister of Bethel African Methodist Episcopal Church in Brookhaven. He died on February 10, 1958. (Margaret Therrell.)

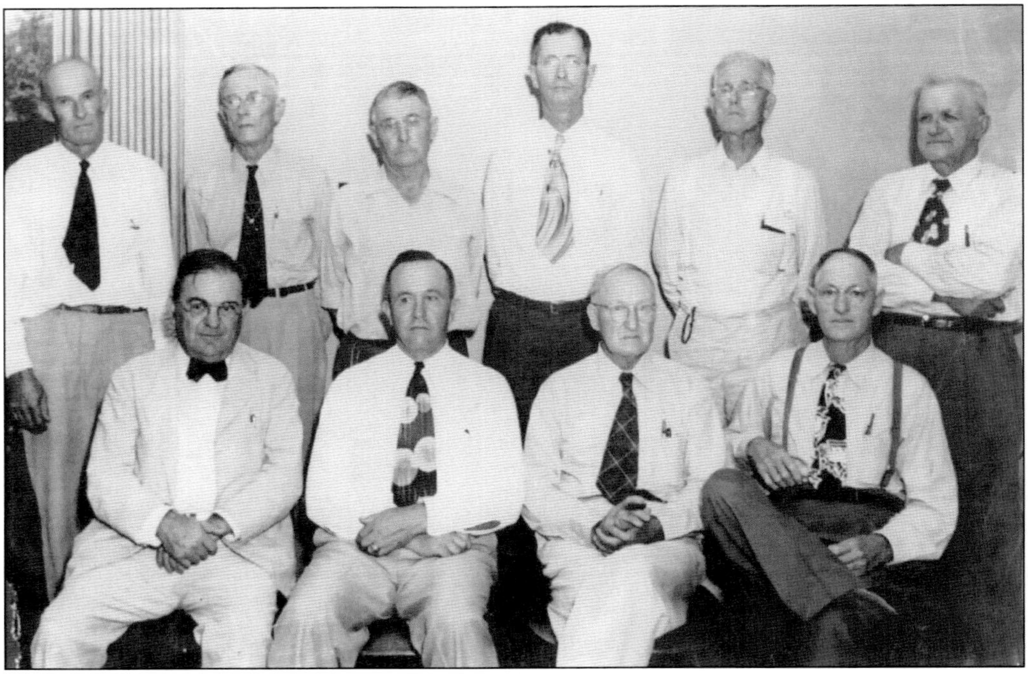

Lincoln County and Brookhaven businessmen got together often for lunch to discuss business matters. Shown here in an undated photograph are, from left to right, (first row) Abe Cohn, Cecil Linton, a Mr. Gordon, and Silas Blackwell; (second row) N.H. Simmons, Acie Brewer, Solomon Causey, C.C. Clark, Dewitt M. Ginn, and Samuel D. Moak. (Martha Sinclair.)

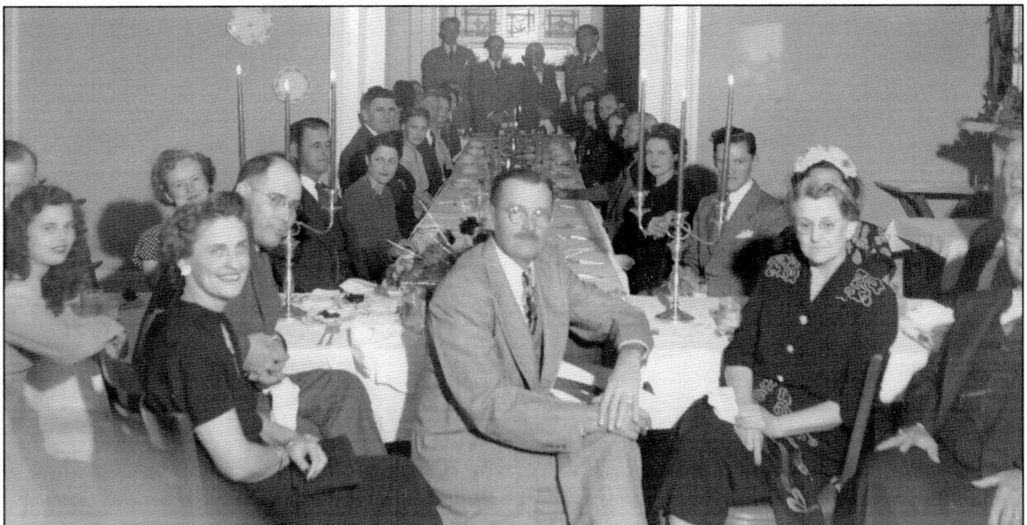

A group of people sits in Magnolia Manor at tables arranged in a "T" formation. Across the front are Laverne Brady (left), Tom Brady (center), and a woman identified as Mr. Brady's mother. In a polka-dot dress behind Laverne Brady is Elizabeth Jones. Seen to her right, behind the candelabra, is Jack Tindall, and next to him is Katherine Swalm. On the opposite side of the table, Katherine Roberts is behind the candelabra, and Owen Roberts is between Katherine and Mrs. Brady. Magnolia Manor, a classical Georgian home, was built in 1863 by Samuel J. Whitworth, son of Rev. Milton J. Whitworth. (LLF.)

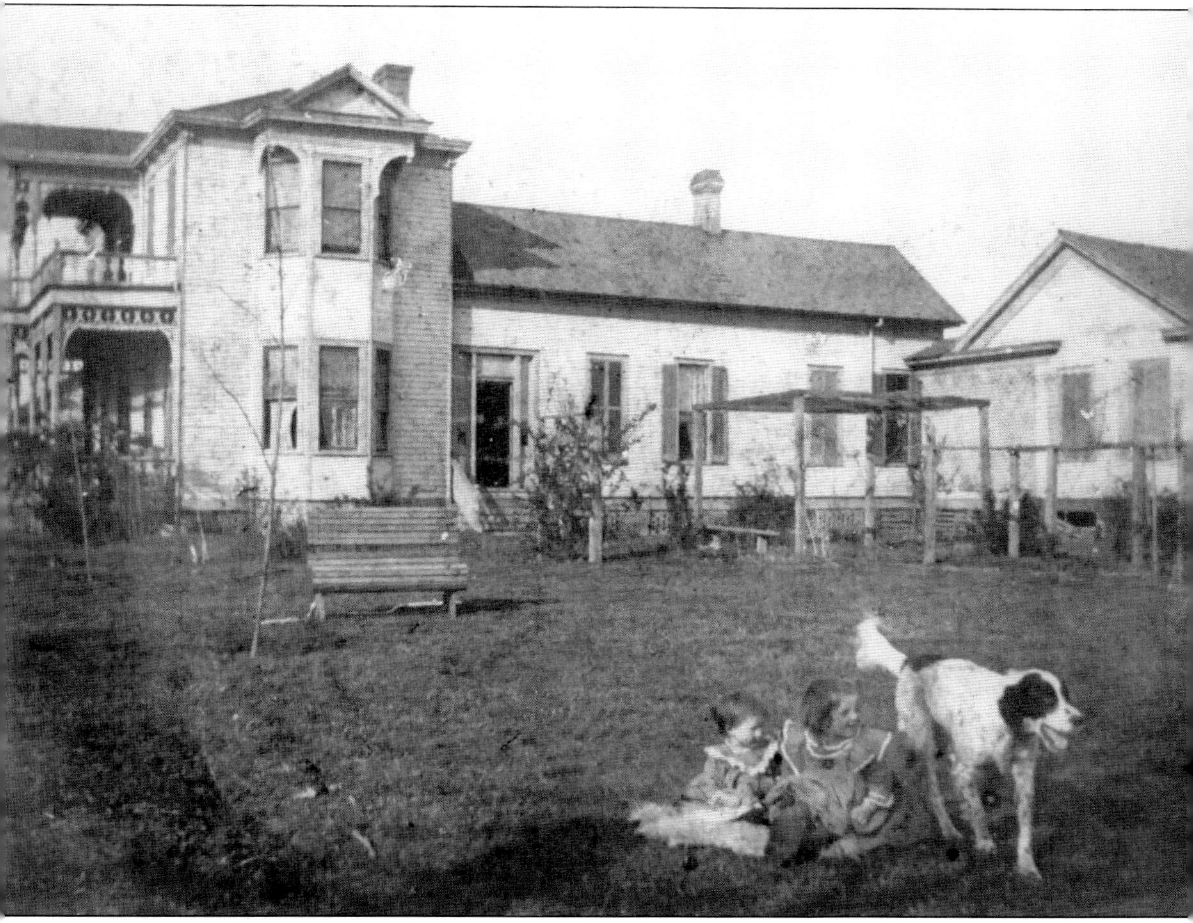

This is the home of Frank H. Hartman and his wife, Mary Eitel Hartman. Frank was born in Osnabruck, Kingdom of Hanover, Germany, in 1840. He came to America with his parents as a young boy. The Hartman family owned a general merchandise store and one of the earliest funeral homes. The children are unidentified. (LLF.)

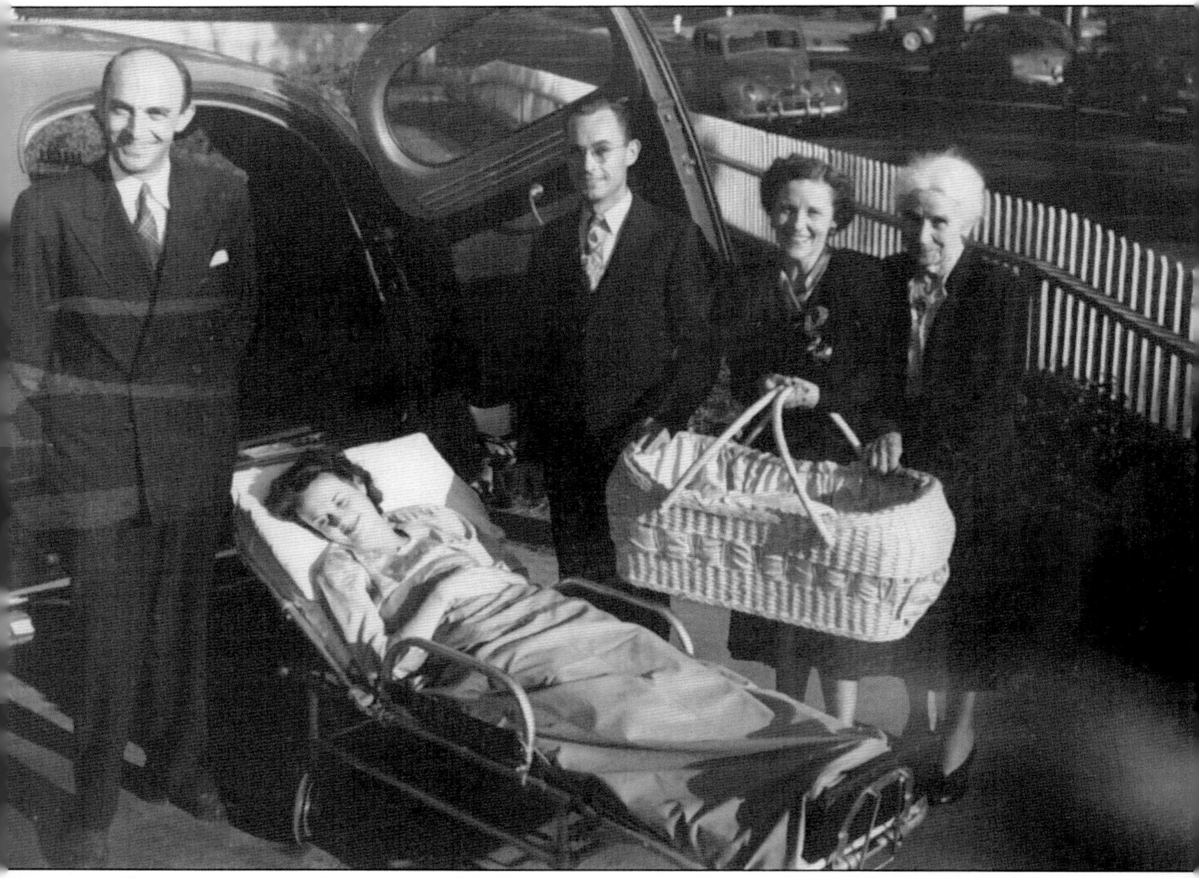

This photograph of an unidentified woman returning home after the birth of her child is part of a group of photographs in the King's Daughters Hospital Collection at the Lincoln-Lawrence-Franklin Regional Library. The photographs were taken in the 1940s to show the new features at the hospital, on North Jackson Street. It was customary for women to spend a week in the hospital after the birth of a child and to then be transported home by ambulance. (LLF.)

Ten

Notable People

A notable person may be defined as one who achieved something significant, interesting, remarkable, or unusual enough to be recorded. Lincoln County has had many people, both in the past and currently, who fall into this category. Some notables do not fit the time frame of this book, while others, like many early settlers, left few records and no photographs. Because of limitations, it is impossible to include them all. The following notables could not be featured in this book.

Ruth Ford, actress, and her brother Henri Ford, writer and editor, left records and images in the hands of corporations, making it impossible to obtain images. Their parents ran the Inez Hotel in the early 1900s. N.B. Bryant, one of the first black editors in the state, operated a newspaper in Brookhaven in 1910 before moving to Jackson. Eli Buchman, born in Russia in 1898, fled the Russian army as a youth alone across Europe and managed to reach the United States. Later, he owned a store, Buchman's Mercantile, in Brookhaven and made a successful home for his family. Noted civil rights workers Hollis Watkins and Addie Cameron Wyatt were born in Lincoln County. They fought for legal and cultural changes. Brookhaven native Janis Moreton Hobbs, the first licensed female pilot in Lincoln County, may also have been the first licensed female pilot in Mississippi.

Not to be forgotten are the many brave men and women who went to war in the American Revolution and the War of 1812 and settled in the area. Those who fought in the Mexican-American War, the Civil War, the Spanish-American War, World War I, World War II, and the Korean conflict fall into this book's time period. The tales of their courage and actions are lengthy.

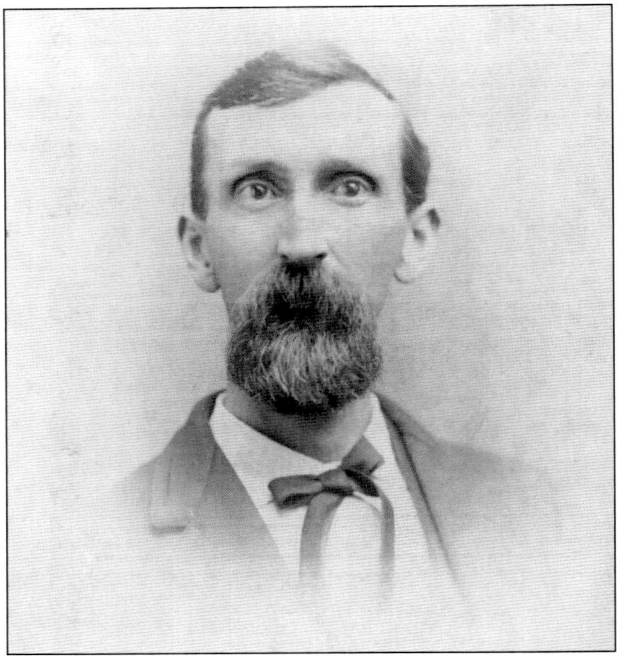

John Evander McNair, lawyer and judge, was born in Richmond County, North Carolina, on August 8, 1808. He met and married Sarah Adaline Watts in Covington County, Mississippi, before moving to the newly formed Lincoln County in 1870, where he first worked as a teacher in the Peabody School. He was elected mayor in 1873 and served in that position until his death on January 4, 1874. (Carroll Montgomery.)

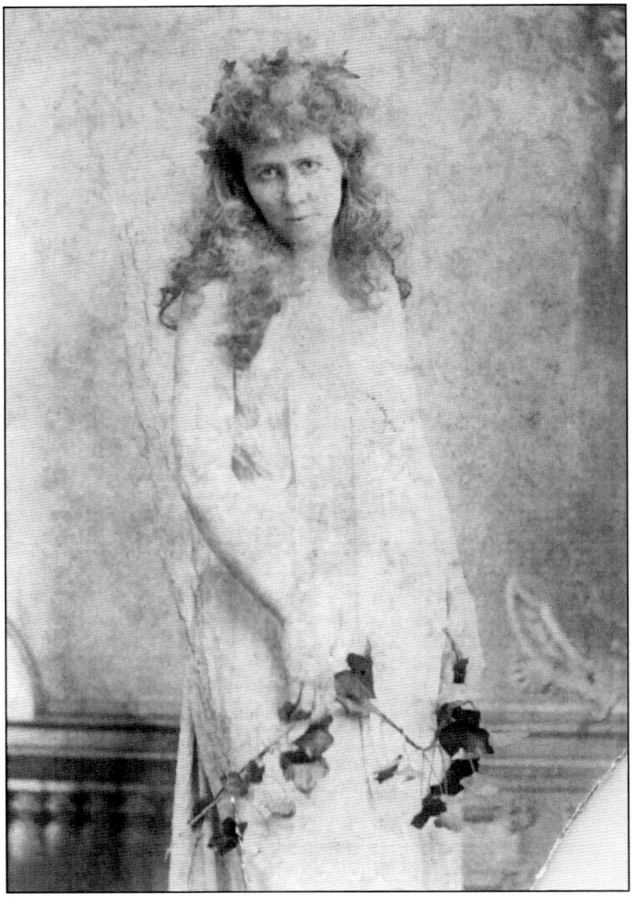

James Lulah "Tallulah" Ragsdale made her stage debut in New Orleans playing Fiordelisa in *The Fool's Revenge*. She came home to write poems and novels and to teach speech and dramatic arts at Whitworth College. Her novel *Miss Dulcie From Dixie* was made into a movie, and her poems were widely published. She was listed in the literary digest *Who's Who in America*. She was born February 5, 1861, in Cedar Hall, Lawrence County (later Lincoln County), Mississippi. Her father was killed in the Civil War and she was reared by her mother, Martha Louise, in Brookhaven. Ragsdale died on December 26, 1953, and is buried in Rosehill Cemetery in Brookhaven. (LCHM.)

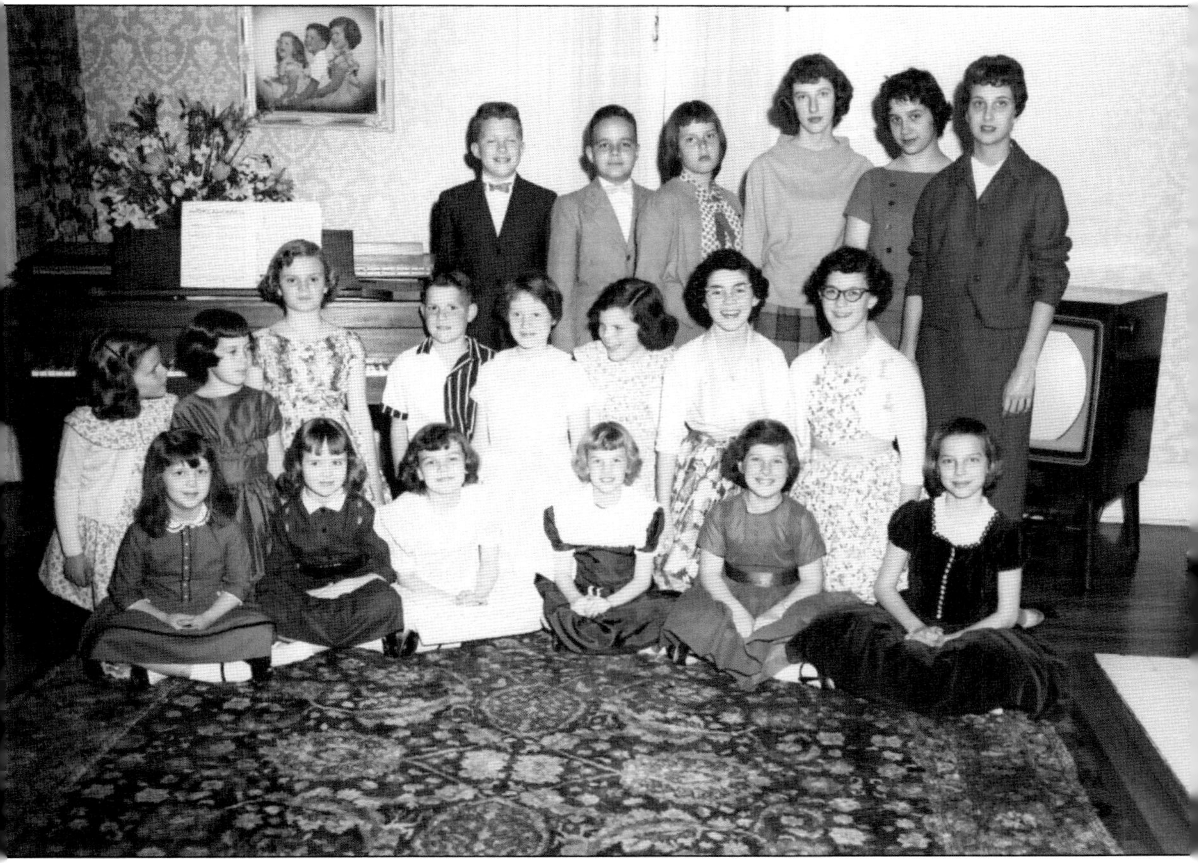

Shown are unidentified students of the three precocious Vardamen sisters—Jemmie, May and Fannie—who shared the spotlight in music from the 1920s until the 1950s. Jemmie and Mae had been instructors at the Cincinnati Conservatory of Music, and Fannie was a student there. In Brookhaven, they were instrumental in creating a foundation for the appreciation of music, organizing the Philharmonic Society, which brought musical artists such as Van Cliburn and the London String Quartette to Lincoln County. (LLF.)

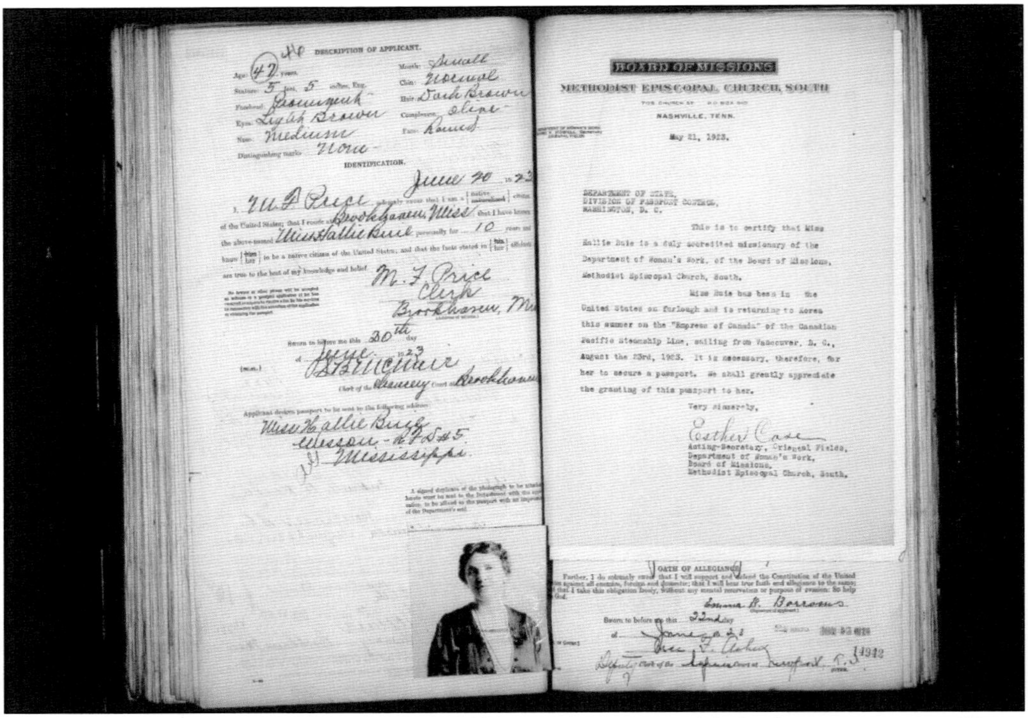

BOARD OF MISSIONS
METHODIST EPISCOPAL CHURCH, SOUTH
NASHVILLE, TENN.

May 21, 1923.

DEPARTMENT OF STATE,
DIVISION OF PASSPORT CONTROL,
WASHINGTON, D. C.

This is to certify that Miss Hallie Buie is a duly accredited missionary of the Department of Woman's Work, of the Board of Missions, Methodist Episcopal Church, South.

Miss Buie has been in the United States on furlough and is returning to Korea this summer on the "Empress of Canada" of the Canadian Pacific Steamship Line, sailing from Vancouver, B. C., August the 23rd, 1923. It is necessary, therefore, for her to secure a passport. We shall greatly appreciate the granting of this passport to her.

Very sincerely,

Esther Case
Acting-Secretary, Oriental Fields,
Department of Woman's Work,
Board of Missions,
Methodist Episcopal Church, South.

Hallie Buie (1878–1949), a native of Caseyville, Mississippi, was a Methodist missionary in Korea for 30 years. During her service in Korea, Buie worked as head of a girls' school. She was also a licensed minister of the Methodist Church in Korea. She coauthored the children's book *K Sooni* with Virginia Fairfax. (Bettie Posey Bullard.)

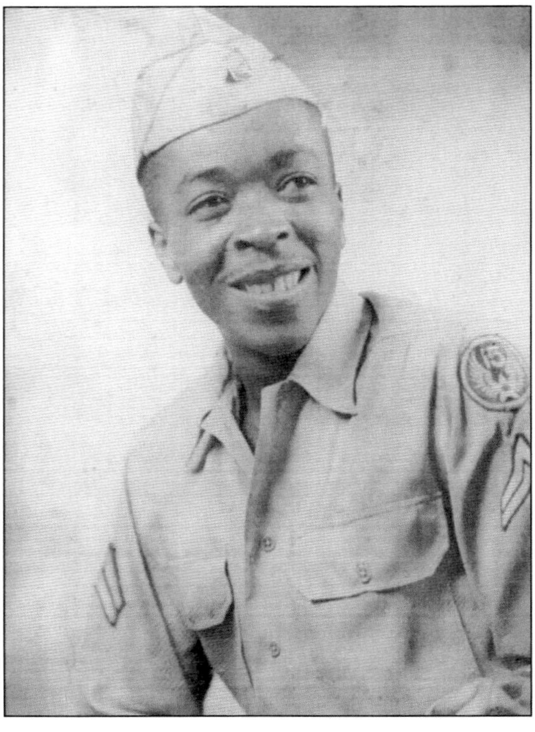

Minyon Gaston of Brookhaven has the distinction of being the first black male to serve as an air-traffic controller. Born on December 24, 1922, he left school to enlist in the Army at age 16. He was a member of the distinguished Tuskegee Airmen, serving in the 332nd Air Division under the commands of Gen. Benjamin O. Davis Sr. and Gen. Daniel "Chappie" James. Gaston received five combat ribbons and two Bronze Stars for distinguished service. Upon returning, he earned a bachelor of science degree in mathematics from Hofstra University and completed work for a master of science degree in guidance from Atlanta University. He is still honored for his support to the Lincoln County Boys and Girls Club. Gaston was married to the former Annie Mae Newton. (Maxine Allen.)

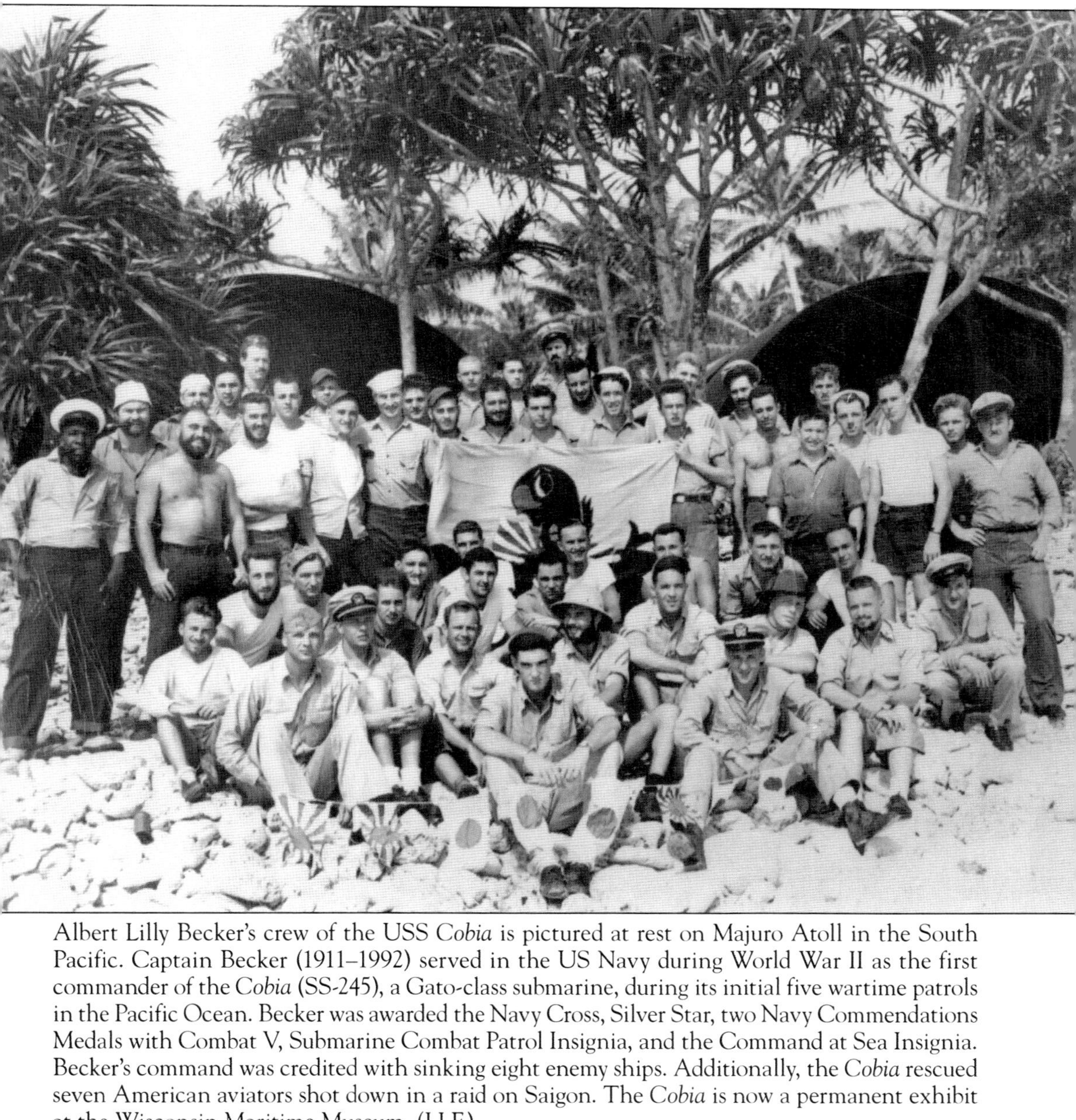

Albert Lilly Becker's crew of the USS *Cobia* is pictured at rest on Majuro Atoll in the South Pacific. Captain Becker (1911–1992) served in the US Navy during World War II as the first commander of the *Cobia* (SS-245), a Gato-class submarine, during its initial five wartime patrols in the Pacific Ocean. Becker was awarded the Navy Cross, Silver Star, two Navy Commendations Medals with Combat V, Submarine Combat Patrol Insignia, and the Command at Sea Insignia. Becker's command was credited with sinking eight enemy ships. Additionally, the *Cobia* rescued seven American aviators shot down in a raid on Saigon. The *Cobia* is now a permanent exhibit at the Wisconsin Maritime Museum. (LLF.)

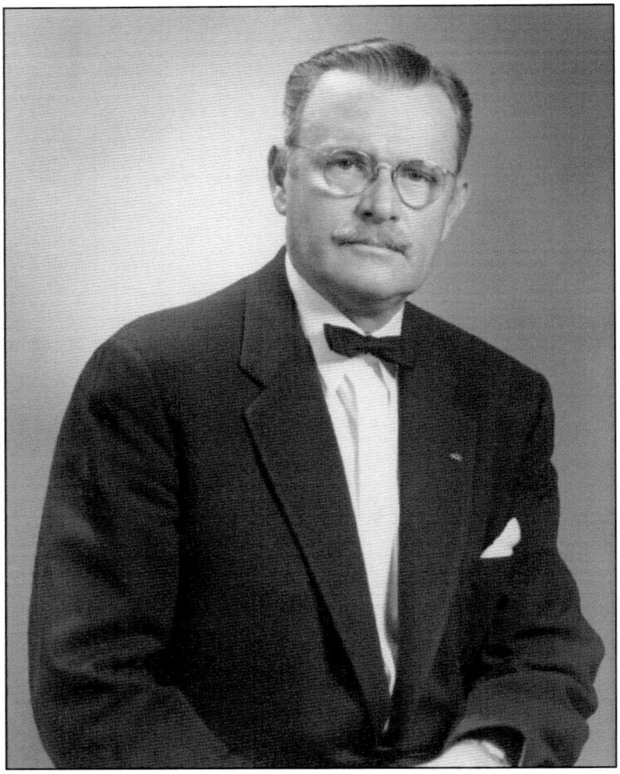

Thomas Pickens Brady was born on August 6, 1903. He married LaVerne Holmes, and they had two sons—Thomas Pickens and Bruce Holmes—and six grandchildren. A graduate of Yale and the University of Mississippi School of Law, he became a member of the firm Brady, Dean, and Hobbs. Brady was commissioner of public safety and director of the Mississippi Highway Patrol from 1940 to 1943. He was a delegate to three Democratic National Conventions and a member of the Democratic National Committee from 1960 to 1964. He served as a colonel on the staffs of four Mississippi governors. In 1950, he became circuit judge of the Fourteenth Judicial District, where he served until 1963, when he was appointed as a justice of the Mississippi Supreme Court, a position he held until his death in 1973. (Becky Taylor.)

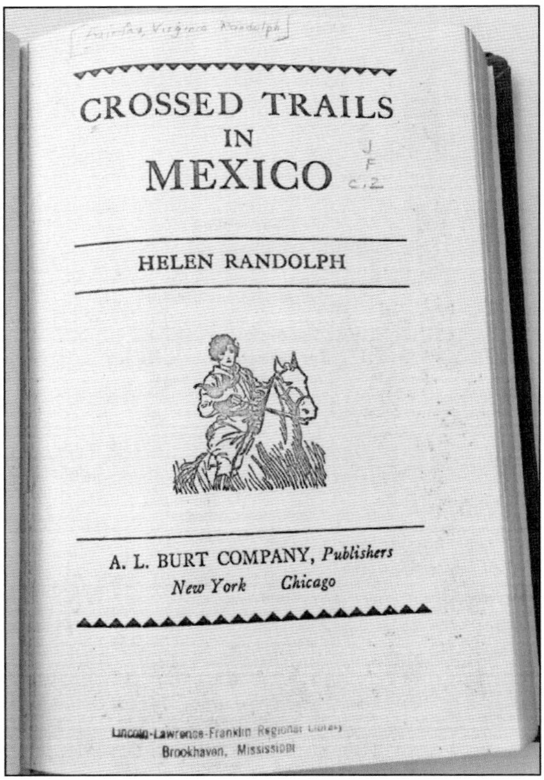

CROSSED TRAILS
IN
MEXICO

HELEN RANDOLPH

A. L. BURT COMPANY, *Publishers*
New York *Chicago*

Lincoln-Lawrence-Franklin Regional Library
Brookhaven, Mississippi

Helen Ripley (1889–1982) was both an artist and a writer. She and Virginia Fairfax (1882–1956), another Brookhaven author, wrote a series of books for girls that served as a forerunner to the famous Nancy Drew stories. The women coined the name "Helen Randolph" from Ripley's first name and Fairfax's maiden name. Some of the stories have Mexican backgrounds taken from Ripley's childhood. Ripley shared leadership duties in the Girl Scouts with Fairfax. She wrote that the response of the girls to the stories they told around the campfires at the annual two-week camp gave her and Fairfax the idea for writing the books. (LLF.)

This handsome young couple, photographed around 1910, are Lamar D. Smith (b. 1892 or 1893) and his wife, Annie Case. In 1955, Lamar was tragically murdered in front of the Lincoln County Courthouse as he attempted to register to vote. The suspects were never arrested, due to lack of proof; all are deceased. His death is one of the FBI's unsolved civil rights cases. Smith served in World War I. (LLF.)

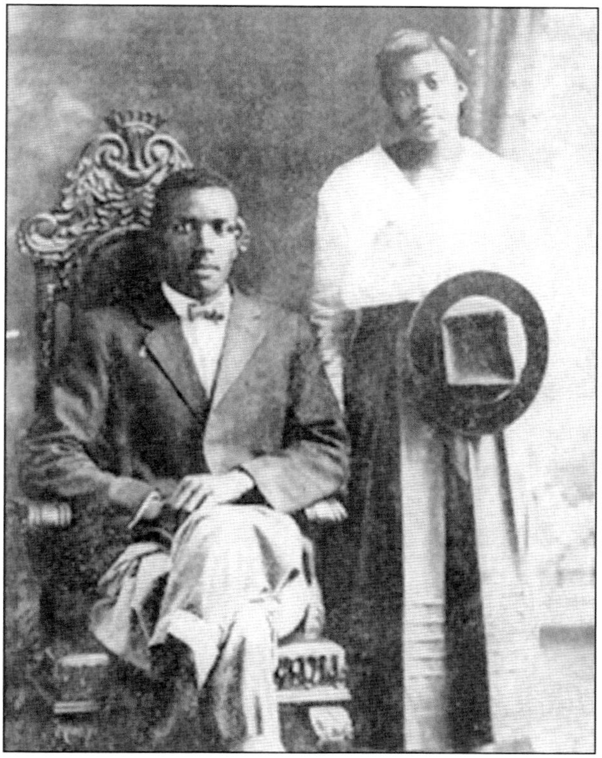

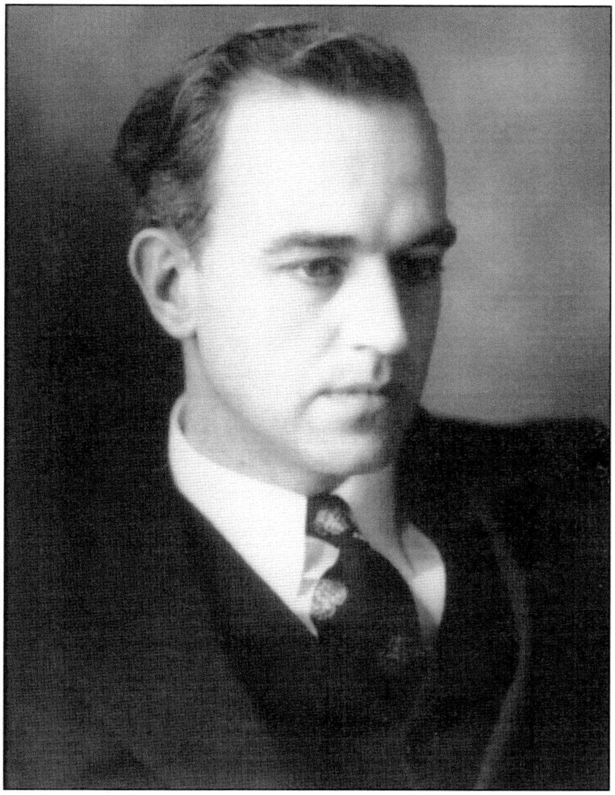

Karl Ferdinand Wolfe (1904–1984) was born in Brookhaven to Wiley Woodard Wolfe and Elizabeth Heuck Wolfe. His uncle Charles F. "Joe Jr." Heuck was elected mayor of Brookhaven a few years later. The family moved to Columbia, where Karl worked in logging camps under his father's supervision. He saved money for education in New Orleans, and was accepted to the Chicago Institute of Art in 1924. He met Mildred Nungester in 1937. The couple married in 1944 and moved to Jackson, Mississippi, opening their studio in a wooded area near the current location of Meadowbrook Drive. Their work is nationally known and honored. (Elizabeth "Bebe" Wolfe.)

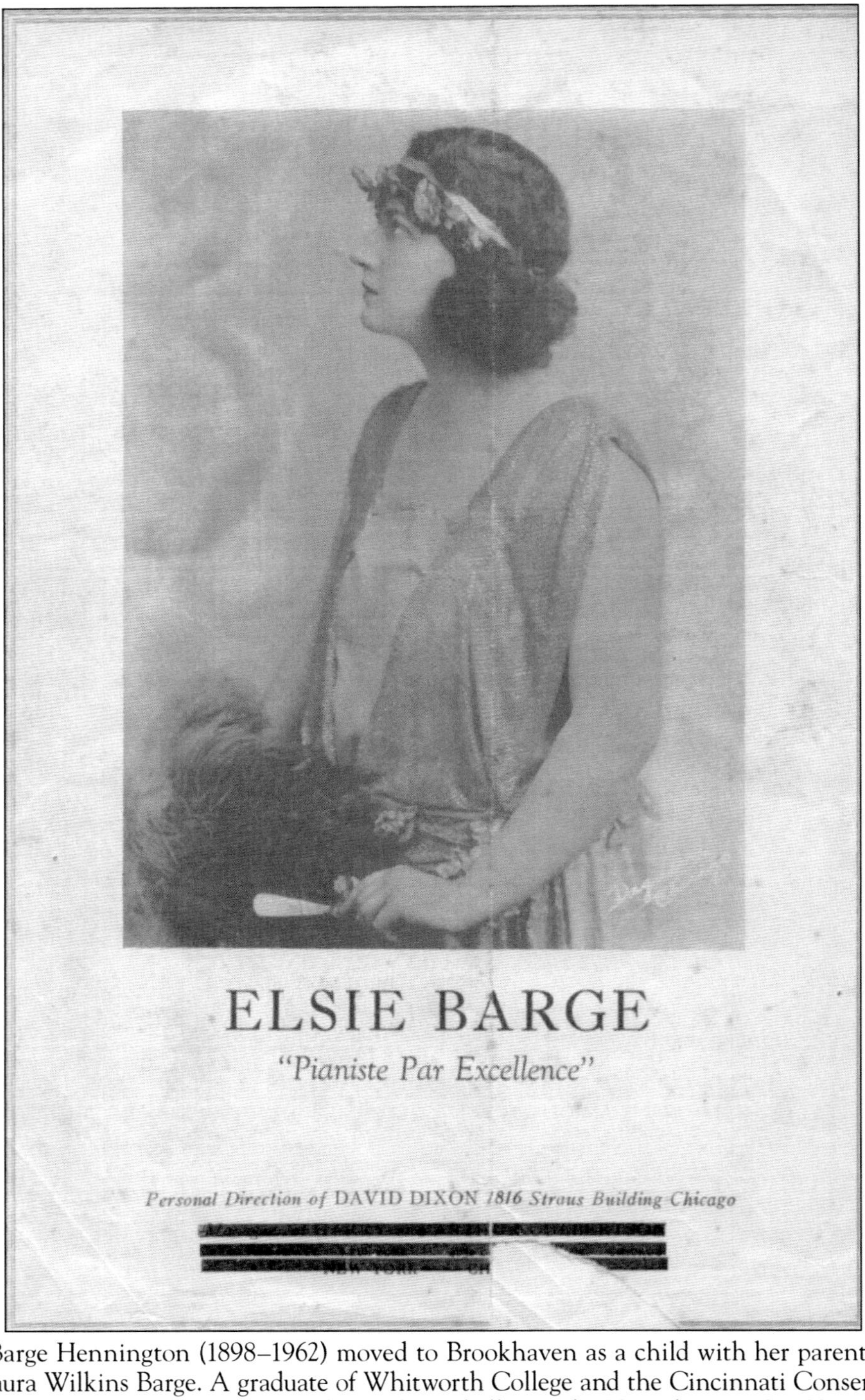

Elsie Barge Hennington (1898–1962) moved to Brookhaven as a child with her parents, T.C. and Laura Wilkins Barge. A graduate of Whitworth College and the Cincinnati Conservatory of Music, she was a concert pianist who performed all over the United States. Dr. Hennington directed a large music school in Florida for several years. After moving back to Brookhaven, she actively promoted cultural and musical programs and events. She taught piano for many years and organized the Crescendo Club for her students. The Mississippi Federation of Music Clubs named a scholarship in her honor after her death. (LCHGS.)

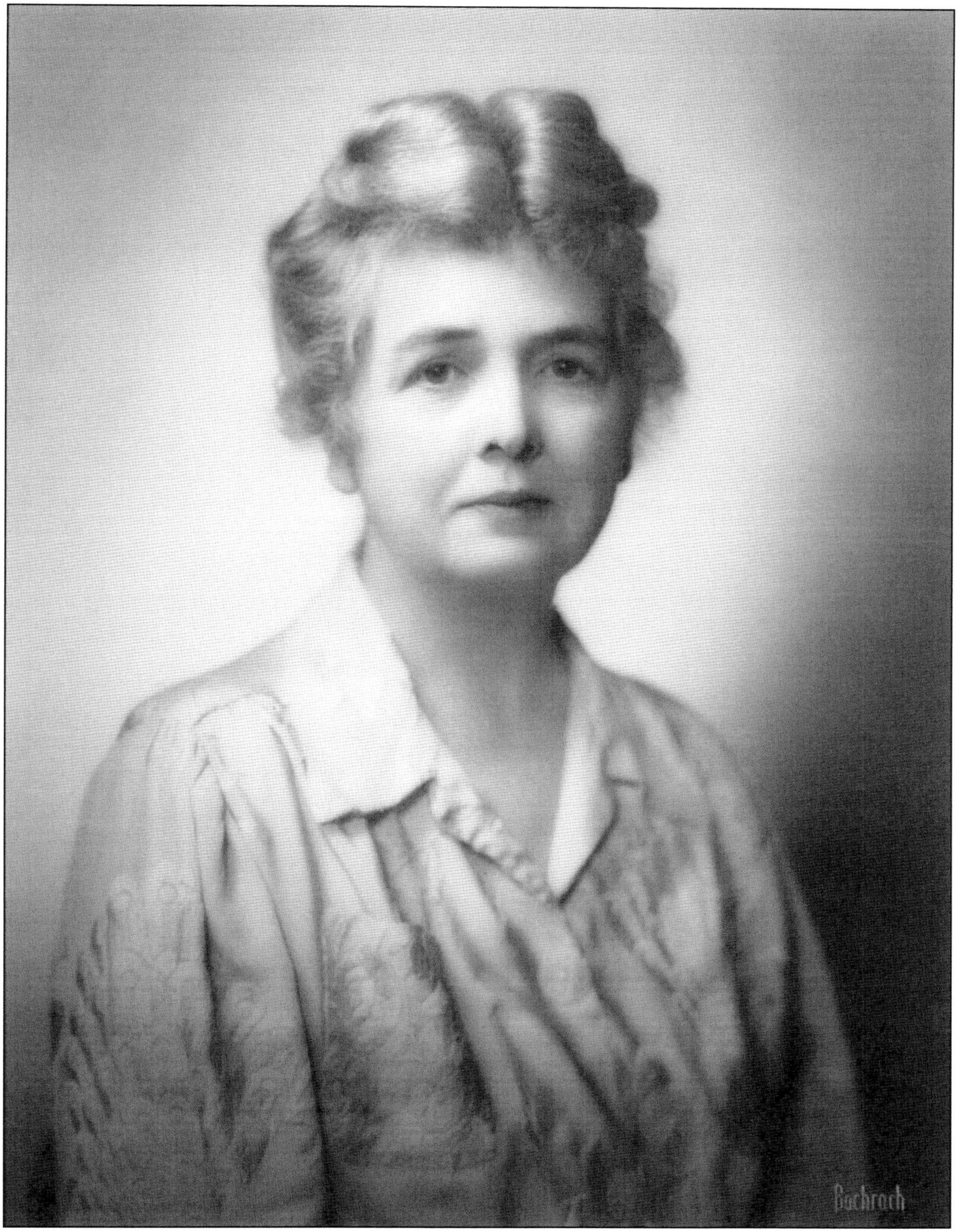

Cid Ricketts Sumner (1890–1970) was born Bertha Louise Ricketts in Brookhaven, Mississippi, to Robert Scott Ricketts and Bertha Burnley Ricketts. Her "placid" nature as a baby earned her the nickname "Cid." The youngest of four, she was the only daughter born to the Ricketts. A writer and an adventurer, she authored 14 books, including *Quality*, which was made into the motion picture *Pinky*. She is best known for her series of Tammy books, from which several films and a television series were made. (Sarah Holcombe.)

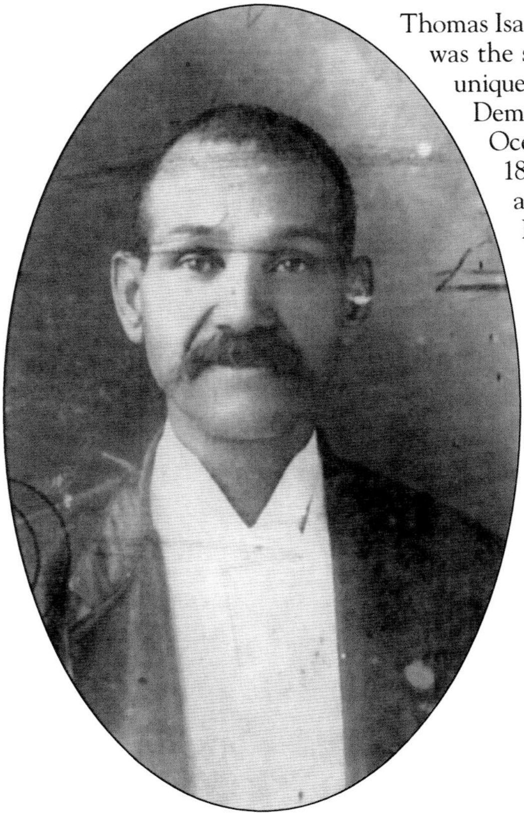

Thomas Isaac "Ike" Keys, born in 1861 in Lincoln County, was the son of Preston Keys and Mary Porter. Ike was unique, in that he was a staunch Republican in a largely Democratic society. He was appointed postmaster in Ocean Springs, Mississippi, serving in that post from 1889 to 1893 and from 1896 to 1911, during the administration of several Republican presidents. He also operated a retail store. Keys died in 1931. (Ray L. Bellande.)

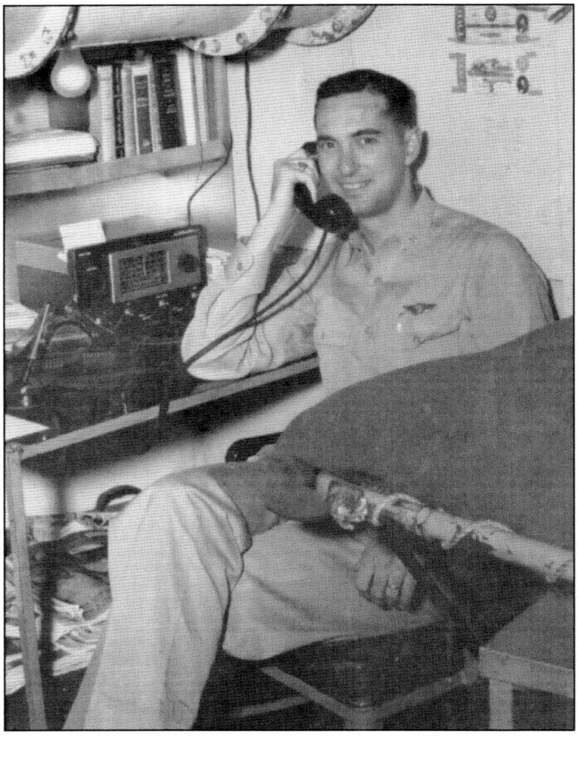

Dr. Jim Barnett served in combat as a Navy flight surgeon with Fighter Air Group 15 during the Korean War, aboard the aircraft carrier USS *Princeton* (CV-37). He received two Battle Stars and was recommended for the Navy Cross. Barnett practiced medicine in Lincoln County for 36 years. He served on numerous local, state, and national boards. In later years, he also served in the Mississippi House of Representatives. (Roberta Barnett.)

Born in 1911, O.C. McDavid knew he wanted to be a newspaperman. His career began when he finished high school, and continued until he retired as managing editor of the *Jackson Daily News*. In retirement, he helped establish the Craftsmen's Guild of Mississippi and spent his time as a sculptor and painter. The Mississippi Press Association honored him by naming an annual meeting the O.C. McDavid Student Journalism Conference. McDavid died in 1998. The University of Houston houses Captain McDavid's World War II letters. (Mississippi Press Association.)

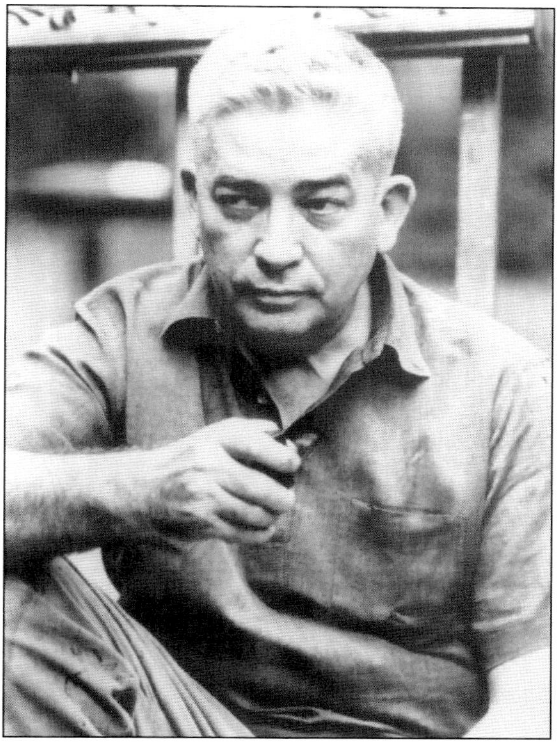

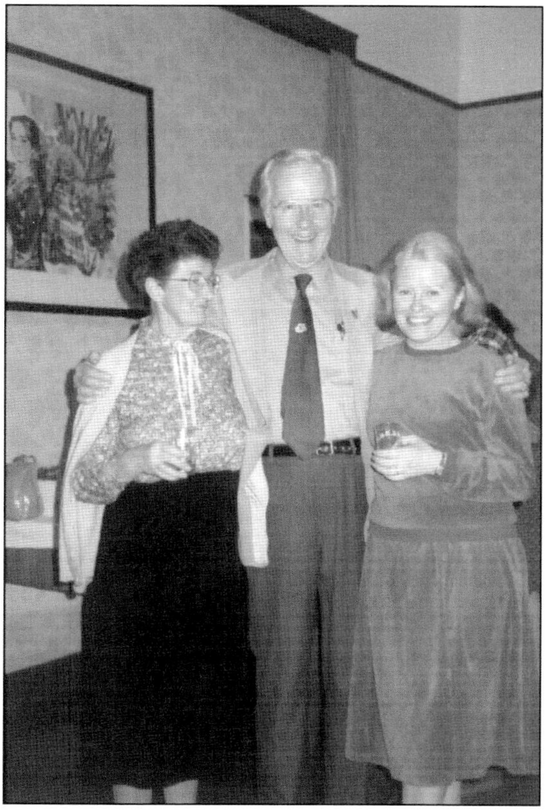

Although Thomas H. Perkins III was a World War II hero at the Battle of the Bulge and recipient of a Purple Heart and Bronze Star, he is remembered most for his passion for camellias. Perkins's brother William began the Camellia Society in Brookhaven, but Thomas became a foremost authority on camellias. He was the first American to be elected to the presidency of the International Camellia Society. His legacy remains in many ways. A camellia is named for him and the camellias he planted throughout the town are still enjoyed by all and win awards in shows. He is shown with two unidentified Camellia Society visitors. (LLF.)

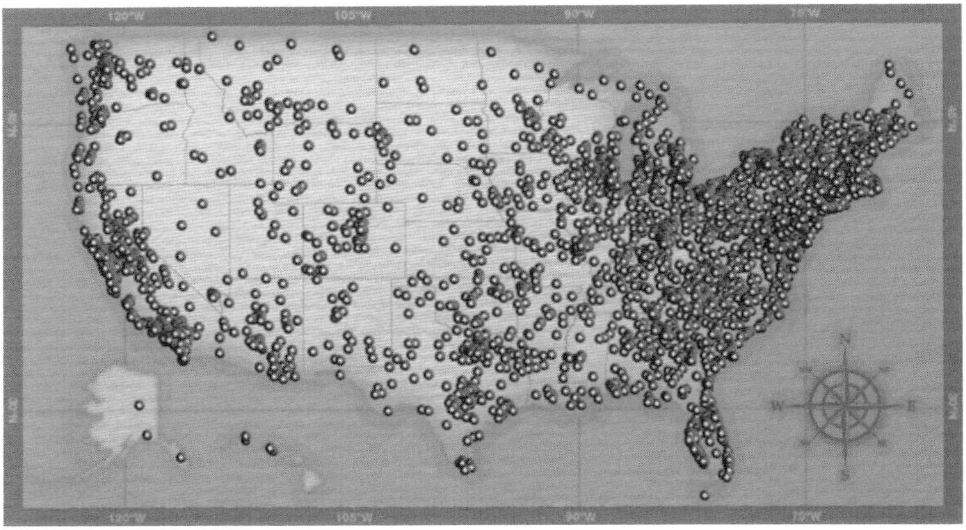